DESIGNING EUROPE

Designing Europe

Comparative Lessons from the Federal Experience

David McKay

OXFORD
UNIVERSITY PRESS

*This book has been printed digitally and produced in a standard specification
in order to ensure its continuing availability*

OXFORD
UNIVERSITY PRESS

Great Clarendon Street, Oxford OX2 6DP

Oxford University Press is a department of the University of Oxford.
It furthers the University's objective of excellence in research, scholarship,
and education by publishing worldwide in

Oxford New York

Auckland Bangkok Buenos Aires Cape Town Chennai
Dar es Salaam Delhi Hong Kong Istanbul Karachi Kolkata
Kuala Lumpur Madrid Melbourne Mexico City Mumbai Nairobi
São Paulo Shanghai Taipei Tokyo Toronto

Oxford is a registered trade mark of Oxford University Press
in the UK and in certain other countries

Published in the United States
by Oxford University Press Inc., New York

© David McKay 2001

The moral rights of the author have been asserted
Database right Oxford University Press (maker)

Reprinted 2003

ISBN 0-19-924213-5

PREFACE AND ACKNOWLEDGEMENTS

This book was inspired by the belief that the recent development of the European Union (EU) more resembles the evolution of some of the more established federations such as the United States and Switzerland than that of other supranational organizations or customs unions. Even in the absence of a definitive constitution, the EU has acquired most of the trappings of statehood. The EU is also highly heterogeneous, so it seems fair to assume that the more power that accrues to the centre, the greater the potential for the development of 'stateness' problems or a reluctance of some of the member states to maintain a loyalty to the central authorities. Just such a sequence has occurred in other federations including the United States and Canada. The main objective of this book is, therefore, to trace the origins of founding constitutions in these countries and to explain how and why attempts were made to adapt these constitutions over time to maintain the territorial integrity of federations.

All five of the federations in this study are developed democracies with political party systems that broadly reflect the balance of central and provincial power. Indeed, parties are the main means whereby dissident states and regions can express their disquiet at central power. They can, in addition, serve as the vehicles for the accumulation of central power and the transformation of federations from decentralized to centralized structures. Money also plays an important part in the evolution of federations. Centrally organized vertical and horizontal grants can be used to placate dissident regions or to build loyalty to the centre. For these reasons special attention is paid to party systems and to the ways in which central grants and fiscal arrangements generally are used by federal authorities to build or maintain national identities.

At all times the analysis places the historical experience of the five countries in a theoretical context that facilitates comparison with the EU. Very generally, the study concludes that the EU should maintain its supermajoritarian decision-making structures, but should adopt a highly codified constitution which can be amended only by popular approval among the member states.

This study has its origins in an Economic and Social Research Council project into fiscal redistribution and party systems in five federations (Award Number R000222125). I thank the ESRC for its support. I also have to thank a number of individuals for their advice and support including Peter Leslie at Queen's University, Michael Keating and Robert Young at Western Ontario, David Cameron and Richard Simeon at the University of Toronto, Peter Merkl at the University of California Santa Barbara, Christian Anglade at Essex, Jonathan Steinberg at Cambridge, Sonja Waelti at Freiburg, and Ulrich Kloti at Zurich. I received valuable research help from Sabine Zanger of Essex

University and Alexander Zamauss of the University of California, Santa Barbara. All the errors and omissions that remain are, of course, my own.

I would also like to thank the Department of Political Science at the University of California, Santa Barbara, for providing such an amenable base for much of the writing up of the research. Thank you, in particular, Stephen Weatherford for your help.

Finally, I should say how important I think it is that the EU should learn from systematic historical comparison. For in spite of frequent claims that the EU is *sui generis*, the fact remains that, like most of the established federations, from the very beginning the European Union has been a conscious political project designed to expand the territorial competence of a central government. I hope readers will agree that the following analysis provides insights into what the EU might learn from these experiences.

David McKay
Mistley, Essex
April 2000

CONTENTS

Contents

LIST OF FIGURES

LIST OF TABLES

1

'Stateness', Federalism, and Institutional Adaptation

THE assertion of national and regional identities in a wide range of countries from Spain to the former Soviet Union has helped to re-establish academic interest in the problems associated with states winning or maintaining the allegiance of diverse populations in multinational societies. Linz and Stephan have called this a 'stateness' problem or the condition that exists 'when a significant proportion of the population does not accept the boundaries of the state (whether constituted democratically or not) as a legitimate political unit to which they owe obedience' (Linz and Stephan 1992: 123). Much of this literature is concerned with transitions to democracy in Latin America, Southern Europe, the Balkans, and the former Soviet Empire (for a review, see Linz and Stephan 1996). But stateness problems also affect—or have affected—the long-established democracies including Canada, Switzerland, the US, the United Kingdom, and Belgium. In these and other democracies, historical differences and antagonisms between constituent parts have been reconciled following extended periods of bargaining and institutional experimentation. In some cases, territorial units have been unable to reconcile their differences and civil war has ensued. Such was the case with the United States in the 1860s. In other cases such as Canada and Belgium institutional reform has averted secession, but only at the cost of the need for constant renegotiation between regions and between regions and the federal government. There is also the example of the European Union (EU) which for many years has been striving to establish a quasi-federal central authority to govern its institutionally and ethnically diverse member states.

Much of the work on transitions to democracy is concerned not only with the obvious question of the conditions under which democracy might develop, but also with the conditions under which multinational regimes may disintegrate. Often, the breakdown of authoritarianism triggers territorial disintegration, as occurred in the Soviet Union and Czechoslovakia and may well occur in such countries as Indonesia or Iraq (for a summary of this literature, see Leff 1999). Much less attention has been devoted to the equally important question of the conditions under which ethnically and socially diverse *democratic* regimes manage to *maintain* their territorial integrity. The major exception is, of course, an influential body of work on the institutional devices employed by such countries as the Netherlands and, more recently, Spain, South Africa, Belgium, the United Kingdom, and elsewhere to reconcile antagonistic ethnic, linguistic and religious groups. Often called consociationalism, such devices are now recognized as crucial to maintaining the legitimacy of governments in diverse societies (for the classic statement on this subject, see Lijphart 1969; 1977). The approach of this literature is, however, essentially instrumental. Institutional devices such as proportional representation and power sharing are seen as means of avoiding conflict within existing nation states. Often this involves adapting centralized unitary constitutional arrangements and replacing them with complex decentralized decision making structures. Consociationalists are less concerned with how diverse societies have developed and adapted over long periods. Countries sometimes do this by adopting consociational institutions and sometimes not. Many states are, moreover, conscious creations forged out of military and political necessity. In such contexts, constitutional framers, if not able to exploit a *tabula rasa*, do have the luxury of being able to create institutions designed to accommodate the interests of diverse peoples and regions. Such was certainly the case with the United States in 1789 and, to a lesser extent, several other states, including Canada in 1867 and Switzerland in 1848.

The position of the EU at the start of the twenty-first century is much closer to that of these nascent federations than it is to that of the Belgium or Northern Ireland. In the latter, politicians have had to struggle to adapt often rigid political traditions and constitutional arrangements in order to stem or to stave off violent conflict. In other words, throughout its history the EU has proceeded to build institutions and policies on the basis of mutual agreements that are acceptable to all parties. However, as EU responsibilities expand it is increasingly likely that the EU will experience the sort of tensions that have affected other maturing federations. This is especially so given the multinational character of the EU and given the fact that, following European Monetary Union (EMU), the participating countries are now locked into the sort of centralized policy imperatives more typical of nation states than of supranational organizations.[1] These new responsibilities highlight anew the problem of the 'democratic deficit' in the EU. Political scientists and others have devoted great effort to identifying the nature of the democratic deficit and it how it might be corrected (see, for example, Weale and Nentwich 1998; Abromeit 1999; Andersen and Eliassen 1996; Hix 1998). However, little in the way of systematic cross-national research has been undertaken that specifically examines the ways in which other federations have developed over time.

The central concern of this book, therefore, is: what lessons can the EU learn from the experiences of those states which were originally forged out of national, ethnic and geographic diversity, but which have subsequently been obliged to adapt constitutional and other arrangements in order to maintain

---

[1] Definitional problems abound in this area, but, as will be shown in Chapter 2, decision making in 'supranational' organizations is typically characterized by unanimity rather than majority decision rules.

the integrity of their unions? Because the EU is founded on the basis of democratic decision making, comparisons will be confined to democratic states. Comparison will also be limited to federations, in part because all federations are consciously created to accommodate diversity. Consequently, they adopt institutional structures designed to achieve a balance between central and provincial power. The five federations selected—Australia, Canada, Germany, Switzerland, and the US—were chosen because they represent a broad spectrum of experience both in terms of constitutional/institutional structure and in terms of ethnic/linguistic/religious/cultural diversity. All five, moreover, have been obliged to use democratic mechanisms to adapt political and other structures in response to changing economic, social, and political circumstance.

Constitutionally, the five range from the highly decentralized arrangements applicable in Switzerland to the relatively centralized constitution of the United States. However, as will be shown in Chapter 2, formal constitutional arrangements are not always an accurate guide to the actual distribution of powers between central and state authorities. Often, bureaucrats, organized interests and, above all, political parties, exploit institutional arrangements in ways that can both increase and decrease levels of centralization. There are, moreover, a number of ways in which centralization can be measured. As Chapter 2 will demonstrate, it can be measured in constitutional/institutional terms and in terms of political, administrative, and fiscal as well as cultural/commercial criteria. Some federal systems—Germany, for example—are politically centralized but administratively decentralized. Others, such as the US, are institutionally centralized but fiscally decentralized. By assigning a major role to institutional structures and processes, this book draws on the 'new institutionalism' which tries to explain economic and political change in terms of how institutions interact with individual actors and the broader economic and social environment to produce particular outcomes (for good examples of this approach, see Alston, Eggertsson. and North 1996). It is the sheer institutional variety and complexity of this sample of federations that makes comparison with the EU apt. Claims that the EU—originally the European Community (EC)—is *sui generis* and can be explained only in terms of its unique structure and evolution look inappropriate given the increasingly state like status of the Union. Indeed, given this evolution, EU institutions and processes can be properly understood only in comparative context. Placing the EU in *historical* comparative context has rarely been attempted, however, perhaps because scholars have been reluctant to draw comparisons between a highly decentralized European Union and what are widely regarded as relatively centralized established federations

However, although the EU is by most criteria clearly more decentralized than any of the sample federations, by some it is not. In central controls over fiscal matters, for example, including minimum value added tax (VAT) rates and controls over national borrowing, the EU is actually more centralized than Canada, the US and Switzerland. And as will be shown in subsequent chapters, at their inception some of these federations were not notably more centralized than is the EU today. The main emphasis of the analysis will therefore be on the circumstances under which different systems have embarked on centralizing policies or decentralizing policies.

Federalism and Stateness Problems

It is clear from a rich and growing literature on nationalism and national identity that the main constraint on the ability of ethnically diverse states to centralize political authority is the strength of provincial/state[2] loyalties in relation to national loyalties. Where provincial loyalty is strong relative to the centre, systems are more likely to be administratively and fiscally decentralized (Riker 1967; 1975; Linz and Stephan 1996). It is also clear, however, that the *ways* in which governments distribute authority is profoundly influenced by the balance of central/provincial power. In Germany and Switzerland, for example, many tax revenues are shared between different levels of government, thus blurring the lines of authority. In Switzerland, although the federal government largely funds social security programmes, they are directly administered by the cantons and *Gemeinde*—local governments. Swiss sub-central governments also have a major say in the granting of citizenship. These variations apply both between countries and within them. In the US, for example, the provision of welfare—public assistance for the needy—has been largely returned to the states, having originally been a state responsibility and, more recently, a shared federal/state programme.

While it is common to identify a 'rational' distribution of functions between different levels of government (for example, see Peterson 1995), it is clear that a considerable tension can exist between such a rational apportionment and what is politically possible. Most commentators argue, for instance, that redistributive transfer payments—welfare and social security, health benefits—should be national responsibilities, on the ground that only central authorities have a sufficiently large tax base to facilitate an equitable distribution. In fact, however, it may be politically necessary to transfer or devolve some or all of these programmes in order to placate state/regional demands. Such has been the case in both Switzerland and Canada.

Within the European Union, there is a tendency to interpret the subsidiarity principle mainly in terms of economic and administrative efficiency (see Begg *et al.* 1993). Hence the main defence of EMU or EU competition policy is based on economic gains. Yet we have already witnessed instances where national—member state—political objections to what is claimed to be economically appropriate have held sway. British, Swedish, and Danish opposition to EMU and British opposition to the removal of intra-EU border controls

---

[2] Nomenclature is always a problem in this area given that different states employ different names for sub-central units. Throughout, therefore, 'state', 'province', and 'region' will be used interchangeably.

are cases in point. As we will see, these modifications to and adaptations of EU policy are very similar to the ways in which public policy has developed in other federations. While it is a truism that public policy often results from a trade-off between what is efficient and what is politically expedient, systematic comparison between the experience of the EU and that of other federations has rarely been attempted. Following the signing of the Maastricht Treaty comparisons with existing federations, including the five systems under discussion in this book, have been the subject of some analysis. But the resulting research has been confined to simple contemporary descriptions or has invoked economic models of decentralization, such as the Tiebout thesis,[3] as analytical tools. None of this work takes a developmental approach or employs an analytical framework which could locate shifting patterns of territorial political power in the argument (see Begg *et al.* 1993; *European Economy 1993* 1993). In this context, for each of the five federations the following topics will be covered.

1. *The origins of founding constitutions.* The circumstances under which constitutions emerge are a major influence on the balance between state and central power. In most of the cases under discussion military and/or foreign policy concerns dominated the original decisions to forms federations. The resulting institutional arrangements were, therefore, largely a trade-off between defence needs on the one hand and the need to satisfy provincial loyalties on the other. Economic concerns—in particular the need to establish a single market in the exchange of goods and services—were also an important factor in deciding on federal political arrangements. European integration has been driven more by economic than defence concerns, and the problem of how to achieve an acceptable central/provincial balance remains the dominant issue in the emerging EU constitution. The experience of other federations is, therefore, apposite.

2. *How constitutions have been adapted over time to accommodate centralist and decentralist forces.* Through change by amendment and interpretation, founding constitutions have been adapted in all cases. In Australia, for example, a decentralized constitution has failed to produce a decentralized polity. In the US, the constitution was re-interpreted to facilitate centralization during the New Deal and Great Society. More recently the opposite has occurred. In Germany, what looks like relatively decentralized arrangements have not prevented the emergence of a relatively centralized polity. In all cases, analysis will concentrate on the growth of economic and social policy and in particular how federal governments have used fiscal tools to satisfy both provincial demands and demands for centralized national action.

3. *The role of political parties in this process.* In democratic societies political parties are the main agents responsible for articulating interests including

---

[3] The Tiebout model argues that political systems with decentralized jurisdictional fragmentation with each unit controlling taxation are more likely to be Pareto-efficient because each will have an incentive to keep taxes low and the efficiency of public services high for fear of losing investment and mobile tax payers (Tiebout 1956).

those based on regional or provincial distinctiveness (Katz and Mair 1995; Ware 1996). Parties can play the major role in constitutional adaptation or in exploiting institutional rules in order to serve the interests of their supporters. They may do this through influence over legislative, executive, bureaucratic, and judicial rules and procedures. Just such a dynamic occurred with the southern Democrats in the US Congress and the Bloc Quebecois operating through a variety of Canadian political institutions.

4. *The role of parties as legitimizing agents in achieving an acceptable balance of central and provincial power.* In governments' attempts both to centralize and to decentralize, political parties can play the key role in legitimizing subsequent policy changes. As Chapter 2 will elaborate, deepening and widening European integration has renewed scholarly interest in legitimacy and particularly in the relationship between legitimacy and the role of parties as mobilizers of interests and opinions.

The ways in which federalism has developed in each of the five countries is, of course, a vast subject in itself. For this reason, the analysis will concentrate on key periods of adaptation when systems underwent centralization or decentralization. In addition and as indicated, the analysis will largely be confined to economic and social policy and consequent changes in intergovernmental fiscal relations. At all times the study will focus on how different federations have attempted to accommodate territorial distinctiveness. In sum, the major concern of this volume is to identify the ways in which politicians and parties representing citizen loyalties at the state and national levels bargain through political institutions to achieve centralizing or decentralizing policies and programmes.

The Chapters to Come

Chapter 2 will place the study in theoretical and empirical context by providing justifications for making comparisons between mature federations and the European Union. The chapter will, first, argue that the post-Maastricht EU has developed into a species of federal state. In addition, the relevance of the above points 2, 3 and 4 to the EU experience will be developed with a special emphasis placed on the legitimizing role of political parties. Chapters 3 through 7 will deal with each of the countries in turn and will focus on key periods of adaptation in each when systems centralized or decentralized. For all countries the analysis will concentrate on the ways in which political parties operating nationally and in states and regions have used constitutional mechanisms and institutional arrangements—for example, in national legislatures—to broker more centralized or decentralized policies. Chapter 8 will bring the analysis together by drawing broad comparisons between the five countries and the European Union. Chapter 8 will also spell out the implications of the analysis for governance in the EU. While in no way claiming that any one of the sample countries can act as a model or template for the EU, the analysis concludes that the greatest parallels exist with the Swiss experience. As will be demonstrated, Switzerland has the most decentralized system and one where the constituent states, or cantons, have the greatest influence on central policy making institutions.

Chapter 9 will conclude the analysis by providing tentative advice on how the institutional design of the EU might be adapted in the light of the comparative analysis and given the particular balance of provincial to central loyalties prevalent in the early twenty-first century European Union. In other words, in light of the experience of other federations, which institutional arrangements are most likely to minimize the growth of a 'stateness' problem in the twenty-first century European polity?

2

The Federal Experience and the European Union

The recent popularity of federal constitutions is not surprising because federalism is one way to solve the problem of enlarging governments—a problem that is one of the most pressing political concerns in the modern world.

William Riker, 1964

Problems of Definition

ALL students of federalism concede that the subject is beset with problems of definition. In many federations power is decentralized and in others centralized. Some nominally unitary systems display many of the characteristics of federations while many do not. General agreement exists, however, that federations differ from unitary systems in terms of the constitutional and political status of lower-level governments in relation to central authorities. Hence, Riker (1975: 101) defines federalism as 'A political organization in which the activities of government are divided between regional governments and a central government in such a way that each kind of government has some activities on which it makes final decisions'. Most observers would accept that, for modern federations, the definition would be somewhat more inclusive. In 1996 the present author claimed federal arrangements were present when 'the principle of the division of powers between centre and regions is established constitutionally and citizens hold an identity at both levels. At the minimum the component states should have the right to territorial integrity, to some representation in the institutions of the central or federal government, and to be protected by the federal government from external aggression' (McKay 1996: 15). A 'minimal' federation, therefore, would be one where all but national defence was in the hands of state or provincial governments. In practice, of course, the delineation of powers between different levels is determined not only by constitutional provision but also by custom, tradition, and politically brokered compromise and negotiation.

In this context, it is easy to see how the post-Maastricht EU can be categorized as a species of federal state. Two distinct levels of government exist, each supreme in a range of policy areas. Citizens hold identities with both levels and EU treaties guarantee the territorial integrity of member states. However, by some criteria, the EU is clearly not a fully developed federal state. For one thing, defence remains primarily in the hands of member-state governments. For another, legislative power at the federal level resembles an aggregation of national decision making authorities rather than a separate federal parliament representing a federation-wide constituency. Notwithstanding moves towards federal arrangements in both areas—a single defence policy is a stated EU aim and the powers of the European Parliament (EP) are steadily increasing—it may be more appropriate to characterize the EU as 'quasi-federal' or as a hybrid between federation and confederation (for a discussion of definitional problems, see Scharpf 1997).

This accepted, categorizing the EU as a variety of federation can be justified on three grounds. There is, first, the fact that the constitution of the EU—in this case the Treaty on European Union or the Maastricht Treaty—has formally accepted the principle of subsidiarity in its allocation of powers between different levels of government. What this means in practice is that the members concede that some policy areas should be the exclusive competence of the EU, and those that are not should be the responsibility of national governments unless other considerations, such as efficiency, make it more sensible for the EU to act.[1] A number of policies have been allocated to the central authorities including, for eleven members, at least, the crucially important area of macroeconomic policy. Along with national defence, control over macroeconomic policy constitutes the minimum requirement for the functioning of the modern state (Birch 1989, part 1; Duchacek 1970: 222–30). Macroeconomic policy is, moreover, under the control of an unambiguously federal institution, the European Central Bank (ECB). The constitution of the ECB insulates it from direct national influence and requires it to operate as an autonomous EU institution.

Second, as earlier suggested, existing federations are characterized by widely varying degrees of centralization. In addition, most have experienced periods of centralization and decentralization. As will be shown in later chapters, by some measures, such as sub-central/national government tax autonomy, the EU already displays a higher degree of centralization than exists the modern United States or Switzerland. It is quite sensible, therefore, to place the early twenty-first century EU at the 'weak' end of a continuum ranging from strong to weak federations.

A third and related reason to categorize the EU as a federation is the fact that it is stated EU policy to move towards 'ever closer union'. As far as the correction of the democratic deficit is concerned, this is usually interpreted as meaning a strengthening of the European Parliament in relation to the Commission

---

[1] Article 3b of Title II if the Maastricht Treaty reads: 'The Community shall act within the limit of the powers conferred upon it by this Treaty and of the objectives assigned to it therein. In areas which do not fall within its exclusive competence, the Community shall take action, in accordance with the principle of subsidiarity, only if and insofar as the objectives of the proposed action cannot be sufficiently achieved by the Member States and can therefore, by reason of the scale or effects of the proposed action, be better achieved by the Community.' Quoted in Bidwell (1993: 23).

and the Council. This in turn will almost certainly translate into a strengthening of the 'federal' government institutions in relation to national government institutions. In addition, the gradual erosion of the unanimity-voting rule in the Council of Ministers represents a move away from a decision rule which is typical of confederations or supranational organizations rather than federations. In the United Nations Security Council, for example, the veto rule prevails. In none of the five federations in our sample, however, can any one state or province exercize a veto in any national decision making forum, although qualified majority voting (QMV) is well developed in Switzerland and in the US Congress. Within the Council of Ministers, QMV voting is now established as the decision rule for a wide range of policy areas, with unanimity confined to areas of fundamental importance such as enlargement, defence and taxation. One way of interpreting the dividing line between unanimity and QMV voting is to see the former as the equivalent of endorsement of constitutional change and the latter as endorsement of policy or legislative change. While in practice there is no hard and fast conceptual distinction between the two, in some federal systems constitutional amendments are subject, if not to unanimous approval, then certainly to multi-layered 'super-majoritarian' decision rules (on super-majoritarianism, see Weale 1998: 53–61). Hence in Switzerland, a double majority of cantons and of popular votes is required for constitutional change. Moreover, as in the Council of Ministers, constitutional approval is required for a wide range of issue areas including taxation and membership of supranational organizations. This double majority, or two-level, principle is certainly a 'harder' decision rule than that implicit in the Council of Ministers QMV algorithm. In this sense it closely resembles a one-level unanimity rule. We will return to this theme in Chapters 8 and 9.[2]

The classification of the EU as a quasi-federal state appears to be confirmed by a more systematic comparison of the EU and the allocation of policy functions between different levels of government typical of federations. As Table 2.1 shows, only in the provision of national defence and social insurance does the EU appear to deviate markedly from typical federations. These exceptions are, however, significant. Protection against external aggression has always been one of the defining characteristics of the nation state. More recently, the provision of social insurance, and to a lesser extent welfare, has taken on a special status as *rights* inextricably linked to national identity (see Scharpf 1997). None the less, the range of responsibilities is impressive and has been growing steadily over time. Table 2.2 provides a somewhat more refined classification of EU responsibilities and how these have changed during the history of

---

[2] In fact, the range of decisions that are subject to a national veto remains much greater than is commonly supposed. As of late 1999, 25 policy areas remained subject to the unanimity rule including revision of treaties, admission of new members, defence, manufacture and sale of arms, international agreements, citizens' rights, free movement of people, immigration, social security, tax harmonization, the excessive deficit procedure, allocation of structural and cohesion funds and sources of budget revenues. For full list, see *The Economist*, 13 November 1999: 52.

Table 2.1. Allocation of policy functions in typical federations and the European Union

	Typical federations[a]	European Union
Macroeconomic policy	F	F
Agriculture (price stabilisation and income)	F	F
Commercial policy (international negotiations)	F	F
International relations	F	S/f
Defence	F	S
Social insurance (pensions, unemployment, health)	F/s	S
Competition policy	F/s	F/s
Environmental policy	F/s	F/s
Labour market regulation	F/s	F/s
Welfare (social assistance)	F/S	S
Immigration and citizenship	F	F/S
Civil rights[b]	F/s	F/S
Civil liberties[b]	F/s	S[c]
Transport (regulation)	F/s	F/S
Universities/research	S/f	S/f
Health (hospitals and primary care)	S/f	S
Transport (provision)	S/f	S
Law enforcement	S/f	S
Utilities	S	S
Elementary and secondary education	S	S

F signifies exclusive or near-exclusive federal competence; S signifies near-exclusive state competence. F/S signifies near equality in function. Lower case s or f signifies a subordinate role for states or federal governments. The S category includes both state and local governments.

[a]An approximate average of the allocation of policies in Australia, Canada, Germany, Switzerland, and the US.
[b]'Civil rights' signifies the rights of women and minorities; 'civil liberties' protection of freedom of speech, assembly, religion, and enjoyment of due process of law.
[c]But all EU governments are constrained by the rulings of the European Court of Human Rights.

Sources: the author and an adaptation from Begg *et al.* (1993: Table 2.1).

European integration. In fact, the classifications in Table 2.2 strongly imply that the EU has already taken on the status of a nation state.

At first sight however, such a conclusion would seem premature. The scores assigned to each of the policy areas constitute imprecise measures. Above all, they fail to determine which level of government is the final arbiter in a number of key areas. As already noted, each of the EU member states can still pursue a separate foreign and defence policy. As recently as 1982, British action against Argentina in the south Atlantic Ocean was an entirely unilateral action and one taken in the face of opposition from some EC members including Italy. Admittedly, since the signing of the Maastricht and Amsterdam Treaties, the EU has embraced a Common Foreign and Security Policy (CFSP), but the EU has no effective sanctions to impose on members taking unilateral action. Greece, for instance, has a historical antagonism against Turkey that could

The European Union as a Federation

Table 2.2. Issue arenas and levels of authority in Europe, 1950–2001

	1950	1957	1968	1970	1992	2001[b]
Economic						
Agriculture	1	1	4	4	4	4
Macroeconomic	1	1	2	3(2)	2	4[c]
Foreign exchange	1	1	2	2	2	4
Competition	1	2	2	2	3	3
Transport	1	2	2	2	2	3
Communications	1	1	1	1	2	3
Labour market[a]	1	1	2	2	3	4
Capital flows	1	1	1	1	4	4
Revenues/taxes	1	1	2(1)	2(1)	2	3
Energy	1	2	1	1	2	2
Industry	1	2	2	2	2	3
Regional development	1	1	1	1	3	3
Money/credit	1	1	2(1)	2(1)	2	4
Socio-cultural						
Health	1	1	1	1	2	2
Social security[a]	1	1	1	1	2	2
Welfare[a]	1	1	1	1	1	1
Higher education/research 1	1	2	2	2	3	
Labour relations	1	1	1	1	1	2
Politico-constitutional						
Civil and property rights[a]	1	1	1	2	3	4
Civil liberties[a]	1	1	1	1	2	2(3)[d]
Citizenship	1	1	1	1	2	3
Voting and participation	1	1	1	1	2	2
Public order/policing	1	1	1	1	1	2
Defence/foreign affairs						
Defence and war	1	1	1	1	2	3(2)
Commercial negotiations	1	1	3	4	5	5
Diplomacy	1	1	2	2	2	4
Foreign aid	1	1	1	1	2	3

1: All policy decisions at national level.
2: Only some policy decisions at EU level.
3: Policy decisions at both national and EU levels.
4: Mostly policy decisions at EU level.
5: All policy decisions at EU level.
Numbers in parenthesis indicate a revaluation by the author over the original Schmitter scores.

[a]Additions to or modifications of the original.
[b]Classifications for 2001 assume full implementation of the Maastricht Treaty.
[c]By 2002 this category will be scored as 5.
[d]This score would be 4 or 5 if decisions of the European Court of Human Rights are included.

Source: Adapted from Schmitter (1996: Table 6.1) which in turn is an adaptation of Lindberg and Scheingold (1970: 67–71).

lead to military action unsupported by other EU members. In addition, EU policy towards the Balkans has typically lacked unity of purpose and action. Instead, the most decisive and effective decisions have been taken by NATO, albeit with the diplomatic support of the EU.[3]

In addition, member states continue to enjoy almost complete control over internal order. The EU has played virtually no role with regard to British action in Northern Ireland, Spanish action in the Basque country, and other national efforts to control terrorism. In no existing democratic federation are state as opposed to national security forces solely responsible for counter terrorism— although they often are with regard to crime control. Table 2.2 also implies an equal role for member states and the EU in the area of citizenship. In reality, however, and until the full implementation of the Amsterdam Treaty, national governments will continue to have the final say in the most important area of citizenship: immigration from non-EU countries. Even should the Treaty of Amsterdam be fully approved and implemented by 2004, special provisions have been made for Britain and Ireland that would leave those countries with broad discretion in this area. Finally, and as already mentioned, the EU plays almost no role in the provision of social insurance and welfare, although it does help lay down a regulatory framework relating to eligibility such as minimum retirement ages for state-provided pensions.

While it is easy to infer that continuing national control over defence, internal order, social welfare, and important aspects of citizenship disqualifies the EU from nation-state status, the historical experience of other decentralized federations suggests otherwise. Until 1812, the defence of the US was mainly in the hands of state-controlled militias. No national police authority existed in the US until the creation of the Federal Bureau of Investigation in the 1920s. States were the key providers of transfer payments to the needy until the 1930s, and in some key areas they remain so today. In Switzerland, many of these functions, including social security and the granting of citizenship, are shared between federal, state and even local governments. In other words, other federal systems display a wide variety of experiences both across systems and within the historical experience of individual countries. The EU is indeed an unusual species of federal state and in many respects remains *'un objet politique non-identifié'*, but then so do some other political systems including, arguably, both the United States and Switzerland. Political scientists have always encountered difficulties in classifying the United States. Indeed, a veritable cottage industry has been created around the theme of American exceptionalism (for a summary, see Lipset 1996). Linz and Stephan (1996: 34) have even gone so far as to label the United States a 'state-nation' rather than a nation-state because of its uniquely diffuse cultural make up. The Swiss political system also defies simple classification. Unlike most nation states, it is very difficult to identify a locus of political authority in Switzerland (for a discussion, see Linder 1998: Ch. 3). Indeed, as with the EU, some have even

---

[3] However, by mid-1999 signs of real cooperation on foreign policy and defence matters were apparent in the Kosovo crisis and in EU declarations on India, Pakistan, and Afghanistan.

questioned the *raison d'être* of the Swiss state (Steinberg 1996: Ch. 7). As will be developed in Chapters 7 and 8, politically and institutionally the EU has sufficient in common with the Swiss system to argue that they are more akin to one another than either is to 'traditional' unitary states such as France or the United Kingdom.

Adapting Federalism: Constitutions, Institutions, and Party Systems

The sometimes radical shifts towards centralization—and, more rarely, decentralization—experienced by federal systems are naturally a function of a complex mix of institutional structure and unique historical circumstances. In all cases, however, the overriding question has been how to achieve a balance between cultural and geographic diversity on the one hand and the military, economic, and social advantages of centralization on the other. What has transpired in individual cases has been shaped by the following three factors.

1. *The institutional framework of constitutions*. At their inception constitutions display varying degrees of centralization. Most constitutions delineate the division of powers between the central and state governments. In addition, some reserve to the states those powers not given to the federal government. Some vest considerable central power in national legislatures while others contrive to establish second chambers as forums for the expression and defence of state interests. If founding constitutions are unable to accommodate strong state/regional loyalties, then constitutions may be amended—a common occurrence—or, in the most extreme case, such as with the US in the 1860s, a region may secede from the union. In some cases replacement constitutions may be required, although new arrangements may not be acceptable to all parties—Canada in the 1980s and 1990s. Constitutional adaptation may, of course, be a response to centralizing rather than decentralizing trends. The Swiss constitution of 1848 replaced a more decentralist version, as did the American constitution of 1789.

2. *The interaction of formal constitutional rules with other institutions and in particular political parties*. From the above discussion we can conclude that the degree of centralization in founding constitutions is not always a good predictor of the level of centralization that develops over time. In some cases, such as Australia, decentralized constitutions are adapted to produce centralized polities. In others, like the US, a relatively centralized constitution led first to a decentralized polity but later to a more centralized system. In other cases again, like Switzerland, decentralized constitutional arrangements resulted in a decentralized polity. What transpires in individual cases depends not only on original institutional design but also on the balance of federal/state or regional power or the relative strength of state/provincial as opposed to national loyalties. In democratic political systems, this balance is always reflected in the nature of bureaucracies and, particularly, in the nature of party

systems. At the central and state/provincial levels, officials often have an interest in maintaining or building institutional bases of power; although in democratic systems parties in government place limits on their freedom of action
(Ware 1996: Ch. 12). As Riker showed some years ago, the structure of the
party system is often an effective measure of the strength of federalism.
Decentralized parties reflect a decentralized polity where state/regional loyalties are stronger and national loyalties weaker. The main indicators of party
centralization are whether the same parties operate at the national and state
levels and the degree of party discipline applicable at the national level (Riker
1975: 130–40). In some political systems, the level of centralization in the
political parties remains roughly the same through time. Political parties in
England, for example—although not, notably, in the rest of the UK—were
characterized by a high degree of centralization for all of the twentieth century. Swiss political parties, however, have remained relatively decentralized
during this period. In most systems parties change and adapt in response to
changing economic, political and social circumstances. Often, pressures for
centralized policy action conflict with provincial/state loyalties. Such was the
case with the development of the US welfare state in the 1930s and 1940s and
the Canadian welfare state in the 1950s and 1960s. In the Canadian case, the
strains on the centralizing political party—the Liberals—were such that parties
exploiting provincial loyalties—in Quebec—emerged or existing provincial
parties strengthened. In the American case, the southern wing of the
Democratic Party was able, at least at first, to exploit institutional mechanisms
in Congress in ways that satisfied the southern policy agenda.

Figure 2.1 shows the relationship between constitutional/institutional centralization and the strength of provincial as opposed to national loyalties. As
already implied, measuring the degree of constitutional and institutional centralization can be problematical. In Fig. 2.1, the category refers both to the
degree of centralization in founding constitutions and to the sort of institutional centralization engendered by parties and bureaucracies. As later chapters will show, the relationship between the two can be complex, although the
usual pattern is for constitutional and institutional centralization to be con-
vergent rather than divergent. In some cases, notably Germany, it is not possible to make an unambiguous classification. Both in structure and in
implementation, the German constitution has some notable decentralist characteristics. The position of the Länder is well protected by the constitutional
position of the upper house—the Bundesrat—and much of the administration
of federal programmes is administered by the Länder. At the same time, centralized political parties and uniform federal rules and standards suggest a high
degree of centralization.

Federations in the upper left-hand box are likely to suffer challenges to the
legitimacy of the regime as dissident regions are unable to satisfy their
demands in an institutionally centralized polity. In such cases a number of
outcomes are possible. The system may break down completely, as in the US
in the 1860s. Alternatively, the dissident region may gradually be assimilated

Level of constitutional/institutional centralization

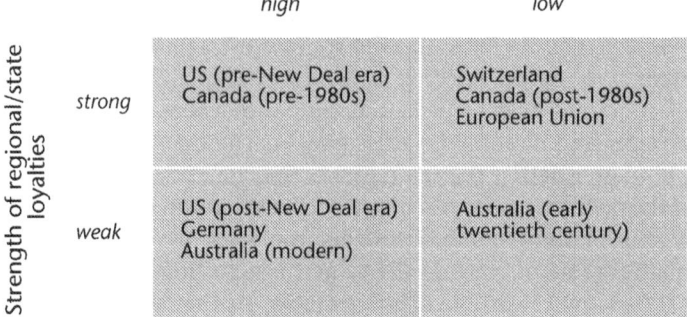

		high	low
Strength of regional/state loyalties	strong	US (pre-New Deal era) Canada (pre-1980s)	Switzerland Canada (post-1980s) European Union
	weak	US (post-New Deal era) Germany Australia (modern)	Australia (early twentieth century)

FIGURE 2.1. Regional/state loyalty and constitutional/institutional form in five federations and the European Union

into a national consciousness. Provincial loyalties may, in other words, weaken in relation to national loyalties. Such was the case with the American south after the 1960s. In the case of Canada, institutional decentralization occurred after the 1970s but in the absence of wholesale constitutional change. Similarly, strong national loyalties in Australia have resulted in a high degree of institutional centralization, especially in the party system, despite a relatively decentralized constitution.

Naturally, Fig. 2.1 fails to capture all the complexities and nuances of the six systems. One missing but very important dimension is the exact spatial distribution of citizen loyalties. In all of the five federations distinctive loyalties, whether based on culture, language, or religion, tend to be spatially concentrated in regions or provinces. Hence most of the Quebecois live in Quebec and the Swiss cantons are generally distinguishable by language and/or religion. Some of the most difficult communal problems occur when such loyalties are spatially dispersed and fail to align with jurisdictional or geographically distinct entities, as is generally the case in Bosnia, Northern Ireland, Malaysia, or the Brussels region of Belgium. Almost by definition, the EU most resembles our sample of federations: citizen loyalties are strongly aligned with national geographic and jurisdictional units.

As will be argued in later chapters, geographically concentrated loyalties are much easier to accommodate than are geographically dispersed loyalties. 'Stateness' problems which are endemic to a number of multiethnic polities including Canada and Switzerland can be ameliorated through decentralization in ways which are much more difficult to achieve in such countries as Northern Ireland or Bosnia.

3. *Political parties as agents of legitimization.* It follows that political parties are the main means not only whereby provincial grievances are aired but also whereby centralist and decentralist trends are legitimized. Students of political

legitimacy have made a distinction between those beliefs which, through the functioning of political institutions, grant the moral authority for governments, and those beliefs which sanction the proper ambit or scope of government action (see, in particular, Beetham 1991). In many federal systems, territorially distinct populations may accept the legitimacy of the central government but only on the condition that what it does in policy terms is limited in some way or other. Clearly, however, the two can be closely related: an increase in central activity or incursions into areas considered the domain of a state or region can reduce the legitimacy of the federal government. In the most extreme cases of all, of course, such as with Kosovo in relation to Serbia, *any* association with the federal entity might be considered illegitimate. Figure 2.2 attempts to place our sample of five federations and the EU in relation to these two dimensions. While such broad classifications can oversimplify— measuring both the moral authority and the scope of government activity can only be approximate—they do help facilitate analytically informed comparison. As will be shown in Chapter 4, for example, it is because citizens in English-speaking Canada broadly accept the legitimacy of the federal government, whether measured in terms of its moral authority or the scope of its activity, that political and economic concessions have repeatedly been granted to the Francophone minority. In a quite different context, most Swiss accept the moral authority of the federal government, but work hard to limit the scope of its activities. Should the scope of its activities increase beyond what is acceptable, then its moral authority would be undermined. In these and other cases, political parties are usually, although not always, the main agents responsible for the articulation of political preferences. By operating through both regional/state institutions and national institutions, parties are the main instruments through which spatially distinct public demands are met. Hence in Fig. 2.2 the state/regions in the upper-left quadrant have all been through periods when political parties with national appeals have instituted national policies and programmes. As far as the EU is concerned, at present the scope of its activities is quite limited and its moral authority relatively low. In other words, citizens in the EU member states hold more of an identity with national, or regional, units than they do with the EU (as measured by opinion poll data, see *Eurobarometer*, various years). These loyalties are, in turn, reflected in an extremely decentralized party system.[4]

In some systems, notably Switzerland and the United States, political parties may not always play this role. Instead, the party function may be augmented, or even replaced, by institutional mechanisms granting to citizens the power to participate directly in decision making through referenda and initiatives. In such cases, the authority and scope of governments may be contained through direct democracy. And in the Swiss case this may take on an

---

[4] Indeed, it may not even be sensible to talk of a European party 'system' in spite of some cohesion in the European Parliament. The fact remains that the composition of the Council and the Commission is primarily determined by national parties operating in national governments. For a discussion, see Hix and Lord (1997).

Moral authority of central government
among state/provinces

		high	low
Scope of federal government activity (in descending order)	high	Australian states German Länder Anglophone Canada Post-New Deal US south	Francophone Canada
	low	Swiss Cantons	European Union Pre-New Deal US south

FIGURE 2.2. Legitimacy of the moral authority of the federal government in relation to the scope of federal activity in five federations and the European Union

important territorial dimension whereby citizens in cantons limit central power. The crucial question for the EU, therefore, is how the EU citizenry and party systems will react and adapt as EU responsibilities grow. They may check the growth of central power through their representatives working in EU institutions. If a democratic deficit inhibits the translation of public opinion into effective institutional and policy change, then a 'stateness' problem similar to that in Quebec may emerge in one or more member states. Alternatively, through socialization and economic and political necessity, the moral authority of the EU may grow and centralizing political forces may prevail, thus pre-empting a stateness crisis. These and other possible alternatives highlight just how relevant is the experience of those countries that have already made such transitions.

In order to facilitate sensible and analytically informed comparison, it is important to establish what *sort* of issues typically mobilize centralizing or decentralizing forces. While these must of necessity differ by country and time period, economic and distributional questions are most often at the heart of intergovernmental change. Hence, during the first half of the nineteenth century, US federal-state relations were dominated by efforts to create a national bank which in turn reflected state fears that the state sources of financial credit would be damaged by national control. Later, during the New Deal economic regulation, social insurance and welfare issues dominated the agenda. These very same issues were at the core of the decentralizing policies of the 1980s and 1990s. In Switzerland, fiscal and welfare state issues have been a constant source of tension between the federal government and the states—cantons— as they have in Canada and Germany. This is not to say that non-economic/welfare state issues have been unimportant in some places and at some times. Language and religion are clearly crucial to central/state relations in Switzerland and Canada, as are culture and region in Germany and, historically, in the United States. But, as will be shown in later chapters, linguistic and other distinctions are often conflated with fiscal, welfare and other economic questions. Hence, linguistically distinctive provinces such as Quebec are not only more likely to claim unfair treatment in the distribution of federal grants and subsidies, but their claims are also more likely to be heeded, for to ignore them may well aggravate stateness problems.

This logic applies not only to language but also to cultural, ideological, religious, and ethnic distinctions. In the American south, for example, antipathy to standardized federal welfare policies led to state-federal matching funding. The resulting programmatic effects were profound: southern states achieved benefit levels far below those prevalent in the northern states. So ideological and cultural distinctiveness led to political mobilization which in turn had important distributional outcomes.

Measuring Centralization

As already suggested, measuring centralization is a complex business. Some systems—the US—are commercially centralized, but culturally quite decentralized. In others—Germany—there is a high degree of centralization in political parties and organized interest representation, but by some measures—the role of the Bundesrat—the polity is constitutionally decentralized. In order to make better sense of this complexity, political scientists have produced multifaceted indicators of centralization in political systems. However, these tend to oversimplify and are rarely good measures of how systems change over time. Hence, Lane and Ersson's institutional autonomy index embraces both constitutional/ political autonomy and the degree of freedom enjoyed by economic interests. As a result, it conflates different sorts of decentralization and therefore fails to capture the degree of regional autonomy in political systems (Lane and Ersson 1991: Ch. 6). Marks et al.'s (1996) regional autonomy index is more useful, mainly because it includes a quite sophisticated measure of federalism.[5] However, they apply it to EU states alone, only two of which—Belgium and Germany—are true federal systems. If applied *exclusively* to federal states, the index would be high for the whole sample and would thus miss those important intra-system differences that are typical of federations. One of the strengths of the Marks et al.'s index, however, is that it attempts to measure the role of regions, or states, in central government. In a sense, this is the most important indicator of all, because in the most decentralized systems—confederations—the governments of the constituent states effectively

---

[5] They assign a score of 0 to 4 to their sample of EU states. 0 signifies no regional government, 1 signifies some regional governments with a limited role, 2 signifies systems with regional government with more extensive competencies, 3 signifies a federal state with high levels of autonomy ,and 6 federal states where regional governments significantly affect national decision making (Marks *et al.* 1996: Table 3.2).

control the central government. Similarly, in the EU the Council of Ministers, which is made up of the representatives of the member states, retains the unanimity voting rule for the most fundamental policy areas: enlargement and revenue sources. For this reason, an attempt will be made to assess the influence of state or provincial governments on each of our five sample federations and to gauge how this influence has changed over time.

Of course, measuring the influence of the states in the national arena constitutes a further challenge. Some years ago Riker and Schaps produced a 'disharmony index' which was specifically designed to measure the degree of centralization in federations. The disharmony index was based on two measures:

1. Whether or not the party in control of the national government is in control of the constituent governments. If the nationally controlling party cannot win in state and provincial elections—as often happens in the United States and usually happens in Canada—then it can hardly hope to bring about a centralized party structure of a centralized constitution.
2. Whether or not party discipline exists on legislative and executive matters. If party members can act together, then they can hope to centralize, otherwise not (Riker and Schaps 1957: 280).

While, strictly speaking, this index is a measure of disharmony rather than decentralization, it is clear that the degree of party control over the national government and the degree of discipline at the centre can be good surrogate measures of the degree of state/provincial control over central governments. In the EU context, for example, party control of the national government is, through party government influence in the Council of Ministers, very extensive. At the same time, party discipline in the EP is low, as it is, by definition, for unanimity votes in the Council (for a discussion and references, see McKay 1999*b*: Ch. 7). Thus by this measure, the EU is highly decentralized. However, there are a number of problems associated with the index. Party discipline may be low at the national level, as it is often the case in multiparty systems, but political and administrative arrangements may none the less be highly centralized, as in the Netherlands or Italy before 1990. Spatially defined party control is a more useful measure, but even here problems abound. In the US, the same parties often control state and national governments, but very little in the way of organizational connective tissue between them exists. In other systems, locally controlled parties may have much in common with the incumbent national party: the CSU and CDU in Germany. Even when the opposition SPD is in government, the CSU shares with it support for the viability of the federal state. In other cases, however, as with the Scottish Nationalists, Sinn Fein and the Parti Quebecois, the regional parties may question the legitimacy of the national party's right to govern.

For these reasons the present study will not employ the disharmony index or any other composite index of centralization. Instead, and following Watts (1996: Ch. 8) it will draw broad distinctions between jurisdictional, administrative, and financial decentralization, and apply quantitative measures only to financial decentralization. Jurisdictional decentralization refers to the allocation of powers between different levels of government, which may be constitutionally mandated or shaped by the interaction of national legislatures and state/regional governments. How programmes and policies are administered is also a function of constitutional and political factors; and the degree of administrative autonomy enjoyed by lower-level governments can be an important indicator of decentralization. The degree of financial decentralization—grants in aid to lower-level governments, transfers to individuals, and other financial flows—is relatively easy to identify and to measure. In addition, the degrees of tax autonomy enjoyed by states and provinces are not only a good indicator of centralization, but, like fiscal flows, are also easy to identify.

While state/provincial autonomy will be measured primarily in fiscal terms, an attempt will be made to assess the *general* influence which states and regions exert on national institutions and decision-makers. This usually translates into how, precisely, decision rules operate in national political institutions. In some instances, notably in Switzerland and Germany, constitutions specifically limit the power of central institutions and delineate the powers of the states. In addition, constitutions often assign powers to upper houses specifically to protect the position of states and provinces. Such was certainly the case with the US, Germany, and Switzerland. In other cases non-constitutional institutions, such as the First Ministers Conference in Canada and the Premiers Conference in Australia, take on this role. Sometimes, custom and convention play a part. In Switzerland, for example, it is customary to limit political conflict by assigning some powers and responsibilities in government to representatives of all the main political parties.

Conclusion

The main purpose of this chapter has been to demonstrate that much can be learnt from systematic comparison between the EU and the five sample federations that are the subject of this study. The EU can be considered an evolving species of federal state, albeit a highly decentralized one. European Union citizenship now exists even if the loyalty of most Europeans remains with national or regional governments rather than with the federal government. The EU has also acquired a constitution, which, like the other federations, delineates central—federal—as opposed to state—member state—jurisdictional and administrative powers. As in the other countries, an institutional framework is in place to ensure the effective representation of the constituent states in the decision making process. The EU also has acquired a complex system of intergovernmental financial relations with centrally administered grants and central control of macroeconomic policy, including member-state borrowing.

What the EU lacks, of course, is an historical experience of state-federal economic and political interaction. If, as many would argue, the federal status of the EU dates only from the implementation of the Treaty on European Union—the Maastricht Treaty—then this historical experience is short in the extreme. It is this fact, above all, which makes comparative study based on the historical evolution of other federations so relevant.

3

The United States: The Rise and Fall of Territorial Politics

Constitutional Origins and the Territorial Dimension

FOLLOWING the experience of the Articles of Confederation, the US constitution was a conscious attempt to centralize political authority in the federal government. Established in 1781, the Articles vested very little power in Congress and failed to establish either an executive or a judiciary. And while the Congress was given the power to declare war and raise an army and navy, it depended on subventions from the state legislatures to finance the armed forces. In addition, each of the 13 states could issue its own paper money and raise barriers to trade with other states. These essentially confederal arrangements greatly restricted the ability of the new country to generate wealth and to raise taxes. Most importantly, national security was compromised given the absence of a strong central authority with the power to finance a war effort: a fact forcefully noted by Alexander Hamilton, in the *Federalist Papers* (Hamilton *et al.* 1961: 25–35).

The primary task for the 55 delegates at the Philadelphia convention in 1787, therefore, was the creation of a federal government with sufficient authority over the states to provide for economic growth and national security. While this is clearly not the place even to attempt to summarize the many millions of words written on the origins of the US constitution, two crucial points on the proceedings need to be made. There is, first, the fact that in spite of strong localist or provincial sentiment in the states, the new constitution produced highly centralized institutions. States were effectively excluded from national decision making. Only with regard to the equal representation of the states in the Senate were the states given access to central power. But, as will be discussed in the next section, the constitution gave to the states no formal means whereby Senators could be mandated or instructed to act on the states' behalf. This formal detachment of state from federal government is further demonstrated by the very specific ways in which the constitution mandated federal institutions, notably Congress and the Courts, to act directly on individual citizens rather than affect them indirectly through the states. So from the very beginning the federal government could tax, recruit, police and judge its citizens free from state influence (for a discussion see Riker 1955:). In addition, the constitution (Article 1, Section 10) expressly forbade the states to enter into treaties or agreements with one another: 'No state shall, without the consent of Congress . . . enter into any agreement or compact with another State, or with a foreign power.' Thus no group of states could come together and formally challenge the authority of the federal government. Finally, although the Tenth Amendment to the Constitution—'The powers not delegated to the United States by the Constitution, nor prohibited by it to the States are reserved to the States . . . '—has often been interpreted as a protection of states rights, the fact remains that the constitution actually assigned a great deal of potential responsibility to the federal government. This included the right to levy taxes, raise armies, and regulate interstate commerce. Article 1 Section 8 actually assigns 18 specific powers to Congress which, in contemporary eighteenth century terms, amounted to the equivalent of the sort of powers exercized by unitary governments at the time.

The federal government's very prominent position in relation to the states did not mean, of course, that power was centralized *within* the federal government. On the contrary, bicameralism and the separation of powers greatly limited what one branch could do on its own. In this sense, the formal arrangements of the constitution clearly represent a compromise between the need to establish central control on the one hand, and on the other hand limiting the ability of both simple majorities and any particular faction or interest from exercizing undue influence on the federal government (Hamilton *et al.* 1961).

All of the above refer to the formal constitutional arrangements between federal and state governments. *Politically*, the late eighteenth-century reality was characterized by what might be called *asymmetric dual federalism*. The system was dual in the sense that both the federal government and the states had distinctive and complete political institutions with each capable of acting on citizens independently of the other (for a discussion, see Kincaid 1996: 30–4). But the state legislatures remained the main focus of authority for citizens. It was the framework of state law and public policy that moulded the relationship between the citizen and political authority. The new federal government actually did very little in policy terms. Indeed, even the defence function was vested primarily in state militias rather than in a federal force; the constitution assigns more space and detail to these militias than to any other policy responsibility (for an extensive discussion, see Riker 1955). From the very beginning, serious disputes emerged on the nature of federal power and these disputes in turn reflected very different conceptions of nationhood among the leaders of the young republic. During these first few years, two distinct views on the nature of territorial power in the new country could be discerned which reflect the ideas of the two the main architects of the constitution, Hamilton and Madison. For Alexander Hamilton, the primary task for the new country was to build what Samuel Beer has called the 'national idea'. Hamilton greatly feared that the size of the country would encourage the growth of state as opposed to national identities. But only in national identity could the country prosper and liberty be adequately defended. As Beer puts it: '[His] nation-alism was 'expressed . . . in his belief that Americans were "one people" rather than thirteen separate peoples' (Beer 1993: 5). Because Hamilton believed that the new constitutional arrangements would fail to prevent such a decentraliz-ing trend, he argued that the new national government should take on the role of nation builder by actively pursuing the construction of national insti-tutions, and in particular a national bank.

James Madison shared with Hamilton a conviction that America needed a stronger federal government, but unlike Hamilton he believed that the particular arrangements arrived at in Philadelphia would achieve a near per-fect balance between central and regional power. The constitution's checks and balances would contain central power, whereas federalism would, by frag-menting power in a large diverse country, prevent oppressive government. In essence Madison was arguing that large units produce greater choice and a 'greater variety of parties' (quoted in Elkins and McKitrick 1993: 87). With more competition no one party or state would dominate the others. It is important to stress that Madison was embracing pluralism rather than sec-tionalism. His vision of what he called the 'Compound Republic' was founded on his conviction that, given the opportunity, economic, religious, and other factions would do all they could to advance their interests at the expense of others. The complex institutional structure of the republic would prevent this.

The political reality in 1789, however, was that the Founding Fathers had produced a constitution which was highly amenable to the accumulation of centralized power. At the same time, localist sentiment remained strong and this became increasingly so as the distinctive socioeconomic structure of the southern states *vis-à-vis* the northern states became ever more apparent. The stage was set, therefore, for a conflict between sectionalist loyalties and a cen-tralized institutional structure.

The National Idea and the Rise of Sectionalism, 1800–61

The most decentralist element in an otherwise centralized constitution was the election of senators by the state legislatures. The potential existed, there-fore, for the legislatures to instruct senators how to vote. In this way, the states could exercise a direct influence on national affairs. In fact, a great debate took place over what was called the 'doctrine of instructions'. A number of states insisted that it was within their prerogative to instruct elected senators on matters of public policy and several did so in the period 1780–1840. Instructions would only work, of course, if effective sanctions against wayward senators were available. Under the Articles of Confederation, national legisla-tors were frequently recalled by the state legislatures, but senators were in a quite different position. Elected for six years and operating in a chamber which was the equal of the House of Representatives, senators soon put the prestige and status of national office before any obligations they may have had to their state legislators, most of whom sat for only one or two years before an election. As Riker notes, some resignations were forced on recalcitrant senators, and especially those from the south; but the sanction became less and less effective after 1840 (Riker 1955: 454–8).

As the United States grew in economic and military strength, so the conflict between the national idea and states rights became more acute. Denied direct access to national decision making in what was a centralized federal polity, the states were increasingly obliged to rely on the support of individual spokesmen in national government and on intellectual debate. During the period down to 1812, nationalizing forces were on the ascendant as the US expanded territorially and fought a war with Britain over the status of Canada. For the next 25 years the question as to whether the US could establish a national bank dominated federal-state relations. The issues involved in the creation of a national bank were very similar to those surrounding the creation of the first national bank in 1791. Those who believed that the powers of the US government were strictly circumscribed—including, originally, Madison and Thomas Jefferson—argued that the Congress had no right to establish a bank as this represented an infringement of states rights. Above all, agrarian interests saw in a concentration of power in a central bank the threat of monopoly power and the prospect of the withdrawal of credit extended to small farmers by state-chartered banks. To this end a Jefferson-dominated Congress refused to renew the bank's charter in 1811.

Congress chartered the second Bank of the United States (BUS) in 1817. Unlike the first national bank, the BUS could establish branches in the various states. It was perceived, therefore, as a direct threat to the much weaker state banks. Almost immediately, the Maryland legislature levied a tax on the notes of the new bank, claiming that it was a 'foreign corporation'. A lawsuit ensued which was eventually appealed to the Supreme Court in the famous *McCulloch v. Maryland* case. In his Opinion of the Court, Chief Justice John Marshall argued that the constitution of the United States emanated not from a compact of the states but directly from the people. As such, the federal government could do anything mandated to it by the constitution. As Marshall put it:

The government of the Union, though limited in its powers, is supreme within its sphere of action . . . Let the end be legitimate, let it be within the scope of the constitution, and all means which are appropriate, which are plainly adapted to that end, which are not prohibited, but consist with the letter and spirit of the Constitution, are constitutional . . . The states have no power by taxation or otherwise, to retard, impede, burden or in any manner control, the operation of the constitutional laws enacted by Congress to carry into execution the powers vested in the general government. (Cited in Morison and Commager 1962: 436)

This decision proved highly controversial, and with the election of states-rights supporter Andrew Jackson in 1828 the BUS along with other nationalizing policies came under constant attack. Eventually, Jackson vetoed the bill rechartering the bank in 1832; and not until the creation of the Federal Reserve in 1913 did the United States acquire a central banking system.

Opposition to the bank was based on a fundamental disagreement on the nature of federal power. For states-rights supporters such as John C. Calhoun of South Carolina, the federal government was a creation of the states and the citizens of the states, not of the American people. Hence:

The very idea of an *American People*, as constituting a single community, is a mere chimera. Such a community never for a single moment existed—neither before nor since the Declaration of Independence . . . [each state is] . . . a separate sovereign community. (Cited in Beer 1993: 8)

Calhoun also supported what he called 'nullification', or the right of what he considered sovereign state legislatures to nullify national legislation judged to be against the interests of the state. In effect, Calhoun and his supporters supported the right of the states to secede should they be faced with an 'illegitimate' exercize of federal power.[1] This extreme position differed markedly from that of other leaders associated with states rights. For such luminaries as James Madison, Thomas Jefferson and Andrew Jackson, limiting federal power was a means of guaranteeing liberty and democracy. For Calhoun, state sovereignty took precedence over other values and it was up to the individual states to establish the appropriate relationship between government and citizen.

From 1820 all the way through to outbreak of the civil war in 1861, this tension between nationalism and state sovereignty dominated political discourse. The issues around which debate took place were slavery and the tariff. Southern plantation owners opposed any extension of tariffs on imported goods, while the increasingly industrial north called for protection from British competition. In 1861 Congress passed the Morrill tariff—the most protectionist measure enacted since 1832—but only because southern congressional delegations had withdrawn from Congress. Slavery was by far the more important issue. It dominated political debate at the time and was the immediate cause of southern secession. Northern opposition to slavery had been growing for some decades and by the 1850s the American party system had become polarized on the issue of slavery.

In the three decades before the creation of a Republican Party in 1854, the party system gradually lost ideological and organizational coherence. Under the banner of equality, democracy, and states rights, Andrew Jackson's Democratic Party had consolidated its strength among agrarian interests, north and south, as well as urban workers in the north. The much less successful Whig Party was created in response to Jackson's egalitarianism and relied on support from northern capitalists and nativists as well as southern plantation owners. This nascent class divide clearly cut across the sectional divide in American politics and as the salience of the territorial issue increased so the appeal of the two main parties waned. The upshot was the emergence

---

[1] The Kentucky and Virginia Resolves of 1798 also claimed state sovereignty but fell short of asserting the rights of the states to nullify national laws. For a discussion, see Riker (1964: Ch. 4).

of a new Republican Party specifically devoted to limiting any extension of slavery to the unorganized territories. It won support from northern elites and, increasingly, northern industrial workers and plains farmers. Meanwhile the rump of the Democratic Party became a predominantly southern party. The landslide victory of the Republicans in the 1860 presidential election sounded the death knell for the viability of the union. Intent on limiting any extension of slavery to the territories, Lincoln and the Republican Congress became anathema to the southern legislatures who were convinced that the Congress was acting unconstitutionally. This is clear from a number of contemporary accounts, including confederate President Jefferson Davis, who claimed that the north was guilty of 'persistent abuse of the powers . . . delegated to Congress' (cited in Beer 1993: 15).

On 20 December 1860, the South Carolina legislature voted unanimously for secession, declaring that 'the Union now subsisting between South Carolina and other states under the name of "The United States of America" is hereby dissolved' (quoted in Morison and Commager 1962: 667). By February 1861 a further six states had seceded and the Confederate States of America was created on 8 February 1861. Lincoln's response was swift and unambiguous. In his appeal to Congress for war powers he declared:

Originally some dependent colonies made the Union, and, in turn, the Union threw off their old dependence for them, and made them States . . . The Union and not themselves separately, produced their independence and liberty. By conquest or purchase the Union gave to each of them whatever independence or liberty it has. The Union is older then any of the States and, in fact, it created them as States. (Quoted in Beer 1993: 13)

What is interesting about this *ante bellum* period is the very limited role played by national institutions, including the political parties, in mediating disputes between the states and the federal government. Indeed, it was a national institution, the Supreme Court, that through the 1857 Dredd Scott decision helped precipitate the crisis. In this infamous case the Court argued that even a slave freed in territories north of the Mason Dixie line remained a slave in law. Thus the Court approved an extension of the slave culture of the south to the unorganized northern territories and declared the Missouri Compromise invalid (for a discussion, see Fehrenbacher 1976). Within Congress, a coalition of northern and southern Democrats, encouraged by a weakened President Pierce, had in 1854 forced through Congress the Kansas Nebraska Act, which gave to the settlers of the new territories the right to decide on slave or non-slave status. This helped weaken the Democrats in the north and, once the new Republican Party captured Congress in the 1858 midterm elections, the party system was, for the first time, unambiguously sectional in nature. In the 1860 presidential election the Democrats could not agree on a candidate and fielded one for the northern states and one for the south. Lincoln's name did not even appear on the ballot in ten of the southern states. Events had come to such a pass that Lincoln's generally conciliatory stance on the slavery issue became irrelevant. In effect the shots were being called not by national leaders and national parties but by the southern *state legislatures*. And once they voted for secession, Lincoln and the Republicans had no choice but to challenge by force of arms what they considered an illegal and revolutionary act.

Secession was a direct result of failure of national leaders and national institutions to reach a compromise on the slavery issue. In the absence of mediating forces, confrontation between the national Republican Party and the southern legislatures became inevitable. The distributional/economic dimension, which was at the heart of the slavery issue, also assumed an ideological dimension that was to prove important for many decades after the end of the civil war. In sum, while the north championed democratic values such as free speech universal male suffrage, the south became increasingly associated with elitist, anti-democratic values (for a discussion, see A. Schlesinger 1953: Ch. 36).

The New Federal Bargain: Accommodating the South, 1870–1940

Following the civil war, there was remarkably little constitutional change. Three amendments to the constitution—the 13th, the 14th, and the 15th— abolished slavery, guaranteed due process and the equal protection of the laws, and gave the right to vote to all American (male) citizens. These apart, the centralized American constitutional structure remained as it was before the war. Following the reconstruction period which lasted from 1866 until the early 1870s, white southerners gradually reasserted their control over southern politics. During the ensuing 60 years two key developments are of note.

First, *paternalism replaced slavery in the southern agrarian economy*. During the 1880s and 1890s all the southern legislatures enacted laws which restricted the freedoms of the African-American population. These ranged from poll taxes and literacy tests designed to restrict voting to laws mandating the formal segregation of the races in education, housing and public accommodations. There was a clear economic dimension to this development: most blacks were poor tenants or sharecroppers in farms leased by white landowners. Abolition had increased the cost of labour; and, to compensate, southern planters created new contracts tying former slaves to former masters. Alston and Ferrie (1999: Ch. 1) show that employers provided a range of benefits, from covering tenants' debts to funding small schoolhouses, in order to keep their labour force intact. Economic and political power was also increasingly concentrated in the planter class. Before the war, smallholders and artisans shared power with the planters. After the war, the south acquired a much more stratified political culture. Southern distinctiveness was founded on its two-class, anti-democratic political system, which in turn derived from the unique character of its agrarian base.[2] Other regions of the United States, including the most of the west and mid-west, remained predominantly agricultural even as industrialization proceeded apace during the last quarter of the century. But nowhere else did agrarian paternalism prevail. The politics of paternalism and race also became indistinguishable from Democratic politics. The civil war had effectively expunged the Republicans from the southern scene. And the reassertion of white supremacy was led exclusively by southern Democrats. Successive Supreme Court decisions, often penned by southern justices, greatly restricted the application of the 14th and 15th amendments to the states and helped legitimize the segregationist 'Jim Crow' laws enacted after 1890. In effect, the US had acquired a two-and-a-half party system. Northern Democrats and northern Republicans continued to compete for the votes of farmers and workers in the north, while in the south a one-party system prevailed. To be sure, there were factions and splits within the south, but the Democrats retained a monopoly of political power (the definitive study of southern politics in this period is Key 1949).

Second, *southern politicians exploited federal institutions to advance their own policy agenda.* The emergence of a one-party south had profound consequences for American politics and American federalism. Within Congress, southerners, with their long tenures in office, began to monopolize the leading parliamentary positions, and especially so with the rise of the standing committees and their sub-committees during the first quarter of the twentieth century. By the 1930s committee chairs were able to set the legislative agenda and wield effective vetoes on specific items of legislation. The centripetal influence exercized by party and party leadership correspondingly declined (on the House, see Polsby *et al.* 1969; on the Senate, Matthews 1960). Committee chairs were, therefore, in the perfect position to bargain both within Congress and with successive presidents for public policies deemed to be in the interests of the dominant southern elites. On the broader electoral scene, northern Democrats could win the presidency only with the support of the south. These developments transformed the role played by the south in distributional public policy. Prior to the civil war, southern political leaders had always opposed, as an affront to states rights, what were called at the time federally-led 'internal improvements'. Usually, this opposition was based on the belief that federal intervention in such areas as banking and transportation would lead to the domination of the southern economy by northern interests (Morison and Commager 1962: Ch. 25). Following the rise of the one-party south, however, Democrats were perfectly placed to use their Washington base to broker federal legislation on their terms. Initially, two issues—economic development and race—dominated this agenda, to which a third—welfare—was added later.

---

[2] The 'south' was, of course, far from being homogeneous whether judged in political, economic, or social terms. Large tracts of the south, including areas in Tennessee, Kentucky, and West Texas, were not part of the plantation political economy. None the less they shared with the other southern states a sense of grievance over the outcome and aftermath of the civil war. For a vivid account of southern culture, see Cash (1969).

Although southern Democratic leaders were conservative on most issues, they generally welcomed federal largesse in the form of grants in aid for infrastructure development and the like. Hence southern members of Congress supported the Federal Highways Act of 1921, which established an interstate network of roads in the south (Billington 1984: 61). Later, in the early New Deal, southern support for the National Recovery Administration and farming subsidies, although weaker than in the north, was substantial. As far as race was concerned, southern preferences were clear: under no circumstances would federal interference with southern racist society be tolerated. They were successful in achieving this objective all the way until after World War II, when close cooperation between northern Blacks and liberals and the southern Democrats became unsustainable.

Later, when New Deal programmes turned to labour relations, welfare, and social security, southern politicians extracted from the Roosevelt administration crucial concessions that helped shape the whole of the New Deal. In the early Roosevelt years, southern political power was enhanced by a tacit deal between Roosevelt and the southern contingent. As Alston and Ferries (1999: 44) note: 'Support for the New Deal was exchanged for a relatively free hand in writing and rewriting legislation to fit the peculiarities of the South.' In specific terms this meant the exclusion of agricultural workers from pensions and other benefits under the 1935 Social Security Act and the institution of state-federal matching funds for public assistance under Aid for Families with Dependent Children (AFDC). The latter resulted in greatly varying benefit levels by state, with the southern states providing the lowest benefits. This system lasted almost until the end of the twentieth century[3] (Table 3.3; for a discussion, see Bell 1965; Skocpol 1995). In addition, southern congressional power assured the abolition in 1943 of the Farm Security Administration, which had provided tenant farmers with a measure of security unacceptable to landlords (Alston and Ferrie 1999: Ch. 4).

So, in contrast to the *ante bellum* period, the years from 1870 through to 1940 were characterized by a steady incorporation of southern influence into national decision making. This was facilitated both by changes in the party system and by institutional changes in Congress. The Democratic Party evolved into two distinct parts, one southern and conservative and the other northern and, after 1932, liberal and interventionist. Democratic presidential candidates were required to accommodate the south in order to guarantee victory. They were also obliged to appoint southerners to leading positions in government, and especially in the judiciary. Within Congress, the rise of committee power and the decline of party leadership greatly enhanced the positions of southern members with seniority. This was especially so in the Senate, where the exploitation of parliamentary rules by prominent southerners gave them an effective veto over national legislation (Huitt 1965). Institutional

[3] Not until the passage of the Personal Responsibility and Work Opportunity Reconciliation Act in 1996 was the AFDC system overhauled. The effect of this law was to devolve almost all responsibility for welfare provision to the states. For an account see Cammisa (1998).

changes in Congress also had the effect of further fragmenting an already complex policy process. In order to achieve results, organized interests were obliged to focus their efforts on individual committees and sub-committees. Lobbying efforts were, therefore, organized by programme or sub-programme rather than across programmes and issues. This fragmentation extended to the new federal bureaucracies created by the New Deal. Congress helped shape the new agencies and bureaus that in turn reflected the complexity of the congressional committee system (on Congress, see Fenno 1973; on the bureaucracy, see Wilson 1989: Ch. 13).

Outside the south, a gradual decline in sectional politics occurred. Most of the states of New England, long a Republican stronghold, voted for Roosevelt in 1936 and by the 1950s as many New England states were in the Democratic as in the Republican camp. Elsewhere, the two 'northern' parties competed for votes more on the basis of ideology than sectional appeal. Even in the midwest and west, where Republican support was, until the 1930s, generally on the ascendant, sufficient party competition existed to prevent the emergence of a territorial rather than ideological politics. It is true that the oppositional Populist—and to a lesser extent Progressive—movements did have strong regional support in the agrarian west and mid-west, but even in these cases it was issues, not region, that dominated their political agenda. And in just a few decades, the populists were reincorporated into mainstream American politics (see McConnell 1969). In sum, the south was different. Not only did southerners carry the historical baggage of the civil war; they also represented a distinctive socioeconomic region. Beginning in the 1950s, however, changes to the southern economy precipitated social and political changes that eventually were to transform the special territorial status of the south within the union.

The Decline of Territorial Politics, 1940–2000

The most enduring legacy of the New Deal was the nationalization of American politics and the centralization of public policy. This can be measured in a number of ways. In terms of regulation, the New Deal greatly increased the role of the federal government in economy and society. This applied both to direct federal influence on individuals and firms and to federal influence on state and local governments. Federal spending also increased from 2.6 per cent of GDP in 1929 to 9.4 per cent in 1939. By 1959, this had increased to 18.5 per cent largely as a result of greatly increased defence spending (Table 3.1). Meanwhile state and local own-source government expenditure rose from 7.4 per cent in 1929 to just 8.1 per cent in 1959 (Table 3.1). Intergovernmental grants in aid also increased during these years. Federal grants to state and local governments constituted just 1 per cent of GDP in 1929, increasing to 1.1 per cent in 1939 and 1.4 per cent in 1959 (Table 3.1). Public perceptions of the federal role also changed during this period. And while no public opinion data exist prior to the 1930s, Fig. 3.1 does show how, during that decade, most Americans viewed the federal government favourably in relation to state government. In effect, the Great Depression had exposed the inadequacies of state provision in social and economic policy. As a result increasing numbers of Americans turned to the federal government for help.

Table 3.1. Federal spending, federal grants, and state/local own-source spending as percentage of GDP, 1929–1979

Year	All federal spending	Domestic spending	State/local own-source spending	Federal grants
1929	2.6	1.5	7.4	0.1
1939	9.9	8.1	9.4	1.1
1949	16.1	7.5	6.9	0.9
1959	18.5	7.7	8.1	1.4
1969	19.8	9.9	10.3	2.1
1979	20.8	15.0	9.9	3.2

Source: ACIR (1988), adapted from Table 1.

The trends established during the period 1930–60 were to continue through to 1980. By 1979 federal spending reached 20.8 per cent of GDP, while grants to state and local governments soared to 3.2 per cent of GDP. Meanwhile, as expressed as a percentage of GDP, state and local own-source expenditures remained almost unchanged at 9.9 per cent of GDP in 1970: almost the same figure as in 1939 (Table 3.1).

What is interesting about this transformed federal role is that it developed parallel to, rather than as part of, the changes that were buffeting sectional politics during the same period. As was stressed in the last section, by the 1940s the unique position of southern politicians in national politics was well established. Public policy had been profoundly affected by southern influence. In particular, the Roosevelt administrations turned a blind eye towards the racial politics of the south in exchange for southern support for a centralizing New Deal agenda. By the 1940s, however, the policy agenda had changed. Migration to the northern industrial cities and military mobilization raised the political consciousness of African-Americans throughout the United States. As Democrats and supporters of an active federal role, they increasingly pressured northern Democrats on the segregation and discrimination issues. Northern white liberals, too, were increasingly uncomfortable with the positions taken by their southern fellow Democrats. The seeds were, therefore, sown for major conflicts within the party.

At the same time, the race issue increasingly dominated the southern Democrats' policy agenda. During the New Deal era—and before—they had supported federal spending on infrastructure and economic development, although they remained firmly opposed to welfare and social security as well as federal interventions in the labour market and anything that might undermine southern tenants' dependence on landlords. After the war, this pattern continued: southerners continued to support infrastructure spending, including investment in defence installations, but they remained adamantly opposed to welfare spending. Moreover, the most rapidly growing item on the federal budget after 1960 was transfer payments to the old and the needy.

Migration and mechanization had by 1960 changed the face of southern agriculture. No longer was the paternalistic landlord-tenant relationship at the heart of southern politics. Even so, southern white politicians continued to defend the subordination of blacks in all aspects of social and economic life. So even while the original economic rationale for the subordination of African-Americans had been greatly weakened, racism remained at the heart of southern politics. It is in this context that the position of southern politicians in national politics should be understood. Within the Democratic Party, the tensions were such that in the 1948 election several southern states split with the Democrats to vote for the Dixiecrats (Table 3.2). Throughout the 1950s, southern Democrats in Congress contrived to veto any effective civil rights and welfare legislation through their command of congressional committees and use of such parliamentary devices such as the Senate filibuster (Sinclair 1999). Once again in national office after 1960, the Democratic Party became increasingly associated with a centralizing liberalism and support for federal intervention in economy and society. In 1968 the deep south broke

Table 3.2. Percentage of state and Congressional seats won by Democrats in the south,[a] selected years 1936–1996

Year	% states won by Democrat candidates, presidential elections, southern states	% House seats won by southern Democratic candidates	% Senate seats won by southern Democratic candidates
1936	100	98	100
1948	100[b]	98.1	100
1960	60	94.2	100
1972	0	68.4	68.2
1980	10	64.5	54.4
1988	0	66.4	68.2
1992	30	61.6	59.1
1996	30	43.2	31.8

[a]Ten southern states.
[b]Four states—South Carolina, Mississippi, Alabama, Louisiana—won by State Rights Democrat candidate Strom Thurmond of South Carolina; six states vote for Harry Truman, the official Democratic candidate.

Sources: Presidential elections: US Department of Commerce, *Statistical Abstract of the United States* (various years). Congressional elections: Ornstein, Mann, and Malbin (1998), adapted from Tables 1.2 and 1.4.

away from the Democrats to support racist presidential candidate, George Wallace. Thereafter, the southern states increasingly deserted to the Republicans in presidential elections, and, slowly but surely, also at the congressional level (Table 3.2; for a detailed account of these changes, see Scher 1997).

Until the 1970s, however, the southerners' institutional base in Congress remained intact. As Ornstein, Mann, and Malbin (1992) note, southern Democrats dominated almost all of the key standing committees in Congress all the way through to the end of the 1960s. As a result, liberal Democrats had to rely on large congressional majorities to ensure the passage of civil rights and Great Society legislation. Not until the elections of 1964 did such a majority emerge. This accounts for the failure of the Kennedy administration to make any real headway in civil rights and social policy in the 1961–3 period. After 1966, when their majority was reduced by Republican advances in the mid-term elections, southern Democrats managed to veto most new liberal initiatives.[4] Until very late in history, therefore, southern legislatures together with southern Democrats in Congress not only managed to delay the legal emancipation of southern Blacks, but also continued to compromise or delay a wide range of social policy legislation. Not until major institutional reforms in Congress greatly weakened the powers of committee chairs and the seniority rule in the early 1970s was the grip of the southern Democrats broken (for a discussion, see Rieselbach. 1986). For the purposes of our argument, two developments in the 1975–2000 period are worthy of note. First, the steady advance of the Republicans in the south dramatically reduced the political distinctiveness of the region. The Republicans were—and remain—the conservative party in American politics, but by the 1980s this conservatism had only a very loose territorial dimension. Republicans had become strong in the mountain and western states as well as the south, but, depending on the election, their appeal could also be national in nature. For the first time since the before the civil war—and possibly since the founding of the Republic—the United States acquired a genuinely national politics. Differences in ideology and interest were increasingly mediated by national politicians operating in national institutions.

The second and related point is that as the Republicans advanced in national politics so many of the values and interests of the south became conflated with those of conservatives throughout the United States. These included fiscal conservatism, opposition to federal spending and intergovernmental aid—especially on welfare-related programmes—and support for defence spending. What was missing from this agenda was the issue that had dominated the old south: the subordination of blacks in southern agriculture. Instead, southern conservatives espoused issues of national concern. Race became secondary to their main purpose: the advance of the conservative

---

[4] A notable exception was the 1968 Civil Rights Act, whose passage was precipitated only in the wake of the assassination of Martin Luther King Jr. See McKay (1997: Ch. 3).

position in national politics.[5] This they were successful in doing. By the 1990s, national conservative leaders such as House Speaker Newt Gingrich of Georgia and Senate majority leader Trent Lott of Mississippi became prominent as *national* rather than *southern* figures.

The Territorial Dimension of Intergovernmental Aid

Southern political and economic distinctiveness was to have what look like quite perverse effects on federal aid to the states. Other things being equal, it would be expected that a rebellious region which had suffered a devastating civil war with the union, followed by a 70-year period of relative economic and social stagnation, would be in a good position to bargain for special treatment from the federal government. Add to this the privileged institutional position of southern members of Congress resulting from the combination of a one-party system and advantageous parliamentary rules, and the scene should be set for the flow of federal largesse to the south. However, rather than bargain for extra federal aid, members instead made the defence of southern paternalism their top priority. Often this translated into opposition to welfare and social spending generally. Indeed, as far as welfare was concerned, southern legislatures took their cues from their allies in Congress and contrived to *reduce* spending on welfare to the lowest in the union. Even by 1990, the south continued to lag the rest of the country in terms of benefit levels. Eligibility rules were also strictest in the region, thus reducing the percentage of the population on welfare below that of much richer regions (Table 3.3). And while after the civil war southern opposition to 'internal improvements' was replaced by an acceptance of the need for federally funded infrastructure spending, such investments took up a smaller and smaller proportion of total federal aid, especially after the implementation of the Great Society programmes.

Paul Peterson has distinguished between infrastructure investment (developmental spending) and welfare/social investment (redistributive spending). Between 1962 and 1990 developmental federal spending increased from 4.22 per cent of GNP to 5.24 per cent, while redistributive spending increased from 4.78 per cent to 10.26 per cent (Peterson 1995: Table 3.2).[6] Admittedly, these figures in part relate to a period when southern congressional power was on the wane, but for most of the social programmes the die was caste by the 1960s. The 1935 Social Security Act continued to form the basic architecture of both welfare and social security through to the late 1990s. And the design of some of the 1960s social programmes, including medical assistance for the

---

[5] While this is broadly true, among African-Americans the Republicans became associated not with overt racist politics but with encouraging policies which would retard the erosion of *de facto* segregation. See Scher (1997: Ch. 4).

[6] Developmental spending includes transport, natural resources, safety, education, and utilities, while redistributive includes pensions, welfare, health hospitals, and housing (Peterson 1995: Table 3.2).

Table 3.3. Average Aid for Dependent Family payments per family in selected regions and AFDC population as a percentage of regional population, 1990

	US	South[a]	ENC[b]	Pacific[c]
Average AFDC monthly payment per family ($US)	396	223	379	606
AFDC recipients as % of total population	6.5	6.6	7.0	8.4

[a]Ten southern states.
[b]East North Central region: Ohio, Indiana, Illinois, Missouri, and Wisconsin.
[c]Washington, Oregon, California, Alaska, and Hawaii.
Source: US Department of Commerce, *Statistical Abstract of the United States* (1996), adapted from Tables 599 and 600.

poor—Medicaid—continued to leave the states with some discretion over benefit levels.

As a result, the south in general and the poorest deep south states in particular lagged behind the national average until the early 1990s (Table 3.4). By 1996, they had just about caught up with the average, although in relation to state personal income they continued to receive a far smaller share of federal spending than would have been achieved in a system based on equity considerations (Table 3.4). This outcome can best be understood in terms of the theoretical framework developed in Chapter 2. What, in effect, the southern Democrats in Washington were doing was building the moral authority of the federal government by limiting the scope of its activities. In this way, a modified New Deal and, to a lesser extent, Great Society legislative agenda served to legitimize federal intervention. The southern Democrats were thus able to

Table 3.4. Per capita federal spending:[a] US and the south, 1981–1996 (current US dollars)

	1981	1991	1996
United States	2,413	4,282	5,179
Per capita income[b]	9,948	18,666	22,788
South[c]	2,301	4,178	5,238
Per capita income	8,339	15,814	19,865
Deep south[d]	2,185	3,867	5,019
Per capita income	7,782	14,863	18,891

[a]All federal spending includes grants to state and local governments and transfers to individuals.
[b]Per capita income figures are for 1980, 1990, and 1995.
[c]Virginia, North Carolina, South Carolina, Georgia, Florida, Kentucky, Tennessee, Alabama, Mississippi, Arkansas, Louisiana, and Texas.
[d] North Carolina, South Carolina, Georgia, Alabama, Mississippi, Arkansas, and Louisiana.

Source: Spending data: US Department of Commerce, Bureau of the Census, *Federal Expenditure by State* (Fiscal Years 1981, 1991, and 1996), computed from Table 8. Per capita data: US Department of Commerce, *Statistical Abstract of the United States* (1996), Table 699.

protect white southern interests and the southern 'way of life' through the 1960s and, in some locales, beyond. Eventually, economic change—first the mechanization of agriculture, then urbanization and industrialization— undermined southern distinctiveness and the special need to legitimize federal intervention. By the 1990s, of course, an ascendant national conservative Republican movement was to incorporate the south in its grand design for a general reduction in the role of the federal government. Part of the Republicans' appeal was, of course, their critique of federal as opposed to state governments: a perspective that reflected the public mood after the late 1970s (Fig. 3.1).

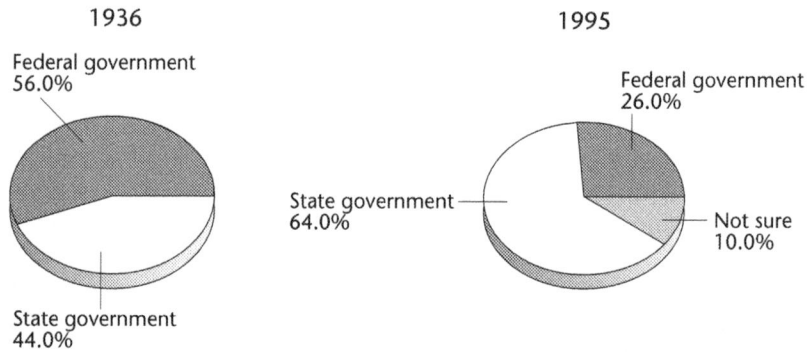

Question asked : 'Which do you favour–concentration of power in the federal government or in state government?'

FIGURE 3.1. Public regard for federal and state governments, 1936 and 1995
Source: Nathan (1996).

    What is interesting about both the rise of the federal role and its relative decline in recent years is that, the south apart, very rarely was the issue discussed in terms of the distributional consequences for *particular* states and regions. And as noted, in the case of the south all the pressures were for a reduction rather than increase in aid. Put another way, at no time has the American system of intergovernmental aid been informed primarily by a nationally agreed redistributive formula based on notions of equity and desert. Formulae do exist, of course, but they are disaggregated into myriad specific programmes.[7] Hence state and local lobbyists for federal aid focus on *programmes* in such areas as transport, law enforcement, education, welfare, and so on. When they attempt concerted action by region or locale, their effectiveness is reduced (Beer 1977; McKay, 1981).

---

[7] The Nixon administration did introduce a formula-based system of general revenue sharing in 1972, but the programme remained relatively small and was eventually abolished by the Reagan administration in the 1980s.

In this respect the United States is unique among the five countries under discussion in this book. In sum, the fragmented nature of the congressional decision making system combined with highly decentralized but national political parties has virtually eliminated regional politics in the US. As a result, the pattern of federal spending by state defies any simple characterization. This is true both of transfers direct to individuals and of intergovernmental aid. Tables 3.5 and 3.6 demonstrate this point well. The net winners and losers from federal spending constitute an almost arbitrary list. The winners include both urban and rural states, northern and southern, rich and poor. There is slightly more rationality to the losing state pattern: mid-western and upper mid-western states are consistent losers. This reflects their relatively healthy economies and relatively small dependent populations. To be fair, the distribution around the mean is relatively low but it remains an oddly unexpected pattern.

Without carefully disaggregating the whole range of federal programmes over time, it is not possible to provide a complete explanation of these figures. The shift towards a less unequal distribution over the period is almost certainly a result of the sizeable cuts in developmental programmes—and also agricultural subsidies—instituted after 1981. Such cuts hit the remoter smaller states such as Alaska and the mountain states hard. This apart, the figures demonstrate the almost complete absence of a distributional politics by section or region in the US. States rarely mobilize to seek redress from these inequalities and the public is barely aware of them. This is all the more surprising when it is remembered just how dependent individual members of Congress are on the support of their constituents. However, while this electoral connection is undoubtedly of great importance (see Mayhew 1974; King 1996), the institutional rules in Congress together with the absence of clear sectional divisions have served to fragment the representative-constituent link by issue and ideology (Shepsle 1994). Typically, then, legislators will exploit the parliamentary rules in both chambers to serve particular constituency interests rather than states or regions. Of course, a territorial dimension to this dynamic exists because some congressional districts are relatively homogeneous. But when advancing positions, members will generally coalesce by issue rather than by region. Even the rise of party voting in the House and Senate over the last several years bears little relationship to clearly definable geographic blocs. Instead, ideology has provided the cues for members (Cox and McCubbins 1993). Members from the south or the mountain states may be more conservative than members from the north-east, but when appealing to voters they refer not to this geographic difference but to differences based on issues and ideology.

Interestingly, this development may actually have been aggravated by the historical role played by southern legislators in Congress. Certainly, in both the periods in recent American history when the potential for nationally agreed spatial redistribution through federal aid was present—the New Deal and Great Society—southerners in Congress worked hard to fragment and

Table 3.5. Net winners from all federal domestic spending 1971–1996, per capita, top twelve states

Winners 1971	$	% difference from US mean	Winners 1980	$	% difference from US mean	Winners 1996	$	% difference from US mean
Alaska	2,251	162.2	Alaska	5,096	122.1	Virginia	7,535	45.5
N. Dakota	1,446	68.5	N. Mexico	3,835	67.2	Mary.	7,302	40.9
N. Mexico	1,444	68.3	Nevada	3,380	66.9	Alaska	7,150	38.1
Nevada	1,337	55.9	Wyoming	3,561	55.2	N. Mexico	7,047	36.1
Hawaii	1,268	47.8	Hawaii	3,284	43.2	Hawaii	6,770	30.7
Colorado	1,188	38.5	Colorado	3,186	38.9	Missouri	6,548	26.4
Mary.	1,183	37.9	N. Dakota	3,161	37.8	Mass.	5,984	15.5
Montana	1,152	34.3	S. Dakota	3,030	32.1	Rhode I.	5,714	10.3
Wash.	1,137	32.5	Montana	2,890	26.0	Montana	5,657	8.8
Arizona	1,110	29.4	Maryland	2,879	25.5	Miss.	5,590	7.9
S. Dakota	1,107	29.0	Wash.	2,874	25.2	N. Dakota	5,543	7.3
Oklahoma	1,080	25.9	Tennessee	2,844	23.9	W. Virginia	5,503	6.2
US mean	858			2,294			5,179	

Sources: 1971 and 1980 figures adapted from Anton (1983); 1996 figures, as for Table 3.4.

Table 3.6. Net losers from all federal domestic spending 1971–1996, per capita, bottom twelve states

Losers 1971	$	% difference from US mean	Losers 1980	$	% difference from US mean	Losers 1996	$	% difference from US mean
Conn.	552	−35.7	Indiana	1,638	−28.6	Wisc.	3,867	−25.3
Indiana	574	−33.1	Michigan	1,672	−27.1	Minn.	4,048	−21.8
Wisc.	575	−32.9	Conn.	1,680	−26.8	Michigan	4,094	−21.0
Ohio	616	−28.2	Wisc.	1,171	−25.2	Utah	4,096	−20.9
Michigan	618	−28.0	Ohio	1,777	−22.5	Indiana	4,145	−20.0
Penn.	674	−21.5	N. Jersey	1,820	−20.7	N. Hamp.	4,303	−16.9
Illinois	677	−21.1	N. Carol.	1,883	−17.9	Illinois	4,324	−16.5
N. Jersey	686	−20.0	Delaware	1,936	−15.6	Oregon	4,423	−14.6
Delaware	717	−16.4	Mass.	1,974	−14.0	N. Carol.	4,475	−13.6
N. Carol.	717	−16.4	Penn.	1,984	−13.5	Ohio	4,487	−13.4
Vermont	721	−16.0	Vermont	2,001	−12.8	Texas	4,521	−12.8
Mass.	739	−13.9	Iowa	2,022	−11.9	Nebraska	4,597	−11.2
US mean	858			2,294			5,179	

Sources: As for Table 3.5.

weaken programmes. The upshot was a pattern of economic and social spending that was less formula-driven and less focused by state and region than otherwise would have been the case.

Policy fragmentation resulting from congressional institutional rules has also served to fragment interest-group activity and the operation of the federal bureaucracies. As a large and rich literature shows, the consequence for public policy has been to make it inordinately difficult to build winning coalitions across issue areas, let alone across states and regions (for a summary, see Ripley and Franklin 1991). In addition, the *administration* of federal programmes displays no consistent pattern. Some, like social security, are administered directly by the federal government while others, such as Medicaid, are shared. Again, this outcome results directly from the fragmented nature of the decision making structure. Unlike some of the countries discussed in later chapters, and in particular Germany, there is no territorially informed *philosophy* of administration in the United States.

Two final points are important in this context. First, the fragmentation of spending by programme and the absence of direct state or regional access to federal decision making have made it much easier for the size and content of federal aid programmes to fluctuate according to fashion and ideology. Hence the great retrenchment of the Reagan years, which was to have lasting effects on intergovernmental politics in the US, was easier to expedite in the absence of solid regional coalitions across state and programmes. Instead, the Reagan administration was able to 'pick off' vulnerable programmes and in particular welfare and capital investment spending (for a review, see McKay 1989: Chs 6 and 7). As Table 3.7 shows, these spending cuts were quite dramatic, with federal aid falling from a high of 15.1 per cent of the federal budget in 1980 to under 11.1 per cent in 1985. As will be shown in later chapters, in some coun-

Table 3.7. Percentage distribution of federal budget outlays, 1970–1999

	Amount in 1982 dollars (billions)	Total %	Defense	Payments to individuals	Net interest	Aid to state and local governments	Other
1970	509.4	100	44.3	29.9	6.8	12.0	7.0
1975	586.0	100	27.3	45.4	6.9	14.8	6.6
1980	699.1	100	23.5	46.4	8.9	15.1	7.1
1985	849.6	100	27.1	44.7	13.7	11.1	3.1
1990	912.2	100	26.4	46.8	14.6	10.7	1.5
1996	1,612.0	100	16.3	55.1	15.9	10.8	1.8
1999[a]	1,733.0	100	15.0	56.5	14.0	11.5	3.0

[a]Estimated

Source: US Department of Commerce, *Statistical Abstract of the United States* (1996: Table 5.14), updated from *Economic Report of the President* (1999).

tries the existence of distinctive regions with effective political access to national decision-making greatly reduces the potential for equivalent fluctuations in the size of the federal government role, and in particular how it relates to the spatial distribution of largesse.

Second, although federal aid has fluctuated considerably over time and the authority and scope of state governments has also waxed and waned through history, the federal government has never made a concerted effort to interfere with the right of the states to raise their own taxes and borrow money. Indeed, the US preserves for its states a degree of fiscal autonomy that is unusual even among federations (Ter-Minnassian 1997). This in part reflects the principle of dual government deriving from the original constitutional compact with the states. Both federal and state authorities were to act separately on citizens, and in no area was this prerogative more jealously guarded than in fiscal matters (Beer 1993: Chs 4 and 5). More importantly, as this chapter has repeatedly stressed, the organizational and institutional 'connective tissue' between state and federal governments has always been weak in the US. For the federal government successfully to challenge the states' fiscal powers would have required the emergence of a national coalition of both state and federal interests operating through federal institutions. But since the effective 'nationalization' of the Senate in the early part of the nineteenth century, no federal institution can facilitate such a process. Federal and state decision making processes are essentially separated. As a result, most of the conflicts between the two levels of government have been brokered through the courts. And at no time have the courts had to arbitrate a fundamental challenge to state fiscal autonomy. Had the federal government and courts made any such challenge, the states would almost certainly have revoked it through constitutional amendment.[8]

Summary and Conclusions

At the inception of the Republic in 1789 territorial issues dominated political discourse and they remained important all the way through to the 1960s. Also from the beginning, however, a centralized constitutional structure and minimal representation of the states in national decision making made it inordinately difficult to mediate territorial disputes between the central authorities and the states. Hence the bitter battles over the founding of a national bank, the tariff and, eventually, slavery. By the late 1850s, unable to accommodate the economic and cultural distinctiveness of the south, the anti-slavery Republican Party found itself on a collision course with the southern legislatures and civil

---

[8] The amendment process is, of course, cumbersome and rarely used. Two-thirds of a vote of both houses of Congress followed by a vote of three-quarters of the state legislatures is the usual method. The states have the right to ask Congress to convene a national convention whose decisions would have to be ratified by three-quarters of the states. This method has never been used, but should the Congress challenge state fiscal rights it would be available to the states as redress. In fact, the need for federal government intervention in this area has been reduced by the fiscal rectitude which most state constitutions require of their governments. For a discussion, see Ter-Minassian (1997).

war ensued. After the war, the southern Democrats emerged as a truly sectional political party. A new federal bargain was struck between northern politicians and the southern Democrats, which came to its full fruition during the New Deal period. Southerners in Congress exploited their privileged parliamentary positions to demand special treatment for the south in exchange for their support of the New Deal. The result was a perverse distributional pattern of federal aid: the poorest region received less in aid, especially on welfare related issues, than many wealthier parts of the country. In other words, a general increase in the scope of federal government activity in the north was legitimized in the south by adapting programmes to fit southern preferences.

The fragmentation of power in Congress not only served the interests of the southern elites but also helped contribute to a generally more fragmented political process. The ways in which organized interests and federal bureaucracies operated reflected in part the complexity and conservatism of the committee structures.

Although, from the 1950s, economic change including the mechanization of southern agriculture helped erode the distinctive position of the south, a newly revitalized national Democratic Party embarked on a further programme of nationalization and centralization during the 1960s. For many southerners, these policy changes were at first conflated with the race issue, but as race receded in importance, so the conservatism of the south became more akin to the Republican conservatism of the north. By the 1970s, therefore, southerners were defecting to the Republicans in presidential elections. By the turn of the century, the south had become a Republican stronghold at the presidential and congressional levels and, increasingly, at the state and local levels.

Intergovernmental aid is disbursed in the absence of a regional dimension. Instead, programmatic issues and ideology determine who gets what. Political parties no longer mobilize on sectional grounds. Legislators, interest groups, and bureaucrats also see the world in these terms. Obviously, programmes do have a territorial dimension, but there is little in the ways of a *politics* of territory. This phenomenon almost certainly relates to the relative absence of deep ethnic, religious, and linguistic divides in the United States. It is, indeed, understandable that Linz and Stephan (1996: 34) characterize the United States as a state-nation rather than a nation-state. However, it also relates to a particular mix of constitutional and institutional arrangements, which, over time, first served to isolate the south, and then, through institutional adaptation, to placate the south. Most recently, economic change and the highly fragmented nature of national political institutions have in combination effectively removed the territorial dimension to politics in the US.

4

Canada: The Unresolved Federal Bargain

The Canadian Confederation is not inherently stable. It is a truism
that divisive forces threaten Canada's national unity.

Steven Muller, 1961

Origins

I N contrast to the American colonies to the south, Canada failed to develop
a strong democratic tradition with the popular will expressed through
regional legislatures. Instead the constitutions created in 1791 for francophone Lower Canada and anglophone Upper Canada established a system of
strong executive power vested in a crown-appointed governor-general. Elected
assemblies were created for both territories, but these had few legislative powers. Government was facilitated through governor-dominated patronage networks which closely resembled the dynastic courts of Europe (Stewart, Victor,
and Jockel 1996).

During the first part of the nineteenth century Canada developed into three
distinctive economic and social units: anglophone Upper Canada centred on
Ontario, francophone Lower Canada centred on Quebec, and the maritime
colonies, which were predominantly anglophone but constituted separate and
fragmented political communities (Wagenberg *et al.* 1990). During this same
period the population of French-speaking Canada grew rapidly to reach
610,000 by 1847 from a mere 70,000 in 1760 (Stewart 1986: 33). While the
economic development of Upper Canada was slower, it too was expanding
rapidly through immigration and natural growth.

Interestingly, in Lower Canada opposition to British rule was based more on
a desire on the part of francophone elites to access the decision making structures of the English-dominated 'court' than to transfer authority to the common people. In this sense, the French Canadians broadly accepted the
prevailing political order which was statist, hierarchical and ordered. Such sen-
timents were reinforced by the Catholic Church, which feared that a move
towards American-style democracy would undermine its own entrenched
position and potentially lead to the destruction of the French language
and culture. In anglophone Canada disquiet at the way in which the US was

developing also led to deep distrust of democracy and popular government. Most Canadians believed that American-style mass democracy would eventually lead to political instability or even to anarchy. They also viewed the United States as intent on expanding its territories to the north as well as to the south and south-west; and fears that an American invasion was imminent were common during the 1830s and 1840s (Stewart 1986: 32). These contrasting interpretations of the threat of American power highlight the fact that from the very beginning Canada was a 'dual society' consisting of a distinctive francophone segment and a distinctive anglophone segment.

While deference and conservatism were much more developed in Canada than in the US, discontent—and more rarely open rebellion—were endemic during the first half of the century. Two issues dominated political discourse. First, in Lower Canada an assembly dominated by francophones was constantly frustrated by English executive power. Second, in Upper Canada, where by the 1840s the powers of the assembly had been enhanced, clear party political lines were drawn between the Conservatives, who wanted to preserve existing constitutional relationships, and the Reformers, who wanted to create a new constitutional order. Consequently, successive elections were fought on the issue of constitutional change. An abrasive oppositional politics ensued which became the hallmark of Canadian politics.

Party tensions were eventually put to one side because of changes in the external environment of Canadian politics. During the 1850s, the British, newly converted to free trade, dismantled the mercantilist system that afforded protection for Canadian goods. At the same time, the expansion of the industrial northern states and the prospect of a victory for the Union in the American civil war heightened commercial and military fear of American power. In 1864, leaders of the main factions in Canadian politics came together with the intent to form a great coalition. Hence the Conservative John A. Macdonald, Reformer George Brown, and the French-speaking clericist George-Etienne Cartier put aside their rivalries and decided to form a political union (Vipond 1991: 16–17). Only a single administration, they argued, could provide for a common defence against the US and guarantee the free exchange of goods and services in a single market. In Rikerian terms, the founders calculated that the costs of ceding sovereignty to a higher authority were outweighed by the benefits of association with such a larger territorial unit. The motives of the three factions differed, but all agreed that federation was a necessity. The French Canadians wanted to control their own affairs in a francophone-dominated regional assembly. What was left to the Canadian government would be matters of defence and commercial cooperation from which the French community would benefit. Reformers saw in federation the possibility of representative government in the form of a popularly elected assembly. They also trusted that a Canadian government would protect them from the large Catholic population to the north. As one of their spokespersons put it at the time, those 'of another language, another race, another country' might eventually rule Canada if the existing constitutional arrangements prevailed (Reform Party leader Oliver Mowat, in Vipond 1991: 19). Support from the Conservatives was more muted. Not surprisingly given their attachment to custom and English political traditions, they preferred unitary to federal arrangements; and their leader; John A. McDonald, fully expected that even if a federal system was adopted it would soon transmute into a *de facto* unitary system (Norrie 1991: 30).

What eventually transpired in the form of the 1867 British North America Act was a highly centralized federal system. In marked contrast to the United States, all the powers not vested in the central government were not left to the states—the original provinces were Quebec, Ontario, Nova Scotia, and New Brunswick, with Manitoba and British Columbia added in the early 1870s.

Instead, sovereignty remained with the federal government which, through centrally appointed lieutenant-governors, retained the power to invalidate provincial legislation within one year of its enactment. A popularly elected House of Commons was created with executive power vested in the majority Commons political party. Moreover, although seats in the Senate were allocated to the provinces, senators were to be appointed by the governor-general—in effect, the prime minister. Hence the Senate, rather than being an independent force, was to become a creature of the incumbent government. Finally, the Imperial Judicial Committee of the Privy Council (JCPC) in Britain was established as the highest court in Canada and therefore became the *de facto* court of judicial review over the constitution. Through its control of the treaty power, Britain remained the final source of sovereignty in foreign affairs. Not until The Statute of Westminster in 1931 was this power formally transferred to the Canadian government, at which time Canada became an independent nation state (see the discussion in Beckton and Mackay 1986: 25–6).

The provinces were also assigned popularly elected assemblies with a parliamentary form of government. As far the powers given to the federal as opposed to provincial governments are concerned, the constitution arrived at an allocation designed to preserve the integrity of the union. Hence, responsibility for shipping, trade and commerce, the currency, the postal service, and banking were allocated to the federal government, as was defence. Agriculture and immigration were assigned a concurrent status, while all other matters, including property, civil rights, education, charitable institutions, health, and the administration of justice, were left to the provinces. The provinces were also assigned a considerable degree of fiscal freedom. They could raise taxes independently of the federal government. As we shall see, this power was to provide the provinces with an important vehicle for the assertion of provincial power during the twentieth century.

While this division of powers is typical of federal systems, the institutional architecture of the new system looks quasi-federal at best, especially as the federal government could in theory invalidate the decisions of provincial governments. There is no doubt that the centralized features of the constitution reflected both a fear that Canada might follow what was considered the disastrous path of the more decentralized United States, and the wishes of the dominant political grouping of the time, the Conservatives. As earlier noted, many leading Conservatives believed that Canada would evolve into a unitary system. As it turned out, however, Canada was eventually to become a relatively decentralized federation—although the route towards enhanced provincial power was halting and erratic.

The Ebb and Flow of Federal Power: Canadian Federalism 1867–1982

Until 1896, a centralizing Conservative Party under the leadership of Sir John A. Macdonald dominated Canadian politics—Macdonald was prime minister for all but nine years of this period. Through an extensive patronage network and use of the disallowance power—the power to invalidate provincial legislation—the federal government became the dominant force in Canadian politics. The federal government also used its constitutionally established power over trade and finance to control the provinces through the issuance of regulations and the distribution of federal largesse in such areas as agriculture and transport. Hence very early in the history of the confederation[1] the federal spending power became a major focus of intergovernmental relations (Muller 1967: 148).

Between 1896 and 1914, provincial power was on the ascendant. This resulted in part from the election of a Liberal government with a French-speaking premier, Wilfred Laurier. Unlike most Conservative leaders, Laurier had a strong provincial base and he convened the inaugural First Ministers Conference of provincial premiers in 1906. This meeting was to develop into the most important intergovernmental negotiating institution in the Canadian system. At the same time two new provinces—Alberta and Saskatchewan—were created in the Canadian west, while Manitoba was enlarged. Provincial loyalties were to prove especially strong in these western provinces, whose economic development was facilitated through a combination of provincial initiatives and federal grants. This period also saw a great increase in immigration from Europe, with most of the new arrivals settling in Ontario and the western provinces.

Quebec remained the most distinctive province, however, with its majority francophone population and assertive provincial government. While the political power of the French Canadians remained firmly entrenched, economic power was concentrated in a small English-speaking elite whose loyalties were firmly rooted in Ottawa. However, francophone Canada was relatively quiescent during the first part of the twentieth century, notwithstanding protests at Canadian involvement in British wars—the Boer War and

---

[1] Canada was officially designated a confederation of states, although it in fact was always a federation. Given that Canadians often refer to the Confederation, the two terms will be used interchangeably in this chapter.

the two World Wars—involving conscription and substantial loss of Canadian lives overseas (see McRoberts 1997: Ch. 1).

Provincial power was ascendant during the 1920s but declined during the 1930s and 1940s as first depression and then World War II greatly enhanced the role of the federal government. In the decade down to 1930, continuing immigration and economic growth fuelled the growth of provincial services. State governments were quick to exploit the fiscal freedom afforded by the Canadian constitution. They could and did raise income and corporate taxes, and although formally prohibited from raising indirect taxes, they none the less did so by defining a direct tax as a tax 'demanded from the very person who it is intended or desired should pay it' (Krelove 1997: 205). In this way provincial sales and other indirect taxes were interpreted as 'direct' taxes. In these and other matters, including interpretation of the disallowance power, the JCPC favoured provincial over federal powers (Russell 1990: 49).

Economic depression brought with it new and greatly enhanced federal programmes. Led by activist liberal governments under the direction of William Lyon Mackenzie King, who held the premiership for an astonishing 22 years between 1919 and 1948, the provinces became increasingly dependent on federal grants and subsidies during these years. Federal dominance in fiscal and other matters was to continue through the 1950s, again under the influence of a dominant Liberal Party with major new federal programmes launched in the areas of unemployment insurance, family allowances, old age pensions, and health insurance. At the same time, the economic and cultural distinctiveness of the western provinces grew, as did that of francophone Quebec, where English-speaking elites continued to dominate economic affairs. What, in effect, was happening during this mid-century period was a growing disjunction between the centralized institutional structure of Canadian federalism and cultural and economic decentralization in some provinces. Moreover, those forces responsible for strengthening regional identity increasingly found a voice in provincial jurisdictions. Hence the party system began to fragment with the emergence of distinctively provincial parties with few or no ideological or organizational links with the national parties. We will return to this point in the next section. Federal-provincial tensions were also apparent in fiscal federalism, with increasing distributional conflicts over the fairness of the federal grant system. With some provinces, notably on the Atlantic seaboard, impoverished in relation to others, a high degree of fiscal asymmetry emerged. By fully utilizing their fiscal independence some provinces became relatively self-sufficient in relation to the centre while others became increasingly dependent. We will also return to this point in a later section.

From the late 1960s through to 1982 Canadian federalism was buffeted by four important developments, three of which strengthened centrifugal forces and weakened the centre.

1. *The increasing dependence of the maritime provinces on federal aid.* Equalization formulae in federal grant programmes were always likely to increase the dependence of the poorer provinces on the centre. However, the

economic dislocation caused by the oil crises of the 1970s aggravated this tendency to the extent that by 1982–3 the four maritime provinces were actually receiving almost as much in revenue from the federal government as they were from local sources (Table 4.1). As a result, the main focus of maritime contact with the federal government was to maintain or increase these subsidies. To this end a regional grouping, the Council of Maritime Premiers, presented a united lobbying front to Ottawa.

2. *Increasing political assertiveness on the part of the resource-rich western provinces.* These same events served to highlight the cultural and economic distinctiveness of the west. Rising commodity prices, and in particular oil prices, greatly enriched some of the western provinces whose fiscal independence permitted them to charge higher royalties on mineral extraction. At the same time, most western provinces received little in the way of federal aid (Table 4.1). These events increased western resentment at having to subsidize the east and helped fuel calls for 'provincial rights' (see Smith 1990: 82–8).

Table 4.1. Total revenue sources, own-source, and federal transfer income, Canadian provinces, percentage distribution, 1982–1983, percentages

	Nfld	PEI	NS	NB	Que	Ont	Man	Sask	Alta	BC
Own-source	52.8	49.9	57.3	55.4	79.4	84.5	68.7	84.8	93.5	86.1
Fed. transfer	47.2	50.1	42.6	44.4	20.5	15.0	31.0	15.1	6.5	13.3
Total	100.0	100.0	100.0	99.8[a]	100.0	99.8[a]	99.7[a]	99.9[a]	100.0	100.0

[a]Excludes small transfers from local governments.

Source: Adapted from Lloyd Brown (1990: Table 9.2).

3. *A 'quiet revolution' in Quebec leading to a resurgence of Quebecois nationalism.* Nationalism in Quebec, which was centred on the use and significance of the French language, grew rapidly from 1969 through to the early 1980s. At the same time, the province experienced rapid economic development and the incumbent Liberal Quebec Government made serious attempts to modernize the province (see Gagnon 1990: 95–108). Quebecois grievances remained, however, and stressed the distinctiveness of a culture threatened by an encroaching Anglo economy and society. Many Quebecois saw the federal government as a party to this process and therefore thought it should be viewed with deep suspicion. Only constitutional change could protect Quebecois society and this meant either the transfer of substantial powers from the federal government to the province or complete independence. After winning the 1976 provincial elections, the Parti Quebecois led by Rene Levesque promised a referendum on 'sovereignty association' for Quebec. Sovereignty association involved transferring control of almost all domestic policy arenas to the province, leaving to the federation responsibility only for macroeconomic policy and defence.

4. *The elevation of the First Ministers Conference to prominence in Canadian politics.* The increasing political salience of the federalism issue also increased the visibility and importance of the First Ministers Conference. From February 1968 the Conference was assigned the job of reviewing basic constitutional arrangements, a process that continued until a new constitutional settlement was reached in 1981 and 1982. Under this settlement the Conference was formally accorded constitutional status.

While all these developments were important, it was the relationship between Quebec and the rest of Canada (ROC) that dominated political debate during these years. Numerous studies have catalogued these events (good accounts are provided by Bothwell, Drummond, and English 1989; McRoberts, 1997) and there is room here for only the briefest of summaries. Much of the impetus to change resulted from the federal response to the rise of Quebecois nationalism. As the Liberal premier from 1968, Pierre Trudeau had a vision of Canada as an independent and united country whose identity could overcome the 'provincialism' of Quebec nationalism. To this end he espoused an official policy of bi-lingualism (a Royal Commission on Bi-lingualism and Bi-culturalism had been set up in 1963) and through the Official Language Act of 1969 he hoped to create a genuinely bi-lingual society devoted to essentially *Canadian* ideas and values. In the event, however, bi-lingualism was resented in many parts of English-speaking Canada and, because it was seen as a standardizing federal policy, it actually helped the cause of Quebecois nationalism (Bothwell 1996). Trudeau was also closely identified with national economic and welfare policies that were viewed as highly intrusive in Quebec. What, in effect, Trudeau was proposing was an end to the dualism that had been the *de facto* basis of Canadian federalism since 1867. In 1968 he dismissed the idea that Quebec should be assigned a special status: 'Particular status for Quebec is the biggest intellectual hoax ever foisted on the people of Quebec and the people of Canada' (cited in McRoberts 1997: 65). Bi-lingualism was quite compatible with this vision, for it was to be imposed equally throughout the country, according no special status to Quebec. Quebec sensibilities were also offended by the way in which the Trudeau Government reacted to a rare instance of political violence in 1970. A splinter nationalist group the *Front de libération de Quebec* (FLQ) kidnapped the British Trade Commissioner and made a number of demands of the government. They later also abducted a Quebec minister, Pierre Laport, whom they subsequently murdered. Trudeau invoked the War Measures Act and effectively imposed martial law in Quebec. The upshot was deep resentment on the part of the Quebecois at the way in which the crisis was handled. The vast majority of Quebecois rejected violence and considered the federal response to the FLQ insensitive and heavy-handed.

Rather than dampen nationalism in Quebec, Trudeau's policies had the effect of arousing it and the referendum on sovereignty association was duly held on the 20 May 1980. Trudeau and the Liberal Party campaigned against a 'yes' vote and sovereignty association was eventually rejected by a margin of three to two.

The final event in this period of Canadian history concerns the patriation of the constitution in 1982. Because the 1949 British North America Act instituted only a partial transfer of sovereignty to the Canadian government, it was necessary to complete the process by legally returning or 'patriating' the remaining parts of the constitution, including, crucially, federal-provincial relations, to Canada.[2] Patriation raised, therefore, the thorny issue of the exact division of powers between the federal government and the provinces. As earlier indicated, the original 1867 settlement had been highly centralist—even if, for the most part, the provinces had developed formidable *de facto* decentralized powers. Quebec in particular was wary of becoming party to any new settlement that permitted, if only in theory, the surrender of these powers to the federal government. Following much debate and controversy, the 1982 constitutional settlement actually changed very little. The existing division of federal and provincial powers remained and no major constitutional change in the status of the major branches was instituted. However, through a new Canadian Charter of Rights and Freedoms, some of the asymmetry of Quebec's place in the federal system was removed including its privileged position in relation to language. From 1982, the official by-word was not biculturalism but multiculturalism: a term which was becoming more and more appropriate to the complex ethnic and linguistic mix that made up Canadian society.

However, unhappy with the new status of the French language, Quebec refused to sign the new constitutional settlement—a situation that prevailed through to the end of the century.

Re-negotiating the Canadian Federal Bargain, 1982–2000

The failure to incorporate Quebec into the 1982 constitutional settlement left the way open for more comprehensive constitutional reforms. This process was aided by the fact that the main participants in the earlier process—Rene Levesque of Quebec and Prime Minister Trudeau—had both passed from the political scene by 1984. Brian Mulrooney and the Progressive Conservatives replaced the Liberals, while in Quebec the Liberals assumed power under the leadership of Premier Robert Bourassa. Three issues dominated constitutional debate: the exact status of Quebec in relation to the federal government; the status of Senate appointments, which remained in the hands of the incumbent government; and the composition of the Supreme Court, appointment to which was also a federal prerogative.

What eventually transpired in the form of the Lake Meech Accord was a set of essentially decentralist proposals, but with special provisions being made for Quebec. Hence, Quebec would be recognized as a 'distinct society' and, in

---

[2] In fact, since the British Parliament always acted at the request of the Canadian government, Canada was already *de facto* independent. It was not so in law, however.

line with the 1982 constitutional settlement, would be guaranteed at least three judges on the Supreme Court.[3] In addition, the provinces could opt out of those federal grant programmes organized on a shared-cost basis that impinged on exclusive provincial jurisdictions. The federal government would compensate them in such cases and the provinces would be required to provide the programmes on their own. The provinces could also veto any constitutional amendment that transferred provincial legislative power to the federal government. Finally, pending more comprehensive reform, the provinces would be given some say in Senate nominations and they could negotiate agreements with the federal government on immigration policy.

In comparative perspective, these reforms appear to be quite radical. Few federal systems formally permit the exercise of an—admittedly limited—state veto over federal legislation, and few allow an opt-out of shared-cost grant programmes. Even more unusual, of course, are provisions naming one state as deserving of special treatment in relation to other states. In Canadian terms, however, the reforms were the culmination of many years of bargaining and negotiation, and as such were not at the time viewed as particularly radical (see the discussion in McRoberts 1997: Ch. 8). None the less, a ratification process that involved not only Parliament but also all eleven provincial legislatures left the way open for the voicing of opposition to Meech Lake in English-speaking Canada. Opposition was centred on the cost opt-out provision—many Canadians feared it would undermine the comprehensive coverage provided by the welfare state—and on the special status accorded Quebec. Led by Pierre Trudeau, opponents framed the accord in terms of the threat of emergence of two distinct and irreconcilable societies—one English-speaking and the other French—which would eventually lead to the break-up of Canada (McRoberts 1997: 198–204). Their fears were aggravated when in December 1988 Quebec passed Bill 178 invoking the 'notwithstanding' clause that had been added to the Canadian constitution as part of the Charter of Rights. This was a truly remarkable provision as it permitted a provincial legislature to invalidate any part of the Charter of Rights. It effectively says 'notwithstanding any of the above'—that is, in the Charter of Rights—a provincial legislature can overrule the Charter. Bill 178 did just this by sanctioning French-only public signs throughout the province. An equivalent Bill—Bill 101—had previously been invalidated by the Supreme Court. But the 'notwithstanding clause' had clear constitutional status and thus effectively overruled any decision by the Supreme Court or other provisions in the Charter of Rights that conflicted with it.

These events galvanized opposition to Meech Lake in many of the English-speaking provinces and in particular in Manitoba, where native rights were central to opposition, and Newfoundland, which actually endorsed then later

---

[3] In fact the 1982 constitution does not *guarantee* three seats for Quebec but requires the unanimous consent of Parliament and the provincial legislatures to change the constitution to include reference to the composition of the Court. As, by custom, three judges are always from Quebec, there is a *de facto* provision for the minimum of three.

rescinded the Accord. Opposition in ROC in turn convinced many Quebecois that they were a besieged society whose only salvation lay in complete independence. Given that the Accord had to be endorsed by all eleven provinces by mid-1990, time quickly ran out and the proposal lapsed. Momentum for further constitutional reform was maintained, however, through a further set of proposals for constitutional reform known as the Charlottetown Accord. Charlottetown generally went further than Meech Lake in terms of reforming the basic institutions of the federal government. The Senate was to be completely overhauled and transformed into a genuinely territorial upper house with six representatives from each of the provinces and one from each of the territories. In addition, Quebec was to be guaranteed a minimum 25 per cent representation in the House of Commons and special provisions were made for the protection of native Canadian rights. On federal-provincial relations, the Accord reserved exclusive provincial control over six areas: urban affairs, tourism, recreation, housing, mining, and forestry. Quebec would continue to be recognized as a 'distinct society'.

These reforms were not, in fact, as radical as they seemed. The powers of the Senate remained peripheral and confined to a very limited veto on some bills and a delaying power on others. Quebec's distinct-society status was, moreover, identified as just one of eight fundamental characteristics of Canadian society and in this respect the provision was weaker than the equivalent clause in Meech Lake. As with Meech Lake, by making concessions to both sides the accord failed to satisfy either. It was subsequently rejected in a national referendum by a resounding 55.4 per cent to 44.6 per cent. The accord received substantial support only in the territories and in the maritimes (Table 4.2; Smith 1990: 58).

Table 4.2. 1992 referendum vote by province from east to west

	Yes	%	No	%
Newfoundland	134,193	62.9	77,881	36.5
New Brunswick	344,010	61.3	145,096	38.0
Prince Edward	48,467	73.6	17,124	25.9
Nova Scotia	218,618	48.5	230,182	51.1
Quebec	1,710,117	42.4	2,232,280	55.4
Ontario	2,410,119	49.8	2,397,665	49.6
Manitoba	198,230	37.8	322,971	61.6
Saskatchewan	203,361	44.5	252,459	55.2
Alberta	483,275	39.7	731,975	60.1
Brit. Columbia	525,188	31.7	1,126,761	68.0
NW Territories	14,750	60.6	9,416	38.7
Yukon	5,354	43.4	6,922	56.1
Canada	6,185,902	44.6	7,550,732	54.4

Source: Williams (1995: Table 2.6).

Failure to settle the constitutional issue and recognize the special status of Quebec fuelled Quebecois nationalism anew. Embittered by what they saw as tantamount to rejection of Quebec itself, pressure was building among the population for a further referendum on Quebec sovereignty. Unlike the earlier referendum, however, the proposal for Quebec sovereignty that was put to the people of Quebec in 1995 implied that approval would result in *de facto* independence. Quebec would continue some association with ROC, but would govern its internal affairs and have the right to negotiate treaties with foreign governments. The economic status of the new entity remained unclear but there was at least the implication that Quebec could go it alone in trade and macroeconomic policy (McRoberts 1997: Ch. 9).

Much to the surprise of most Canadians, a mere 1.2 per cent of the vote on a 94 per cent turnout rejected the sovereignty proposal. For many in ROC this result indicated that the whole question of Quebec independence was now firmly on the agenda and was likely to dominate political discourse for many years ahead. Within Quebec, however, the prospect of independence, and in particular the possibility that Quebec may lose its close economic association with ROC, led many to question the wisdom of the option. For many, a Quebec outside the Canadian dollar zone was particularly disquieting (see Young 1995). In fact surveys have repeatedly shown that only a bare majority of Quebecois favour independence. And as Table 4.3 shows, even at the time of the referendum only 29 per cent failed to hold some Canadian self-identity.

Table 4.3. Self-identification of Quebec francophones

Quebecker only	29.0%
Quebecker first, but also Canadian	29.1%
Quebecker and Canadian equally	28.1%
Canadian first, but also Quebecker	6.7%
Canadian only	5.4%
None of these	1.2%
Don't know/refuse	0.5%

Administered 23–6 October 1995.
The question was 'Personellement vous considérez-vous: Québecois(e) seulement; Québecois(e) d'abord; Québecois(e) et Canadien(ne) à part égale; Canadien(ne) d'abord, Québecois(e) ensuite; Canadien(ne) seulement; rien de cela; ne sait pas /refus?'
Source: McRoberts (1997: Table 5).

In the years immediately following the referendum, other forces were at work which served to reduce the political salience of the secession issue. Canada's increasingly complex ethnic and linguistic mix brought into question the historical characterization of Canada as a 'dual society'. 'Anglo' Canada was less and less identifiable in cultural and economic terms. As important was the increasing assertiveness of Canada's indigenous population, which culminated in the creation of a new territory, Nanavut, on 1 April

1999. Quebec may indeed be a 'distinct society', but so too were many other parts of the complex ethnic and cultural mix that made up modern Canada.

While at the time of writing Quebecois secession seems much less likely than during the mid-1990s, the fundamentals of the Canadian federal system remain open to renegotiation. In contrast to the United States a permanent settlement has yet to be achieved.

A Changing Party System

As would be expected in a decentralized federation, the Canadian party system is territorially fragmented. Different parties often operate at the provincial as opposed to the federal levels; and within individual parties considerable organizational and ideological variations exist both vertically—between the provincial and the federal level—and horizontally—between provinces (for a discussion, see Carty and Stewart 1996). This is particularly true of the most successful party, the Liberals, whose faction in, for example, Quebec has relatively little in common with its counterparts in Ontario or the other provinces.

The renegotiation of Canadian federalism, which has dominated politics in the post-1968 period, was both a result of party fragmentation and a cause of further changes in the party system. Already by 1950, the two-party—Conservative and Liberal—dominance that was the hallmark of the federation's early years had broken down with the emergence of the Union Nationale in Quebec, the Social Credit Party in Alberta, and the Cooperative Commonwealth Federation—the CCF, a socialist grouping which later was to evolve into the New Democratic Party—in Saskatchewan. By that year, in fact, provincial as opposed to national parties controlled four of the ten provincial governments (Table 4.4; see the discussion in Muller 1967). By the 1970s the emergence of the Parti Quebecois as a specifically sectionalist grouping with an agenda that included possible secession from Canada showed the extent of party fragmentation in the system. Concomitant with this development came a new volatility in party politics at the national level culminating in the famous 1993 election result when the Liberals ousted the Progressive Conservatives by winning 177 House of Commons seats to the Conservatives' two. In the same election the revitalized Reform Party won 60 seats in the western provinces, while the Bloc Quebecois won 54 seats in Quebec to the Liberals' 19. The pattern set by the 1993 elections was to be repeated during the 1997 general elections when the Liberals were returned to power with 155 seats to 60 for the Reform Party, 20 for the Progressive Conservatives, 21 for the social democratic New Democrats, and 44 for the Bloc Quebecois. What is significant about the last two elections is that while the Liberals remain dominant, three of the four opposition parties now have sectional as opposed to national bases. In the west, the conservative Reform Party is the main opposition grouping, while the New Democrats provide an alternative leftist focus.

Table 4.4. Percentage of Canadian provincial governments controlled by political parties with national bases, 1905–1980[a]

Year	%
1900	100
1925	78
1950	60
1980	60

[a] Nine provinces until 1949, ten—with Newfoundland—thereafter.

Source: Reproduced from Dunn (1996: Appendix 1).

Meanwhile the Progressive Conservatives remains the major party grouping in Quebec although it lost seats to the Liberals under the leadership of Prime Minister Jean Jacques Chretien in 1997.

Only the Liberals remain as a party with genuinely national strength, and, as mentioned, even this party more resembles a coalition of interests than an ideologically and organizationally unified movement. In sum, fragmentation in the party system mirrors the traumas and tribulations of Canadian federalism over the last 30 years. In the general area of federal-provincial relations political parties have been the main vehicles both for the articulation of grievances and for attempts at crisis resolution. In one sense this is a truism, because the key institution in this process has been the First Ministers' Conference which, like the EU Council of Ministers, is made up of provincial premiers all of whom have been provincial party leaders. Canada's first-past-the-post electoral system, together with its parliamentary arrangements, has guaranteed the domination of national government by one national party. A feeble upper house—the Senate—appointments to which are in the gift of governments has, if anything, added to the insulation of national institutions from the provinces. We will return to this point later, but first ask how the important question of intergovernmental fiscal relations fits into the equation.

Fiscal Federalism: The Politics of Intergovernmental Bargaining

As earlier noted, the federal government has long been active in the economic affairs of the provinces. The constitutional rationale for intervention was the 'federal spending power' or the capacity of the central government to finance shared-cost programmes, usually on a 50/50 basis, in established areas of exclusive provincial competence. Although no specific reference is made to this power in the constitution, it has been inferred from federal taxation powers and control over the public debt and property (Leslie 1993: 24–5). Originally, this role was mainly confined to infrastructure expenditure and agricultural supports. After World War II, however, interventionist liberal governments extended the federal role to such areas as health care insurance, education, pensions, and unemployment insurance. By 1970 Canada had acquired a large and complex system of intergovernmental grants and tax subsidies. There were four main programmes.

1. *The Canada Assistance Plan and Medicare*. In 1966 the four largest welfare programmes were combined into a single programme, the Canada Assistance Plan, which provided matching funds for unemployment, low-income and disability benefits. In the same year the federal government passed the Medical Care Act, which extended some existing smaller programmes to create Medicare health insurance on a matching basis for the provinces. Provided the provinces met certain conditions, they were eligible to receive up to 50 per cent of the total costs of the scheme if benefit levels in any one province were less than the national per capita cost of health insurance. The programme was, thus, open-ended in nature (see Norrie 1993).

2. *Pensions, hospital insurance and higher education*. Similar subsidies were available for hospital construction and insurance, higher education, and aspects of the federal old-age pension programme introduced in 1951.[4] In all these cases, provinces had the option of participating or not. Not surprisingly, almost all provinces opted in rather than out. In Quebec, however, these new programmes were regarded as an infringement of provincial autonomy. It therefore chose to run its own pensions programme, although still with federal subsidies. It also opted out of many of the matching programmes and instead received tax credits from the federal government.

3. *Established Programmes Financing*. In 1965, many of these programmes were rationalized as Established Programmes Financing, which included both the tax subsidies and the 50/50 funding for health insurance and post-secondary education. In 1971 the 50/50 funding formula was replaced by a conditional per capita subsidy made up of a tax transfer—known as tax points—and a cash transfer. The value of the tax transfer is linked to GDP per capita growth. In both cases the programmes were driven by equity considerations. With regard to health care, the aim was to ensure that all citizens had access to uniform and comprehensive health benefits. Should provinces fail to meet these criteria their subsidies would be reduced (see Shah 1995: 239–40).

4. *Equalization*. The final component in the system of intergovernmental aid also stemmed from the interventionist 1940s and 1950s, when the prevailing philosophy was that all provinces should provide similar levels of public service at similar levels of taxation. Hence, in 1957 an unconditional formula-led transfer programme was instituted which provided subsidies to the less well-off provinces. The 1982 constitutional settlement formalized this

---

[4] The Old Age Security Act of 1951 provided federal financed and administered pensions for all Canadians over 70, but pensions for those aged 65 to 69 were financed on a federal-provincial 50/50 basis (Norrie 1993: 101–2).

process and declared: 'Parliament and the Government of Canada are committed to the principle of making equalization payments to ensure that provincial governments have sufficient revenues to provide reasonably comparable levels of public services at reasonably comparable levels of taxation' (cited in Shah 1997: 249). The actual formula adopted is highly complex and based on the fiscal capacity of individual provinces. Using both GNP and an average measure of five of the larger provinces' revenue sources, an equalization per capita measure is calculated for every province (details in Shah 1997: 247–54). Predictably, the resulting formula provides no subsidy to Ontario, British Columbia, or Alberta, and subsidies of varying sizes to the remaining seven provinces (see Fig. 4.1).

Dollars per capita

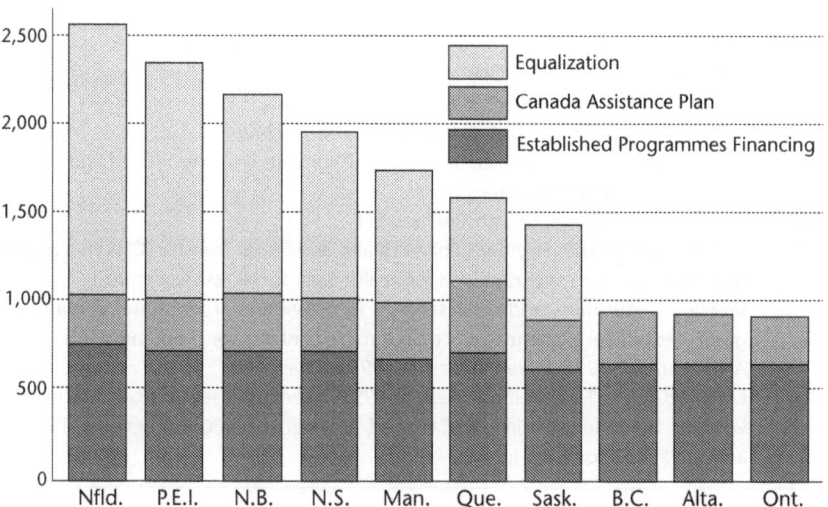

FIGURE 4.1. Major federal transfers to the provinces, 1994–1995
Source: Shah (1995: Table 4b).

In comparative context, these policy changes are notable in a number of respects. First, they are all informed by an equalizing philosophy. Formula-driven territorial equalization is at the very heart of the Canadian system. This obviously applies to equalization and cash transfers, but also to the tax transfers, which involve increasing provincial taxes by the amount that federal taxes are reduced. In this way, the taxpayer in rich provinces is subsidizing the taxpayer in poorer provinces. Second, although the federal role is considerable, the actual *administration* of programmes is largely left to the provinces. Moreover, provinces can elect not to participate. The system does, at least in theory, make some concessions to provincial autonomy—although in the case of the poorer maritime provinces the open-ended nature of some of the

redistributive formula greatly increased dependence on the federal government.

Between the 1960s and the 1990s internal and external economic and political forces buffeted the whole structure of intergovernmental aid. The asymmetric effects of the 1970s oil crises put great strains on some provinces and
on the federal government. Fiscal crisis at the national level led in turn to
major changes in some of the programmes and in particular to the formula
funding bases. These are summarized in Table 4.5.

Table 4.5. Retrenchment in federal transfer programmes, 1982–1996

1982	GNP per capita escalator applied to Established Programmes Financing (EPF) entitlements rather than cash.
1983	EPF cash transfer therefore became a residual.
1984	Post-secondary education portion of EPF limited to 6% and 5% growth for 1983–84 and 1984–85 under the federal anti-inflation programme.
1986	EPF growth reduced form GNP to GNP minus 2 indefinitely.
1989	EPF growth reduced to GNP minus 3 from 1990–91.
1990	EPF per capita transfer frozen for 1990–91 and 1991–2.
1991	EPF freeze and Canada Assistance Plan (CAP) growth limit introduced and extended for three more years.
1994	Further budget limitations on CAP and EPF.
1995	EPF and CAP replaced by the Canada Health and Social Transfer (CHST), a block-grant programme covering funds for health care, social assistance, post-secondary education, and social services. By converting programmes into a block grant, the federal government acquired more control over spending levels. Allocations for 1996–7 were frozen at 1995–6 levels.
1996	For 1998–9 CHST entitlements kept at 1995–6 levels but set to grow through to 2002–3. The reductions in EPF, CAP, and, in particular, in CHST between 1993 and 1999 are shown in Fig. 4.2.

Sources: Various, including Department of Finance, Canadian Government, http://www.fin.gc.ca/FEDPROVE/

As can be seen from Table 4.6, federal grants to the provinces did rise
sharply from 1955 to 1975, increasing from 1.5 per cent to 4.4 per cent of GDP.
Note also the effects of retrenchment during the 1980s and early 1990s. By
1991, grants had been reduced to 3.9 per cent of GDP. The politics of fiscal
retrenchment involved both general disquiet at what many saw as an erosion
of the Canadian welfare state and concern in Quebec and among the richer
provinces at the territorial inequities inherent in the system. In fact, compared
with equivalent changes in the US (see Chapter 3, p 42), the reductions in
grants were relatively modest. This no doubt reflects the fact that territorial
politics are well developed in Canada. Formula-driven redistribution is central
to the relationship between the federal government and the provinces and is
at least in part protected through frequent meetings of the First Ministers
Conference. Unlike other federal systems, where the states are represented

Fiscal year ending 31 March ($ billions)

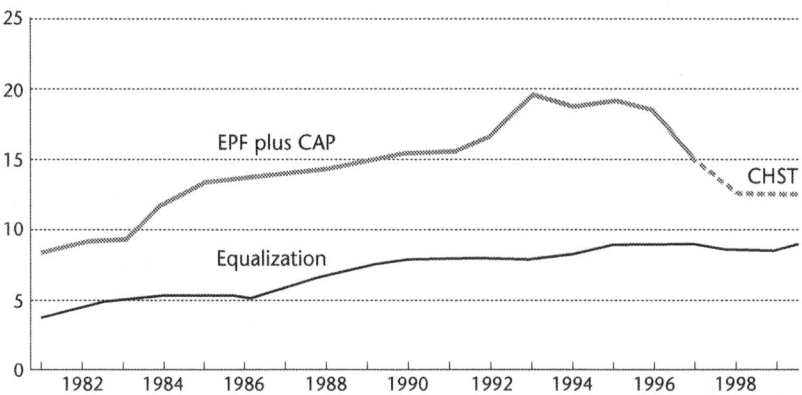

FIGURE **4.2.** Major federal transfers to the provinces, 1981–1999

Source: Government of Alberta at www.treas.gov.ab.ca/ fed1gif, p. 1

EPF: Established Programs Financing

CAP: Canada Assistance Plan

CHST: Canada Health and Social Transfer

Table **4.6.** Canadian public expenditure as a percentage of GDP by level of government, 1939–1991

Year	Federal, including grants to provinces	Federal grants to provinces	Federal, excluding grants to provinces	Provincial and local[a]	All governments[b]
1939	8.2	1.3	6.9	13.6	20.5
1943	39.1	1.3	37.8	6.7	44.5
1950	12.4	1.3	11.1	10.3	21.3
1955	16.4	1.5	14.9	10.7	25.6
1960	17.1	2.4	14.7	14.3	28.8
1965	14.9	2.4	12.6	16.3	28.7
1970	17.2	3.7	13.5	21.4	34.9
1975	20.8	4.4	16.4	23.1	39.9
1980	19.8	4.0	15.7	23.8	40.3
1985	24.0	4.4	19.5	25.9	46.8
1989	21.5	3.9	17.6	24.5	44.0
1990	22.9	3.9	19.0	26.4	47.3
1991	24.2	3.9	20.3	28.0	50.4

[a]Including expenditures of public hospitals.

[b]Including expenditures of the Canada Pension Plan and the Quebec Pension Plan, which together amounted to 2.2% of GDP in 1991. Other columns *do not* include payouts under these compulsory public pension plans but do include pensions paid out of general government revenues (noncontributory schemes, funded from current taxes).

Source: Peter M. Leslie, 'The Final Crisis of Canadian Federalism', in Leslie, Norrie, and Ip (1993: Table 2).

within central institutions, the federal authorities in Canada negotiate with the provinces in the context of a parallel institution. A 'federal government position' exists which is often quite distinct from the position of the provincial governments. Compare this with the situation in the US, where the role of the state legislatures in national decision making is close to non-existent.

Disputes over the general level of intergovernmental aid were, however, minor compared with controversy over the distribution of federal benefits between provinces. Table 4.7 shows the distribution of transfers as a percentage of provincial revenue in 1989–90 and 1999–2000. Note the much greater dependence of the poorer Maritimes on federal aid and the relative independence of the three richest provinces, British Columbia, Ontario, and Alberta. Note also that, in spite of the retrenchment of the 1990s, there were very few significant changes to this pattern during the decade. *Proportionately*, the pattern of dependence remained roughly the same. In absolute terms, however, a general reduction in expenditures at all levels of government has meant that provincial economies are less dependent of federal aid than they were. Indeed, Table 4.8 shows the distributional pattern in dollar terms, per capita and as a percentage of provincial GDP between 1995 and 1998. As is clear, even in this relatively short period, dependence on federal largesse was reduced significantly from, for the whole of Canada, 5 per cent to 4 per cent of GDP.

Table 4.7. Major federal transfers[a] as percentage of provincial revenues, 1989–90 and 1999–2000

Province	1989–1990	1999–2000
Newfoundland	42	43
Prince Edward Island	43	41
Nova Scotia	39	40
New Brunswick	39	37
Quebec	28	25
Ontario	19	19
Manitoba	30	33
Saskatchewan	29	22
Alberta	18	16
British Columbia	20	19

[a]1989–90: Canada Assistance Plan, Established Programmes Financing and Equalisation. 1999–2000: Canada Health and Social Transfer and Equalisation.

Sources: 1989–1990, Leslie (1993: Figure 2); 1999–20000, Federal Finances, http://www.fin.gc.ca/FEDPROVE/

While the western provinces have long resented the fact that their tax dollars are used to subsidize the east (Anderson and Bonsor 1986), their objections have not acquired the stark political dimension associated with Quebecois objections to the federal grant system. As part of a general disenchantment with what they considered was an intrusive and insensitive federal govern-

Table 4.8. Major federal transfers to provinces and territories ($Cm),[a] per capita ($C), and as a percentage of GDP, 1995–1998

	1995	1996	1998
Newfoundland	1,502	1,484	1,440
Per capita	2,582	2,646	2,648
% of prov. GDP	14.6	14.2	12.7
Prince Edward Is	311	311	317
Per capita	2,314	2,284	2,329
% of prov. GDP	12.4	11.2	11.2
Nova Scotia	1,933	1,938	1,960
Per capita	2,069	2,083	2,094
% of prov. GDP	10.4	10.0	9.5
New Brunswick	1,610	1,585	1,619
Per capita	2,126	2,105	2,152
% prov GDP	10.6	9.6	9.4
Quebec	11,658	11,036	11,018
Per capita	1,600	1,518	1,503
% of prov. GDP	6.9	6.1	5.7
Ontario	10,536	9,651	9,453
Per capita	964	871	830
% of prov. GDP	3.4	2.9	2.5
Manitoba	2,134	2,053	1,870
Per capita	1,891	1,812	1,640
% of prov .GDP	8.3	7.3	6.3
Saskatchewan	1,293	1,009	1,151
Per capita	1,278	1,151	1,123
% of prov. GDP	5.3	3.5	4.0
Alberta	2,512	2,314	2,324
Per capita	925	833	800
% of prov. GDP	2.9	2.4	2.2
British Columbia	3,574	3,343	3,343
Per capita	975	863	833
% of prov. GDP	3.6	3.1	3.0
Yukon	319	316	326
Per capita	10,698	9,930	10,275
% of prov. GDP	35.0	27.8	30.4
North West Territory	964	965	954
Per capita	14,374	14,310	14,059
% of prov. GDP	40.5	38.4	37.8
Total Canada	38,345	36,005	35,775
Per capita	1,312	1,215	1,182
% Canadian GDP	5.0	4.3	4.0

[a]Canada Health and Social Transfer (CHST), which consists of tax transfers and cash, and the federal equalization programme which benefits seven provinces. Data for the new territory, Nanavut, are available only from 1999.

Sources: Statistics Canada, http://www.english/Pgdb/People/Population/ (population data), http://www.stat-can.ca/english/Pgdb/Economy/Economic (GDP data), and http://www.fin.gc.ca/FEDPROVE/ (financial data).

Canada

ment, many in Quebec have criticized federal aid programmes and the general structure of federal taxation as favouring ROC and discriminating against Quebec (see, for example, Belanger and Campeau 1991; Ethier 1986). However, as Table 4.8 shows, in recent years, at least, Quebec has received substantially more per capita in federal transfers than has Ontario or most of the western provinces. Of course, equalization transfers are only part of the cost-benefit calculus. A different picture may emerge should the spatial impact of *all* federal taxes and expenditures be taken into account. Such a cash flow or fiscal-balance approach shows the net winners and losers resulting from all federal fiscal transactions including those involving taxes and expenditures on exclusively federal activities.[5] In the most careful cash flow study to date, Mansell and Schlenker (1995: 6–7) conclude that

Quebec has been the largest net beneficiary in absolute terms over [a] . . . 32 year period. It received $168 billion more than it paid to the federal government. Alberta, on the other hand, has been the single largest contributor, paying $139 billion more than it received. For the period as a whole, only Alberta and Ontario have been net contributors. However, British Columbia was also a significant net contributor during the period 1962–1976 and in 1991 and 1992, and Quebec was a net contributor from 1961 to 1970.

These results are summarized as a percentage of provincial GDP in Table 4.9.

Table 4.9. Federal fiscal balances as percentage of provincial GDP, 1960–1992

Period	Nfdl	PEI	NS	NB	Que	Ont	Man	Sask	Alta	BC	Terr	Can
1960–9	16.8	28.8	21.2	14.3	–1.5	–2.6	3.6	4.0	–1.1	–2.5	50.3	–0.3
1970–9	26.0	36.9	28.3	21.3	4.2	–1.1	6.1	4.0	–10.6	–1.6	30.0	1.2
1980–9	32.6	38.3	29.7	27.1	8.0	1.0	12.1	8.2	–10.4	2.8	54.8	3.7
1990–2	31.2	33.6	21.2	20.1	4.6	–1.6	12.1	14.0	–1.1	–0.4	44.2	2.7
Average	26.0	34.8	26.1	21.1	3.8	–0.9	7.8	6.3	–6.9	–0.4	44.8	1.7

Source: Provincial Economic Accounts as calculated by Mansell and Schlenker (1995: Table 2).

These figures clearly show the asymmetric effects of the economic crises of the 1970s and the 1980s, when those provinces most vulnerable to changes in the business cycle received much more in the form of federal largesse while those with energy resources and/or more resilient economies became large net contributors. Perhaps the most remarkable feature of these figures is that at precisely the time—the 1980s—when Quebec was in receipt of the most federal monies, nationalism in the province was rising as never before. While it is true that on a capita basis the redistribution in favour of the province was

---

[5] In fact, a true cost-benefit calculation would include not just fiscal flows but also the consequences of such things as trade, energy, and foreign exchange policies. For a discussion, see Mansell and Schlenker (1995).

smaller, it remains a net beneficiary (Mansell and Schlenker 1995: Table 1).[6] This demonstrates just how detached many Quebecois were from the whole Canadian federal project. By far the largest net contributor by whatever measures employed was Alberta. This does, of course, partly stem from the province's great energy resources, whose value was greatly enhanced during the 1970s and 1980s. Ontario, too, has been a significant contributor, as has British Columbia. In contrast, the maritimes and, naturally, the territories have been very substantial net beneficiaries. This pattern of fiscal flows demonstrates nicely the stateness problems that Canada has experienced since the 1960s. Although not always completely happy with its donor role, politicians and public in Ontario have, for the most part, been willing to subsidize other provinces including Quebec. Alberta has been less compliant, but has yet to generate a political movement intent on challenging the integrity of the union. In British Columbia, advances by the New Democratic Party highlight the fact that politics in that province are aligned more along ideological than along sectional lines (Carty and Stewart 1996: 83–4). In sum, the three donor provinces have been prepared, albeit reluctantly, to subsidize the others. The distributional crisis of Canadian federalism, while serious, has not developed to the point where a constitutional breakdown would involve not just Quebec's secession but also a general disintegration.

There is a final dimension to Canadian fiscal federalism that is of great importance at the turn of the millennium. Put simply, the prevailing economic orthodoxy that has forced Canadian governments at all levels to reduce debt and public expenditure has had the effect of reducing the importance of federal aid relative to private provision. The question of which province gets what is now conflated with the question of the distribution of governments benefits among social groups. This has made the issue of intergovernmental transfers even more complex and hard to resolve.

Summary and Conclusions

The original Canadian constitution was forged out of military and economic necessity and created an institutionally centralized system of government. The provinces were given no privileged access to national decision making. Central institutions never developed into forums for the representation of provincial interests. Instead, the party with the greatest national electoral strength dominated the House of Commons. As the creature of government patronage, the Senate became the antithesis of a 'chamber of the states'. It was, and remains, an enfeebled, indeed almost insignificant, upper house. Judicial power was originally vested in the British JCPC, which was eventually replaced by the Canadian Supreme Court. Although the convention that three of the

---

[6] Again during the 1960s, Quebec was a small net contributor and a net beneficiary thereafter. On a per capita basis the province benefited most during the 1980s. During the early 1990s its relative position declined somewhat (Mansell and Schlenker 1995: Table 1).

Court's judges are from Quebec potentially establishes some territorial dimension to the institution, its constitution remains essentially non-territorial. Neither are provincial interests represented at the national level through the party system. Canada's first-past-the-post parliamentary arrangements have assured that a single national party has dominated national politics. Parties at the provincial level have little in common with national parties; indeed, in the case of some provinces, quite different parties operate at the provincial level.

The absence both of constitutionally established national forum for the expression of provincial interests and the lack of the sort of central-local connective tissue that is engendered by strong party ties has meant that, as far as intergovernmental relations are concerned, Canadian politics has always had a confrontational and even combative character. Confrontation has, of course, been encouraged by the linguistic, economic and geographic distinctiveness of many of the provinces. This applies *tout force* to Quebec, whose relationship with ROC has been particularly traumatic over the last 30 years. Since the 1970s, secession has always been a possibility. As a result, several attempts have been made to renegotiate the fundamentals of the constitutional settlement. None has thus far succeeded. Instead, the special status of Quebec as a 'distinct society' has been recognized in numerous ways, from the composition of the Supreme Court to opt-outs by Quebec from full participation in such federal programmes as old-age pensions—for which the government of Quebec has been compensated.

Intergovernmental fiscal relations have been the focus of much of the tension between the federal government and the provinces. Some time ago, the provinces negotiated the right to shape and administer most of the federally funded programmes in such areas as health care and education. And special additional funding and administrative powers have been devolved to Quebec. But most of the battles have concerned 'who gets what' rather than how programmes are organized, and these have been much sharper and more territorially focused than similar debates in Germany, Switzerland, or Australia. This fact, above all, demonstrates the extent of Canada's stateness problem. The fact remains that even after more than 130 years, many of the citizens of Quebec continue to question both the moral authority of the federal government and the scope of its activities. And this applies even though the province administers most of the federally funded programmes and even though Quebec remains a net beneficiary of federal largesse.

Given the continuing distinctiveness not only of Quebec but also the western provinces, and the absence of central institutions for the representation of provincial interests, it is not surprising that grievances are aired and positions negotiated through the First Ministers Conference. The fact that such a body has become so crucial to mediating disputes speaks volumes for the status of Canadian federalism. Such institutions are more typical of interstate bargaining in confederations or in such bodies as the EU than they are of mature federations.

Perhaps the most significant development for the future of Canada is that the ethnic and linguistic dualism that has dominated the country's history is now being replaced by a much more complex set of relationships, including those between native and non-native Canadians. This new complexity does not, of course, remove the pressures for or the need for constitutional change. Stateness problems remain and as long as they do pressures will continue to exist for a new constitutional settlement, which may or may not involve secession by Quebec.

5

Australia: Party Discipline and Fiscal Dependence

As the power of the purse in Great Britain established by degrees the authority of the Commons, so it will in Australia ultimately establish the authority of the Commonwealth.[1] The rights of self-government of the States have been fondly supposed to be safe-guarded by the Constitution. It has left them legally free, but financially bound to the chariot wheels of the Commonwealth.

Alfred Deakin, 1902

Origins

THE territory that makes up modern Australia was first settled by the British as a penal colony in 1788. By the 1820s colonists from Britain were arriving in significant numbers and in 1823 the British government granted the largest colony, New South Wales, a constitutional charter authorizing the creation of a council with some legislative powers. By 1842, the powers of the Legislative Council had been extended, with two-thirds of the members elected by a limited franchise. In 1850 the British government passed the Australian Colonies Government Act, which allowed the colonies to establish full legislatures and to determine voting rights. By 1859, New South Wales, Tasmania, Victoria, South Australia, and Queensland had acquired constitutions with representative legislatures and executive power vested in governors-general. Because it insisted on retaining its penal colony status, Western Australia's transition to self-governing colony was delayed until 1890.

Although the idea of forming a federation had been supported by British Secretary of State Earl Grey in the 1840s, and received fresh impetus from colonists opposed to transportation during the 1850s (see the discussion in McMinn 1994: Chs 3 and 4), it was not until the 1880s that changing internal and external conditions provoked widespread support for federalist ideas. Externally, the rush for colonies among the European powers had spread to the Pacific. Australians and New Zealanders were concerned that the French,

---

[1] The Australian federal government is officially known as the Commonwealth Government. The terms will be used interchangeably throughout this chapter.

the Germans, or possibly the Italians might have designs on New Guinea, Fiji, and proximate island groups. A common defence among English-speaking Australasians might act as a bulwark against aggression by the European powers—a fear that was aggravated by explicit German designs on New Guinea. (McMinn 1994: Ch. 4). There was also an increasing awareness that a central authority might facilitate free trade and communications between what were very widely scattered and thinly populated self-governing colonies. The first initiative involved not only four of the Australian colonies[2] but also New Zealand and Fiji. Hence the Federal Council of Australasia was given legislative power over a range of external affairs, fishing, and relations with the Pacific islands. In addition, at the request of a colony, the Council could legislate on defence matters concerning that colony. The Council achieved very little, however. It lacked executive power and, above all, populous and prosperous New South Wales, suspicious of the motives of Victoria, refused to participate. (McMinn 1994: 110–11). The second initiative, stemming from the first Australasian Federal Convention that met in 1891, also excluded New South Wales. A draft constitution was formulated but the initiative came to nothing. In effect, any meaningful move towards federation required the participation of New South Wales, whose reluctance was based on a widespread belief that the state's stability and prosperity would be threatened through association with Victoria whose economy was racked by land speculation and other scandals (McMinn 1994: Ch. 8).

More meaningful moves towards federation were taken towards the end of the century. Impetus towards federation was fuelled both by the economic depression of the 1890s with its associated falling commodity prices and by Japanese success in the Sino-Japanese war, which resulted in the Japanese annexation of Korea. From the mid-1890s, therefore, European imperial ambitions in the Pacific were joined by Japanese expansionism (Riker 1964: 28). Australians also feared the mass migration of Japanese into their country and had specifically legislated to restrict entry in 1896. Concomitant with these events came a rise in Australian nationalism, not least in New South Wales, where republican ideas were particularly influential.

By 1897 the parliaments of New South Wales, Victoria, South Australia, and Tasmania had passed bills calling for the election of delegates to a constitutional convention whose findings would be subject to popular referendums. Eventually, Western Australia also nominated delegates to the convention, but Queensland and New Zealand did not take part. Following conventions in 1897–8, a draft constitution was issued which was subject to popular approval. Although approved by referendums in five of the states—Queensland later decided to participate—the 'yes' vote in New South Wales fell short of the 10,000 majority required by the state's enabling legislation (Galligan 1995: 27). A further draft was produced in 1899 and was successfully put to the people in all the states bar Western Australia. The British Parliament subse-

---

[2] Victoria, Tasmania, Queensland, and Western Australia. South Australia became a member briefly between 1889 and 1891.

quently passed the Commonwealth of Australia Constitution Act, which sanctioned the creation of a federal state. Western Australia eventually agreed to hold a referendum, which approved forming a union with the other states. On 1 January 1901 the Commonwealth of Australia was created as a federation of six states. Note that this process was subject to popular approval through referendums in each state. From the very beginning, therefore, referendums were established as an important instrument of public approval, and they remain so to this day.

The constitutional framers opted for a parliamentary system of government with the House of Representatives, the lower house, sharing power with the Senate, the upper house. Apart from money bills, the constitution assigned equal power to the Senate and the House.[3] As in the United States, the Senate was intended to be a 'house of the states'. Senators were given six-year terms with half elected every three years; and states could decide on the method of election. Originally, each state was allocated six seats; today each state elects twelve Senators and each of the two territories—Northern and Australian Capital—two. Also as in the US, the House is elected on a population basis, and has a shorter—three-year—term than the Senate. Finally, a High Court was created with the power of judicial review over the acts and actions of the states and the other branches, including adjudicating disputes between the states and the federal government.

As is clear from this brief description, the Australians specifically copied many of the provisions of the US constitution. Indeed, only in their adoption of a parliamentary rather than a presidential system did the essentials of the two documents differ. In contemporary terms, therefore, they favoured what they saw as the relative decentralism of the American system in 1900 over the more centralised Canadian federal arrangements. As far as the allocation of powers is concerned, the constitution laid down few powers that were the exclusive competence of the federal government, although one of these was to levy customs and excise duties. Others powers were designated as concurrent with the states, but with the proviso that, in event of a conflict, federal legislation would prevail. In effect, this has meant that Commonwealth legislation had *de facto* competence over:

- communications, including lighthouses and telegraphs;
- free internal trade, including uniform customs and excise duties and the power to arbitrate inter-state industrial disputes;
- international affairs, international trade and the protection of Australian borders;
- uniform standards of measurement and classification;
- aboriginal affairs—added by referendum in 1967; and
- social security—added by referendum in 1946.

---

[3] But the senate does have the power to defer or reject all bills, including, according to most experts, money bills. See the discussion in Aitkin, Jinks, and Warhurst (1988: 26–7).

In addition, the federal government was granted those powers needed for it to function effectively as a 'governmental entity'. All other powers were to be left to the states. However, as in the US constitution, these powers were residual in nature. This can be inferred from the somewhat indirect language of Sections 106 and 107:

The constitution of each State of the Commonwealth shall, subject to this Constitution, continue as the establishment of the Commonwealth, or as at the admission or establishment of the State, as the case may be, until altered in accordance with the Constitution of the State . . . Every power of the Parliament of a colony which has become or becomes a State, shall unless it is by this Constitution exclusively vested in the Parliament of the Commonwealth or withdrawn from the Parliament of the State, continue as at the establishment of the Commonwealth, or as the admission of the establishment of the State, as the case may be. (Government of Victoria, Federal State Relations Committee 2000)

The constitution also created an Interstate Commission, a federal body designed to ensure fair and free trade between the states; but it was not intended as an agency for federal-state coordination or adjudication. In the event, the Commission proved to be something of a constitutional white elephant. It lapsed in 1920 following a High Court judgement; it was reconstituted in 1975, and was finally abolished in 1989. At no time has it played a significant part in federal-state relations.

Perhaps the most important policy dimension to the constitutional settlement concerned finance. As already noted, the constitution transferred exclusive powers over customs and excise duties to the federal government. As these were the most important taxes at the time, this transfer constituted a major change in the balance of tax revenue between the two levels of government. Indeed, the failure to agree on federal political arrangements during most of the decade of the 1890s resulted from a failure to agree on this issue. As Galligan notes: 'Even before the conventions were underway, devising a common tariff for colonies that championed diverse free trade and protectionist policies was considered the most challenging issue and was widely billed as the "lion in the path" of federation' (Galligan 1995: 216). As it turned out, the transfer of customs and excise duties to the federal government constituted the first in a series of events that weakened the fiscal position of the states in relation to the centre.

Although the Australian constitution was in some respects centralist, in others it was quite decentralist. The Senate had at least the potential to become a council of the states; few powers were unambiguously assigned to the federal government; it was assumed at the time that the states would retain most policy functions (see the discussion in Galligan 1995: Ch. 1). The constitution was, of course, modelled on Australian conceptions of the American model circa 1900. At that time the US Supreme Court was active in favouring state over federal power, and there was general agreement that the US had a decentralized federal system. The various Australian states were, moreover, distinctive both in geography and in political culture. Western Australia was dependent on mineral extraction, was remote from the eastern states, and agreed to join the federation only at the last minute. In agrarian New South Wales (NSW), radical and populist ideas were widespread, not least in a growing labour movement. The people of NSW were, moreover, distrustful of the more commercially minded elite that governed Victoria. (For accounts of the politics of the Australian colonies towards the end of the nineteenth century, see Irving 1999.) There was, therefore, little expectation at the time that Australia would become a highly centralized federal system. However, that is precisely what it became.

Centralizing Trends, 1901–72

From around 1910 the balance of power in the Australian federal system began to shift away from the states and towards the national government. This change, which continued for most of the century, resulted from a combination of political, financial, and judicial forces. By 1910 a two-party system had emerged at the national level. The Australian Labor Party (ALP) supported an enhanced federal role in economic and social affairs, while the Liberal Party favoured a limited government role. From the very beginning, therefore, party conflict in Australia was centred on the role of the national government. But neither party was sectional in nature, in spite of the fact that the ALP's strength was initially concentrated in NSW. Instead, it was the balance of state versus national power *throughout the federation* that aroused the fiercest controversies. This partisan debate applied not just the House of Representatives but also to the Senate. Indeed, rather than develop into a council of the states, the Senate almost immediately became as partisan as the lower house.

With both houses operating according to the formal and informal rules of party discipline, the stage was set for the formal erosion of state power. The first important change occurred in 1910, when the federal government, rather than returning to the states the 'surplus' revenue accruing as a result of the transfer of customs and excise taxes to the centre, replaced the surplus with a lump-sum grant whose value was soon eroded as a result of inflation (Spahn and Shah 1995: 53). As a result, the states found themselves with very limited fiscal resources. After World War I, economic dislocation increased their indebtedness further and they became more dependent on the federal government. Following a referendum in 1928, a federal Loan Council was created that gave the federal governments powers to control state debts (Aitkin, Jinks, and Warhurst 1988: 29). By the early 1930s the collapse in commodity prices and the ensuing economic depression produced a crisis in intergovernmental fiscal relations during which the state of Western Australia actually voted to secede. Eventually a new system of fiscal equalization was introduced policed a new body, the Commonwealth Grants Commission. We will return to this subject in a later section.

High Court decisions also encouraged the growth of federal power. Until 1920 the constitution was interpreted in terms of 'implied' prohibitions on the activities of the Commonwealth. In other words the courts tried to infer the intentions and motivations of the framers from the wording of the document. In the famous *Engineers* case,[4] however, the High Court claimed that literal interpretation of the constitution was required. This had the effect of expanding Commonwealth powers. In 1932 federal power was further enhanced by the *Garnishee* case, which sanctioned the 'attachment' of state revenues to enforce a law made under the constitution. New South Wales had refused to pay interest on loans, claiming that the money should be used elsewhere. In a series of 'excise' cases during the 1920s and the 1930s, the Court gradually expanded what was meant by an excise tax to include most sales taxes. By the end of the 1930s the states were left with a very limited tax base made up primarily of franchise taxes, stamp duties, and motor vehicle taxes (Petchy and Shapiro 1997: 208–10). Finally, in 1942, the *Uniform Tax Case* established the income tax as an exclusively federal revenue source. Pressed by the unusual demands of the war effort, the Commonwealth introduced a series of acts giving it a monopoly of income tax for the duration of the war. Unhappy that they were losing the right to collect income tax, the states sued. But the High Court not only upheld the right of the Commonwealth to take over income tax for the duration of the war, it also sanctioned the right of the federal government to maintain exclusive control of income taxes after the war. In this way the states were obliged to rely on the federal government to return a proportion of centrally collected income tax revenue (for a discussion, see Bird 1986: 110 et seq).

The creation of the Commonwealth Grants Commission in 1933 and the *Uniform Tax Case* opened the door to a rapid increase in federal vertical grants. As can be seen from Table 5.1, federal grants as a percentage of states' own-source revenue increased from 15 per cent in 1938–9 to 37 per cent in 1948–9 to 53 per cent in 1972–3. This explosion of federal largesse was fuelled by the dominant Keynesian welfare state model of economic and social organization prevalent after World War II. For although the relatively non-interventionist Liberal and National Parties were in office for 23 years between 1949 and 1972, pressures for the extension of the welfare state and the role of the federal government in economic affairs continued to mount.

Dependence on federal aid led to the convening of premiers' conferences at which state and federal delegations meet annually to discuss federal and associated matters. These conferences were not, however, designed to facilitate hard bargaining between the states and the Commonwealth over funding levels—although they were often portrayed as such. Typically, the federal government will already have decided on funding allocations before the

---

[4] *Amalgamated Society of Engineers v. Adelaide Steamship Co. Ltd* concerned a dispute between the union and the Western Australian government's sawmilling and engineering works. The court decided that a literal interpretation of the constitution meant the dispute could be dealt with under federal law. For a discussion, see Galligan (1995: 173–4).

Table 5.1. Vertical fiscal imbalance, Australian states, 1938/39–1994/95

	1938/39	1948/49	1972/73	1975/76	1982/83	1994/95
T/E	48	19	28	26	24	37
R/O	71	28	42	37	37	56
G/E	15	37	53	62	47	41

T/E: Own-source taxes as % of total expenditure.
R/O: Total own-source revenue as % of own-purpose expenditure.
G/E: Grants from the Commonwealth as % of total expenditure.

Source: Matthews and Grewal (1997: adapted from Table 14.5).

conference meets. Instead, they provided an opportunity for the airing of state grievances and for providing the federal government on information on the implementation of federally funded programmes. Often the conferences were used—and indeed still are—to legitimize the positions of state political leaders who can return home claiming victory over federal domination and insensitivity (for a discussion, see Holmes and Sharman 1977: Ch. 5).

Crisis and Change in Intergovernmental Relations, 1972–2000

On coming to power in 1972 after more than 20 years in opposition, the Labor government of Gough Whitlam greatly increased federal grants to the states. Not only was the total amount distributed increased but the method of distribution was modified. Specific-purpose grants were favoured over general-purpose grants and a number of commissions were created in such areas as education, health, and land use to supervize the spending of federal grants. These were areas of public policy the administration of which had traditionally been left to the states, so the new commissions were regarded as an attempt by the Labor Government to centralize power in Canberra (Aitkin, Jinks, and Warhurst 1988). In addition, the government proposed a new system of grants involving federal aid direct to local governments. Not surprisingly, the states objected to this new arrangement, and the proposal was subsequently defeated in a referendum.

Following the Whitlam interlude, when federal-state relations deteriorated badly, a Liberal coalition government under the leadership of Malcolm Fraser came to power in 1975. Fraser immediately announced a 'New Federalism', or a new deal for the states involving the return of a percentage of income tax collections to the states. At the same time, the government was intent on reducing the size of the federal government and reducing federal taxes. But these policies coincided with international economic crisis and rapidly rising oil prices that prevented the full implementation of the Fraser reforms.

Ultimately, the government was not prepared to devolve tax responsibilities to the states and the states were unwilling to put in jeopardy their share of federal grants (Matthews and Grewal 1997: 371).

A Labor government under Bob Hawke—later under the leadership of Paul Keating—replaced the Fraser government in 1983. In marked contrast to the Whitlam government, both Hawke and Keating pursued a neo-liberal policy of reducing government expenditure, lowering taxes and privatizing Commonwealth-owned industries. As far as aid to the states was concerned, grants were drastically reduced. As a percentage of GDP federal grants to the states fell from 9.7 per cent in 1982–3 to 7.1 per cent in 1994–5 (Table 5.2). These cuts were, predictably, opposed by the states, and by 1990 the Labor administration was actively seeking not to confront the states but to collaborate with them on the implementation of economic and political reforms. To this end, a number of important initiatives were launched which were labelled 'New Federalism' or Collaborative Federalism'. In particular, starting in 1990 the federal government convened a Special Premiers Conferences (SPC) and in 1992 created the Council of State Governments (COAG) to facilitate closer cooperation between the federal government and the states. These new institutions created several collaborative bodies, including in 1996 a Treaties Council which gave the states the opportunity to express their views on international treaties affecting state policies in such areas as the environment and labour law. However, the new bodies were predominantly advisory in nature, and neither the Hawke nor the Keating administration was able successfully to reform the one area that dominated federal state politics: intergovernmental fiscal relations (see the discussion in Painter 1998: Chs 3 and 4).

After a long period of abrasive and often confrontational federal-state relations, all the states agreed that it was necessary to present a common front to the federal government. Differences based on size, income, and geographic proximity were to be put aside in a new institution, the Leaders' Forum, which first met in 1994. The Forum was committed to reforming the intergovernmental system and in particular 'to provide the states with a guaranteed revenue base to match their expenditure responsibilities' (Painter 1998: 54). By the mid-1990s the Forum was regularly meeting on a twice-yearly basis. The new initiative did little to smooth federal-state relations, however, although by this time there was general agreement on the need to reduce government expenditures at all levels. In 1996 Labor lost the election to a Liberal/National Party coalition, which proved as determined to pursue a policy of fiscal orthodoxy as its Labor predecessors. In addition, the new Prime Minister, John Howard, preferred to by-pass the new institutional structure of federal-state relations, including the COAG. Instead, he preferred to negotiate by policy sector, thus keeping collaboration with the states as a unit at arm's length (Painter 1998: 189–90).

Table 5.2. Payments to or for the state and territories, 1972–3 to 1994–5

Payment	1972–3		1975–6		1982–3		1994–5	
	$Am	% GDP	$Am	% GDP	$Am	% GDP	$Am	% GDP
General revenue grants	1,700.9	3.8	3,111	4.1	9,221.8	5.3	15,073.8	3.3
Specific-purpose recurrent grants	390.0	0.9	2,315.9	3.0	3,918.2	2.3	14,496.2	3.2
Specific-purpose capital payments	541.5	1.2	1,836.3	2.4	2,098.9	1.2	2,544.6	0.6
General-purpose capital funds	982.0	2.2	1,291.0	1.7	1,493.6	0.9	224.5	(a)
Total gross payments	3,614.4	8.1	8,554.8	11.2	16,732.50	9.7	32,339.1	7.1
Less: Repayments of advances	32.6	0.1	46.2	0.1	325.2	0.2	2,017.2	0.4
Net payments	3,581.8	8.0	8,508.6	11.1	16,407.4	9.5	30,321.8	6.7

(a) Below 0.1%

Source: Matthews and Grewal (1997: Table 14.4).

Political Parties and Adversarial Politics

As has already been implied, political parties dominate Australian politics at all levels. The parties are also highly disciplined, operating as they do in parliamentary contexts in both state and national politics. As in similar systems, control over candidate nominations is the main means whereby party discipline in maintained (Holmes and Sharman 1977: Ch. 4). For all of its history the system has been dominated by two parties—the ALP and the Liberals—with a third minor party, the Country Party, now known as the National Party, sometimes sharing power with the Liberals. A further distinctive feature of the system is that almost at no time have any of the major parties appealed to the voters on a sectional or territorial basis. Indeed, for much of its history the ALP supported the abolition of federalism. Federalism, so the argument ran, fragmented power and thus stood in the way of the implementation of the ALP's radical and socialist programme. Hence the official position of the party was to support:

one sovereign national parliament possessing unfettered powers to pass laws for Australia and the creation of subordinate provincial or State governments possessing delegated powers in the same way as local councils in the states now possess authority delegated from the State parliaments. (Cited in Galligan 1995: 105)

Labor also supported the abolition of the Senate and the direct election of all houses at the state level—presuming that federalism remained. The ALP is unique among the political parties covered in this book in its advocacy of such radical constitutional change and in particular the abolition of the institution of federalism itself. Not until the 1970s did it modify its position. In 1971 its position changed to give '. . . the Parliament of Australia . . . such plenary powers as are necessary and desirable to achieve international co-operation, national planning and the Party's economic and social objectives' (cited in Galligan 1995: 105). Labor's centralist philosophy was further diluted in the 1980s and the 1990s when it became an active supporter of collaborative federalism, or closer cooperation with the states.

Although the Liberal Party has always supported federal institutions, it too has been, at various points in its history, a centralizing influence. This was particularly true in the 1950s and 1960s when, in spite of its traditional emphasis on individual enterprize, Liberal governments legislated to increase the size and scope of a welfare state controlled largely by the federal government. As its name suggests, the National Party appeals to agrarian interests and its support is concentrated in the less urban states of Queensland and South Australia. In recent years it has been in coalition with the Liberals at the national level and in Queensland.[5] All national parties have exercised strong party discipline.

---

[5] There is also a Country Liberal Party which is strong in the Northern Territory, but insignificant in national politics.

As would be expected in a federal system, the parties are organized on both a national and a state basis, but candidate nominations are state-based for both state and national offices. This peculiar feature of the Australian system means that all politicians have to establish a state base before standing for national office (Holmes and Sharman 1977: 108–9). Even so, at both the state and the national levels, *ideology* and *interest* rather than territorial identity have been the key determinants of political behaviour. This applies to all legislative bodies at all levels. And with specific regard to the Senate—the house that, institutionally, most resembles a chamber of the states—party loyalties rooted in ideology predominate. As one prominent official[6] has put it:

Having observed the Senate over the past 20 or 30 years, I know the Senators have never voted on state lines with state interests as against voting on party lines. The states now have no reliance on the Senate as a House of review to protect their interests. It may act as a house of review to protect what the members perceive to be their electorates' interests, but I am not sure that it is fulfilling the states' interests. (Government of Victoria, Federal State Relations Committee 2000: 14).

Professor Cheryl Saunders has put this point more graphically:

[I]n practice the Senate has not operated as a states' house, and that my experience has been that many Senators do not even understand the question when it is put to them. (Government of Victoria, Federal State Relations Committee 2000: 14)

Given this it is not surprising that for most of its existence the Senate followed the lead of the party in control of the House of Representatives, that is, the government of the day. Since the introduction of proportional representation for the election of Senators in 1949, the Senate has been controlled by a party different from the governing party on a number of occasions. Even so, ideological rather than territorial differences have prevailed. This has moved the Australian system some way from the 'ideal' model of an efficient parliamentary democracy, but has done little to serve state representation at the national level (see the discussion by Uhr 1999). None of this is to deny distinctive state political cultures which are reflected in state party systems. There are marked differences within state Labor parties, for example, ranging from the conservative stance of the Tasmanian party to the ideological tone of the Victoria party. The Liberal Party is very much a coalition of centre and right-of-centre interests and the National Party in Queensland is both more populist and successful than the National Party in, for example, NSW (Holmes and Sharman 1977). But none of these distinctions has been translated into a strong sense of territorial identity articulated by state political parties. Indeed, as is shown in Table 5.3, there has been a close coincidence of party representation between national and state levels in recent years, and this during a period of great political upheaval involving efforts to reduce the role of government in society by adopting neo-liberal policies. As in other parliamentary

---

[6] Ken Baxter, former Secretary to the Department of Premier and Cabinet in Victoria.

Table 5.3. Party control of national and state governments, 1990–1997

Year	Federal	NSW	Vic	Qld	SA	WA	Tas	NT
1990	ALP	Lib/NP	ALP	ALP	ALP	ALP	ALP	CLP
1991	ALP	Lib/NP	ALP	ALP	ALP	ALP	ALP	CLP
1992	ALP	Lib/NP	ALP	ALP	ALP	ALP	Lib.	CLP
1993	ALP	Lib/NP	Lib	ALP	ALP	Lib	Lib	CLP
1994	ALP	Lib/NP	Lib	ALP	Lib	Lib	Lib	CLP
1995	ALP	ALP	Lib	ALP	Lib	Lib	Lib	CLP
1996	Lib/NP	ALP	Lib	Nat/Lib	Lib	Lib	Lib	CLP
1997	Lib/NP	ALP	Lib	Nat/Lib	Lib	Lib	Lib	CLP

ALP: Australian Labor Party
CLP: Country Liberal Party
Lib: Liberal Party
Nat/Lib: National-Liberal Coalition
NP: National Party

Source: Adapted from Painter (1998: Table 3.1).

systems, a change of government at the national level is usually preceded by a shift to opposition parties at the state/local level.

The Politics of Dependence: Fiscal Federalism in Australia

Earlier sections have stressed just how important the fiscal dimension is in Australian federalism. The original transfer of most tax revenues to the federal government immediately transferred the responsibility for infrastructure and other investments from the state to the federal government. This was no easy task given that the fiscal capacity of the original states was highly asymmetrical. Western Australia (WA), in particular, received substantial revenues from the extraction of gold; and had the federal tax revenues been handed back on a simple per capita basis the state would have found itself substantially worse off. Tasmania, on the other hand, was seriously in debt. The eventual compromise involved a per capita distribution with special terms provided for WA. Both WA's and Tasmania's problems were to be solved by a provision in the constitution—Section 96—which mandated the distribution of federal grants to the states on its own terms: 'To grant financial assistance to any state on such terms and conditions as the Parliament thinks fit' (cited in McMinn 1994: 261). Grant distribution to WA began in 1910 and to Tasmania in 1912. South Australia became a recipient in 1927. The whole arrangement lent itself to the growth of central controls on how money was spent and in particular the requirement that the states match the federal contribution. Also in 1927 the per capita distribution was replaced by a federal contribution towards the interest charged on the states' public debts. A Loan Council to control state debt levels was also created. When economic depression hit in the early 1930s, the wool and wheat growers in the Australian east were badly affected, thus increasing pressures for the extension of federal largesse. WA considered itself badly enough done by that it actually voted in a referendum to secede from the Commonwealth. However, the vote was more of gesture than anything else: no one seriously expected the state to leave the federation. Instead it was a *cri de couer* designed to attract attention to the state's plight (McMinn 1994 : 262–3). Partly as a result of these events the federal government set up a Commonwealth Grants Commission (CGC) in 1933 to rationalize and oversee the distribution of grants to the states. The CGC instituted the first financial equalization grants based on state fiscal capacity: a system of inter-governmental aid that remains to this day.

Federal Grants and Equalization: How the System Works

Federal assistance to the states consists of general-purpose assistance—block grants—and specific-purpose assistance—categorical grants. More than 50 per cent are general-purpose grants provided for recurring expenditure and for capital expenditure. Most of these are formula driven with population and consumer prices constituting the main indicators. Specific-purpose grants are provided for a range of services including, in order of importance, education, health, social welfare, housing, and transport. Some of these grants are chan-nelled direct to the states and some are channelled 'through' the states to local governments and universities. The breakdown of total Commonwealth pay-ments to the state/local sector is shown in Fig. 5.1. Australian local govern-ments have few independent tax sources and their own-source revenue amounts to a mere 5 per cent of all public spending. The major criticism of specific-purpose grants has been their use by federal governments to imple-ment politically popular national policies. In other words, the size and com-position of the grants has been changed to suit national political purposes—often against the states' wishes (Spahn and Shah 1995: 60). Given that many of the grants are funded on a matching basis, the upshot had been an increase in state and local taxation. During the period of fiscal expansion—early 1970s to late 1980s—the proportion of federal aid given in the form of specific grants increased from around one quarter to over one half (Spahn and Shah 1995: 60). Since then, however, there has been substantial retrenchment with very considerable reductions in specific-purpose recurrent grants and in general revenue funds. These changes are shown graphically in Table 5.4. Under the Hawke and Keating governments, general revenue grants fell by 40 per cent relative to GDP; specific-purpose capital funds fell by 50 per cent. General-purpose capital funds were all but abolished. Only specific-purpose recurrent grants increased in size. Even so, the Australian system is still char-acterized by a high degree of vertical fiscal imbalance with states dependent on federal largesse. The only concession granted to the states in this area was

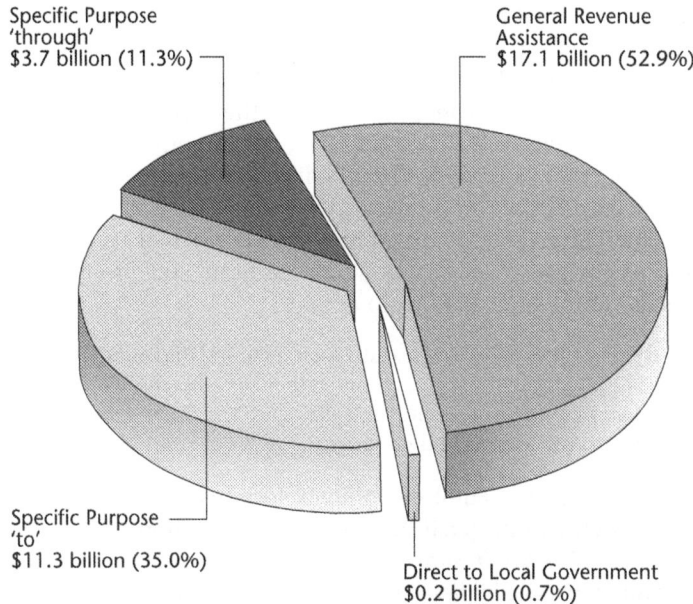

Specific Purpose
'through'
$3.7 billion (11.3%)

General Revenue
Assistance
$17.1 billion (52.9%)

Specific Purpose
'to'
$11.3 billion (35.0%)

Direct to Local Government
$0.2 billion (0.7%)

FIGURE 5.1. Payments to the state/local sector in 1998–9 (estimated)

Source: Commonwealth of Australia (1999: Chart 5).

the transfer of payroll taxes to the states in 1971. This followed a legal battle over the right of the federal government to levy a tax on its own wage expenditures (Holmes and Sharman 1977: 146–7). However, payroll taxes remain relatively unimportant, representing just 9 per cent of total state revenues (Spahn and Shah 1995: 57). In no other major federal states does such an extreme degree of fiscal imbalance exist.

Intergovernmental grants have been subject to a number of changes over the last 30 years, many of them involving complex funding formulae including revenue sharing (for details see Mathews and Grewal 1997). As already noted, the federal government has also used the grant system to shape public policy in the states, and there has hardly been a time when the states have not been in conflict with the Commonwealth in this general area. All the institutions of intergovernmental cooperation, including regular and Special Premiers Conferences, COAG, and the Leaders' Forum, have been used specifically to try and resolve these problems. Interestingly, pressures emerged during the 1990s to replace the consensus, or unanimity, voting rules typical of COAG and the Leaders' Forum with majority or other voting rules providing the Commonwealth with greater leverage over the states. This applies in particular to so-called Ministerial Councils created to deal with specific problems with an interstate dimension. Most these bodies have dealt with substantive areas of public policy such as agriculture or crime, although some meetings have concerned financial relations (Painter 1998: Ch. 5).

But a further unusual feature of the Australian system is that responsibility for the *equalizing* effects rather than the size of grants is allocated to an independent body: the CGC. In other words, while the federal government decides the *amount* of financial assistance to the states, the CGC provides recommendations on the *distribution* of the grants. The CGC was originally established in 1933 and its operations have been rationalized a number of times since. Its methodology for distribution is reviewed every five years. A Commonwealth-appointed chairperson and three members oversee a staff of around 50 and the Commission is widely regarded as a non-partisan and professionally run agency. As Rye and Searle (1997: 163) note:

The Commission has always placed great stress on retaining the confidence of the states and other parties to its inquiries, however much they may disagree with its findings. To this end it fosters a culture of openness and dialogue. The states and other parties are given every opportunity to present their views.

As suggested, the CGC employs complex formulae for the distribution of grant money (outlined in detail for the 1993 distribution in Rye and Searle 1997: Appendix, 173–83). In sum, the Commission weights each state's population according its *disabilities*. *Disability* is a measure of factors that are beyond each state's control and which requires it to spend more than states on average must spend to reach a particular standard of public service or which reduces its relative ability to raise revenue. The resulting formula is symmetrical: states which have less than average disability or greater than average revenue-raising powers have their grants reduced in relation to needy states. Equalization has its roots in Section 96 of the constitution, which gives the federal government the power to distribute grants to the states as it sees fit. Since 1933 this has been interpreted as an equalizing function, so much so, in fact, that by the 1980 Australia had in place ' . . . the most extensive and elaborate system of Horizontal Financial Equalization in the world' (Government of Victoria, Federal State Relations Committee 2000).

In practice the equalizing effects are very substantial for the Northern Territory, both for specific grants and for General Revenue Assistance (Table 5.4; Fig. 5.2). However, for the other states the effects are relatively modest. This is because no great inequalities in terms of population growth and wealth, and hence tax revenues and the relative costs of public services, exists between the states. Indeed, if the Northern Territory is excluded the standard deviation for the relative costs of public service has been calculated at just 7 per cent (Spahn and Shah 1995: 63). Table 5.5 shows the pattern of net distribution of all forms of federal aid per capita and in relation to gross state product (GSP) in 1994–5 (for earlier GSP figures, see Ahmad 1997: 162). Perhaps the most noteworthy feature of the table is the generally high level of federal aid received by all states and territories. The national average amounts to 8 per cent of GSP and even in the richest jurisdiction—Australian Capital Territory—the total comes to 6.2 per cent of GSP.

A final feature of Australian intergovernmental relations is the existence of

Table 5.4. Impact of horizontal fiscal equalization in the distribution of the pool of financial assistance grants and health care grants in 1998–9

State/territory	Distribution using CGC[a] relativities (1) $Am	%	Distribution on an equal per capita basis (2) $Am	%	Difference in distribution, (1)–(2) (3) $Am	Distribution on the basis of personal income tax paid (4) $Am	%	Difference in distribution (1)–(4) (5) $Am
NSW	6,546	29.7	7,467	33.8	-920	8,084	36.6	-1,538
Vic	4,814	21.8	5,474	24.8	-660	5,518	25.0	-704
Qld	4,174	18.9	4,089	18.5	85	3,496	15.8	678
WA	2,117	9.6	2,157	9.8	-40	2,199	10.0	-82
SA	2,131	9.7	1,746	7.9	385	1,554	7.0	577
Tas	855	3.9	552	2.5	303	471	2.1	384
ACT	345	1.6	363	1.6	-18	545	2.5	-200
NT	1,091	4.9	227	1.0	865	206	0.9	885
Total	22,074	100.0	22,074	100.0		22,074		

[a]Commonwealth Grants Commission.

Source: Commonwealth of Australia (1999: Table 3).

Table 5.5. Distribution of federal grants,[a] Australia, 1994–5 (Australian dollars)

	NSW	Vic	Qld	WA	SA	Tas	ACT	NT	Total
Total (billions)	9.31	6.85	5.61	3.13	3.51	1.00	0.54	1.07	31.1
Per capita	1,531	1,526	1,739	1,829	2,039	2,114	1,797	6,269	1,702
% GSP[b]	6.7	6.9	8.7	7.6	8.9	11.7	6.2	24.8	8.0

[a]General Revenue Assistance, General Purpose Capital Assistance, Specific Purpose Payments (direct to states), Specific Purpose Payments (through the states).
[b]Gross state product.
Source: computed from Commonwealth of Australia (1994; 1995).

an official body responsible for monitoring the indebtedness of the states. Thus, the Loan Council which was originally set up in 1927 and approved by a referendum in 1928. Each state has one vote on the Council, the Commonwealth two plus—as the chair—the casting vote. Originally the federal government actually lent money to the states should any state not be able to meet the Council's strictures. In this way Commonwealth control of state finances was further enhanced. However, since the mid-1990s the Council's rules have been relaxed with a voluntary code now in force. This new arrangement was made possible by an agreement among the states to find other ways to control borrowing (Painter 1998: 104–5).

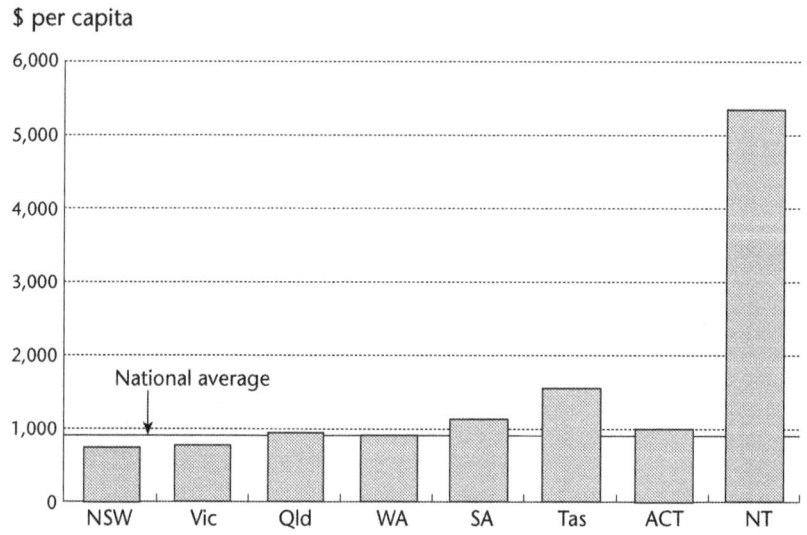

Figure 5.2. General revenue assistance, 1998–1999
Source: Commonwealth of Australia (1999: Chart 6).

Summary and Conclusions

Australia is not a country associated with 'stateness' problems. On the contrary, with the minor exception of the symbolic vote for secession in WA in 1933, throughout its history it has been a model of democracy and political stability. In spite of its vast size and great geographic diversity, modern Australia is relatively homogeneous in economic and social terms. The Northern Territory apart, no great spatial disparities in wealth and income exist. In spite of this, Australian politics do have a clear territorial dimension. Indeed, conflicts over the allocation of taxes between different levels of government and over the distribution of federal grants to the states have dominated federal-state relations from the very beginning. During the first 40 years of the Commonwealth these disputes were as much to do with interstate economic disparities as with state opposition to the federal role. More recently, economic convergence among the states has changed the nature of the debate away from 'who gets what?' towards 'how much do we all get?' Throughout this process, states have lacked a constitutionally mandated institutional base for the representation of their interests. The Senate is anything but a council of the states. Instead it simply mirrors the party politics and party discipline that dominate the House of Representatives. In addition, and in contrast to the United States down to 1937, the Supreme Court has generally favoured federal over state power. These political and institutional arrangements have, in combination with the original fiscal emasculation of the Australian states, led to an unusual degree of federal domination and control.

Intermediate organizations ranging for the Premiers Conference to the COAG to the Leader's Forum have helped fill the institutional gap in federal-state relations. None of these serves as a permanent source of representation for the states in federal decision making, however. Instead these devices act more as public forum for the airing of grievances and the formation of common policy positions among the states. In fiscal relations, the most important body is the CGC, which was set up specifically to depoliticize the equalization component in grant distribution. Significantly, state governments broadly accept the decisions of the Commission.

Indeed there is little evidence that Australians question the legitimacy of the federal role. On the contrary, one of the two main political parties, the ALP, which has a highly democratic organizational structure, was, for much of its existence, committed not only to increasing the federal role but also to abolishing the very institution of federalism. And during the 1950s and 1960s the other main political party, the Liberals, systematically enhanced federal power while in government. Recent political battles have been centred on the question of the *general level* of federal spending, especially on social programmes. The distribution among states has been of secondary importance. None of this is to deny that the extreme vertical fiscal imbalance characteristic of the Australian system is not a source of concern. Among state politicians and officials it has been a constant worry. But this concern has typically been expressed as much in terms of erosion of public sector programmes *per se* as in terms of the erosion of state political and economic autonomy (see, for example, the extensive analysis in Mathew and Grewal 1997).

One important indicator of the status of the federal role is the pattern of constitutional referendum outcomes over the last 100 years. Of those carried— a mere eight out of more than 40 down to 1988—most have approved the extension of federal power. None has specifically devolved power to the states (Aitkin, Jinks, and Warhurst, 1988: Table 2.1).

Australia provides a good example of a country where, for the most part, territorially defined social and economic differences have broadly been reduced through time, and where politics has been increasingly dominated by nationally articulated distributional issues rather than by distinctively state-centred issues. The role of constitutional arrangements in this process Australian is complex. On the one hand, the original transfer of the major sources of taxation to the federal government immediately weakened the capacity of the states to act independently. On the other hand, the Senate had the potential to become a powerful instrument for the representation of the states. The fact that it failed to develop in this way reflects the importance of adversarial party politics in Australia which, from the very beginning, were aligned on ideological rather than territorial lines. Given this, the ensuing centralization of the party system and parties' exercize of power through highly disciplined control of both legislatures, and especially the lower house, is in no way surprising. The existence of a parliamentary as opposed to presidential system no doubt further aided this process. Australia has been fortunate, therefore, that its constitutional and institutional arrangements have been adapted in ways that have facilitated the centralization of power in the federal government without at the same time provoking resentment among the peoples of culturally or economically distinctive states.

6

Germany: Adaptation and Change in a Centralized Federation

Germany Unified: A Tribute to the Success of the Federal Idea

Neville Johnson, 1999

Origins

F EDERAL-LIKE institutional arrangements have been a feature among the German peoples of Europe for many centuries. This phenomenon stems from one simple fact: a continuing disjunction between, on the one hand, a common language and culture and, on the other, fragmented political and institutional arrangements. Hence until unification in 1871 the more than 20 German states and city states, most dominated by the Hohenzollern and Hapsburg royal houses, had entered into a variety of cooperative arrangements mainly with regard to public law and economic affairs (R. Schlesinger 1998: Ch. 4). During the nineteenth century liberal support was concentrated in the smaller western states and was soon overwhelmed by the Greater Prussian Tendency, which combined appeals to German nationalism with the promise that political enlargement would bring with it rapid economic progress. From 1862, Bismarck exploited the military strength of Prussia to extend his control over the rest of Germany creating first the North German Confederation in 1867 and eventually the Empire in 1871, which consisted of a confederation of 25 German-speaking states. Although representation of the states was facilitated through the Bundesrat, the system was both undemocratic—political parties were banned—and autocratic—the Prussian elites dominated politics and the army. In effect, the Empire consisted of a Prussian-dominated alliance of princely states. Even so, the new German Reich was never subjected to administrative centralization. Instead, a relatively small central bureaucracy relied on the states to implement policy. Efficiency was achieved in part because some institutional linkages were already in place—for example, the Commercial Code was adopted in 1861—and in part because most Germans shared a broad cultural acceptance of nationally established standards in public services (Johnson 1998: 26–8).

Following World War I, federal arrangements were also adopted in the new Weimar Republic. However, and as is all too well known, the Weimar Republic

was flawed both institutionally and politically. Institutionally, the main concern of the framers was controlling Prussian irredentism. To this end, Prussian
representation in the upper house, the Federal Council or Reichsrat, was
restricted to two-fifths of the total vote. In addition, and uniquely among the
Länder (states) half of the Prussian Reichsrat representation was to be
appointed not by the Prussian government but by the diets of the 13 Prussian
provinces (R. Schlesinger 1998: 107–8). Although much of the administration
of policy was left to the Länder, most legislation in such areas as the economy
and agriculture was to be jointly formulated by the states and the federal government. Crucially, however, the federation could overrule measures adopted
by the Länder. Moreover, Article 9 of the constitution gave to the federation
the power to overrule Länder competence in internal order and welfare when
there was a 'need for unified direction' (R. Schlesinger 1998: 103). In their
efforts to weaken state power, and in particular the power of Prussia, the
framers gave to the federal government great potential for the centralization
of authority. The dominant political forces in the Weimar Republic—big business and the army—quickly exploited these institutional arrangements and, in
the context of deepening economic crisis, they centralized power in the federal government. In contrast, within the Länder governments, radical left and
right-wing factions, whose allegiance was to national rather than provincial
political forces, replaced the weak, mainly conservative political parties, which
had held majorities in most of the Länder in 1923. So well represented were
these radical forces in both the lower house—the Reichstag—and in the
Federal Council that the Council's constitutional ability to veto any Reichstag
measure with a two-thirds majority vote was never invoked. Instead, the
Reichstag enacted centralizing measures through simple majority votes
(Brecht 1967: 188–9). By the end of the 1920s Germany more resembled a unitary than a federal state. Interestingly, however, even after the advent of
Hitler's Third Reich a federal institutional and administrative framework was
retained. No independent political authority was vested in the Länder, but
they remained important administrative units for the implementation of Nazi
policies.

The Founding Constitution: Germany's Basic Law

Following a conference between the American, British and French authorities
and Länder representatives in 1948, the founding constitution of West
Germany was formulated by the Land minister-presidents of the Allied-
occupied Länder and approved in 1949. Although these ministers were
instructed by the Allies to follow certain principles when creating the constitution, they were given complete freedom over the formulation of detailed
provisions. The Allies insisted only that the new West German state be democratic, with specific guarantees for the protection of individual rights. In addition, the Allies required that a federal system of government be instituted.

Given the experience of Weimar, which had been characterized by a steady drift towards centralization and authoritarianism, the requirement that central power should be limited through a genuinely federal system was unsurprising. Federal arrangements also allowed for territorial expansion in the form of the eventual absorption of East Germany into the system.

It is also unsurprising that the minister-presidents followed principles of governance that had been features of the German states for many generations. They therefore created an upper house—the Bundesrat—which would be a genuine council of the states with Länder delegations chosen by state cabinets. Although not exactly mathematically proportional in size, delegations varied according to the population size of the Länder.[1] The Bundesrat was not the legislative equal of the popularly elected lower house—the Bundestag—as its approval was required only in those domestic policies which were of vital interest to the Länder. In practice, however, this included all the major domestic policy arenas including employment, education, law and order, transport, and welfare.

The original intention in 1949 was that there would be a fairly strict delineation of functions between the federal government and the Länder. In other words, such areas as defence and foreign policy, citizenship, immigration, and macroeconomic policy would be federal responsibilities, while education, law and order, health, regional, culture, and environmental policy would be Land responsibilities. In addition, it was envisaged that tax revenues to finance these tasks would be collected by the responsible jurisdiction, although from the very beginning a single tax code and revenue-collection service would prevail throughout the country. However, and again in line with German tradition, the Länder were to be responsible for most of the *implementation* of federal law. Thus in those areas such as employment law, where the federal government was assigned the main responsibility, Land governments administered the law. A system of extensive cooperation between the federal and state governments was therefore built into the legislative process, with the Bundesrat functioning both as an essential part of the legislative process and as a representative of Land interests. These cooperative arrangements stemmed not only from German tradition but also from the simple fact that in the immediate postwar period the Länder had already built up an extensive system of liaison and communication with each other (Leonardy 1989).

Commentators have always found it difficult to place this German system in a taxonomy of federal states (see, for example, Riker 1964: 123–4). On the one hand the prominent position of the Bundesrat as a council of the states implies a decentralized federation, as does the apparently quite strict division of responsibilities between the two levels of government. On the other hand,

---

[1] Representation in the Bundesrat is not unlike that in the EU Council of Ministers. The largest states have greater representation than the smallest but in the absence of anything approaching exact proportionality. Hence the largest state, North Rhine-Westphalia with 21% of the population, has just 8.7% of the Bundesrat vote, while the smallest, Bremen with just 0.8% of the population, controls 4.3% of the vote.

the decision to opt for a parliamentary form of government implied a degree of centralization, as did Articles 35 and 91 of the Basic Law, which sanction federal intervention in Länder affairs to ensure law and order and maintain the democratic order (Klatt 1999: 41). It became quickly apparent, however, that the Federal Republic was destined to become a centralized rather than a decentralized federation.

Centralized Cooperative Federalism: The Federal Republic 1950–90

The Federal Republic represents a excellent case of how institutional arrangements were exploited by nationalizing political and economic forces to produce a much more centralized system than that originally envisaged by the framers. This accepted, the uniquely German arrangements of territorial power sharing have maintained the essentially federal nature of the system. And as the next section will show, cooperative power sharing was to prove vital to the successful incorporation of the eastern Länder during the 1990s.

Centralization during the 1950s and the 1960s was facilitated by a strong sense of common purpose among the German people that in turn was reflected in the party system. During the Empire and Weimar periods the main territorial divisions involved differences between the politically and/or culturally distinctive Prussia and Bavaria and the other German states. After 1945 Prussia was dismembered and although Bavaria retained its political distinctiveness through the Christian Socialist Party (CSU), a national coalition with the Christian Democrats (CDU) meant that, in most issue areas, Bavarian preferences were subsumed under national CDU objectives. The Federal Republic was also fortunate to enjoy rapid economic growth for the whole of the 1950–70 period. Inter-Länder income and wealth inequalities were small and mainly confined to differences between the older industrial areas and the booming south and south-west. The relative absence of territorial inequalities smoothed acceptance of one of the principle canons of the Basic Law: that the Länder should enjoy 'uniformity of living conditions' (see the discussion in Spahn and Fottinger 1997). To this end, the federal government soon put in place a system a system of vertical and horizontal financial equalization. We will return to this question and how it relates to unification later. Below is a summary of the main centralizing trends during the period:

- creation of federal armed forces, 1954–6;
- air transport and nuclear energy assigned to the federal government, late 1950s-early 1960s;
- federal government given the power to invoke emergence powers in state of emergency,1968;
- separate tax and spending powers largely replaced by joint or shared

income, and corporate taxes, 1950s. Value added tax (VAT) instituted as shared tax, 1969;

- vertical grants to Länder and federally mandated horizontal transfers to speed equalization greatly expanded, 1960s and 1970s; and
- constitution amended so that 'joint tasks' in regional policy, planning, research university construction, and agricultural structural policy can be undertaken, 1969–70. This constitutional change is important, because for the first time Land and federal government were *jointly* responsible for *implementation*. Fritz Sharpf characterised this as the 'enmeshment' of the two levels of government (cited in Klatt 1999: 45).

These changes were facilitated by an increasingly nationalized political party system with the same parties operating at the national and the Land levels. In 1949 ten parties were represented in the Bundestag; by 1961 this had fallen to three. The same development applied to the Bundesrat and the Land legislatures. Moreover, the two dominant parties—the CDU/CSU and the Social Democrats (SPD)—were recognized as *Volkspartien* or 'catch all' peoples' parties whose appeal was to the whole German people rather than to section, whether determined territorially or by ideology. Naturally, the coalition in power at the national level was often different from that in power at the state level, and this was sometimes reflected in different parties controlling the two national legislatures. However, the number of territorially based disagreements was small. As Table 6.1 shows, the Bundesrat exercized very few effective vetoes in the 1949–72 period. They increased somewhat during the 1970s,

Table 6.1. The Bundesrat veto, 1949–1998

Legislative period	Number of bills subject to final veto[a]	Vetoes as a percentage of all bills
1949–53	9	1.6
1959–57	6	1.2
1957–61	2	0.5
1961–65	3	0.7
1965–69	2	0.4
1969–72	0.5[b]	0.1
1972–76	9	1.7
1976–80	11	3.1
1980–83	3	2.2
1983–87	0	0
1987–90	1	0.3
1990–94	10	2.0
1994–98	11	2.0

[a]Following failure to win approval in the joint Bundestag-Bundesrat mediation committee.
[b]One bill was split in two, one half was passed and the other vetoed.

Source: Adapted from Silvia (1999: Table 1).

mainly because of conflicts over equalization programmes, which will be catalogued later.

While the 1960s and 1970s were undoubtedly marked by centralizing policies, these were not the exact functional equivalent of similar policies in
Australia, the United States, and Canada. For in Germany the increased and
extensive use of inter-ministerial committees gave to the Länder an effective
veto over some aspects of federal policy. As one commentator has put it : 'The
evolutionary pattern of federalism in Germany is characterized by the increasing legislative and substantive policy making authority of the federal government, but in exchange for greater co-determination over policy substance by
the Länder' (Deeg 1994: 4). Crucially this system of joint or interlocking policy making often proceeded on the basis of unanimity voting rules, thus
greatly increasing the ability of the Länder to shape federal policy (Lehmbruch
1989: 222).

Two important further developments marked the 1970s and 1980s. First,
the economic dislocation resulting from the oil crises affected the economies
of the Länder asymmetrically. States such as North Rhine-Westphalia and the
Saarland were hard hit, While Hesse and Baden-Württemberg fared relatively
well. These discrepancies put considerable strain on the system of intergovernmental aid instituted and expanded during the 1960s, and eventually they
were to lead to the first serious signs of inter-Länder tensions over resource
allocation. Second, these events took place in the context of a sometimes
unsteady SPD-Free Democrat (FPD) national coalition which was often obliged
to operate in partnership with a CDU/CSU-dominated Bundesrat and
CDU/CSU Land governments. When forced to cut spending on the Joint Tasks
that were funded by federal/Land financing programmes, the first true crisis in
the short history of West German federalism occurred. All parties agreed that
for the system to survive intact, some 'untangling' of the tasks performed by
the two levels of government was necessary. The problem was not resolved,
however, until the election of a new CDU/FDP government in 1982 under the
leadership of Helmut Kohl. Kohl immediately proposed that, as in the
European Community, German intergovernmental relations should follow
the principle of subsidiary. In other words, policy functions should be separated out in ways that result in the most appropriate level of government
being given responsibility for particular tasks. What this meant in practice was
the exclusive allocation of some tasks to the Länder—notably, university construction, aid for schools, hospital construction, urban renewal, and public
housing. At the same time the federal government sugared the pill by increasing intergovernmental aid and increasing the Länder share of the sales tax by
two per cent (see the discussion in Klatt 1999: 50).

As Hartmut Klatt notes, this new phase of what might be called devolved
cooperative federalism was short-lived. By the mid-1980s the federal government was once again legislating in urban renewal and education and some of
the joint tasks were effectively reinstated (Klatt 1999: 52–3). Indeed, disputes
over the allocation of federal funds intensified throughout the decade,

although these rarely reached the point of dominating political discourse in the West German federation. Put another way, a form of territorial politics certainly existed in Germany, but for the most part these were absorbed into national political debates on taxation and resource allocation. We will return to this point in the next section.

Therefore, by the time of the unification events in 1989 and 1990, German intergovernmental relations could still be characterized as centralized cooperative federalism. Inter-ministerial committees designed to ensure consensual decision making remained in place, even if they were not as successful as during the 1960s and 1970s. Federal-Land conflict was contained and mainly confined to financial matters. It had no distinctive cultural or religious dimension. For the most part the German people accepted increasingly uniform national standards in economic and social life. Administration remained predominantly devolved to the Länder even as federal standardization proceeded apace. The same political parties operated at all levels and when the Bundesrat deviated from the national party line it did so more on ideological than territorial lines. When territory did become important, the Bundesrat as often acted as a forum for *all* the Länder as it did on behalf of individual or groups of Länder—although as far as intergovernmental fiscal relations are concerned inter-Länder tensions increased throughout the 1980s. But the real test for German federalism lay ahead. As will be shown in the next section, unification changed the terms of debate on resource allocation and a produced a more territorially based politics.

Intergovernmental Fiscal Relations and the Challenge of Unification

As[2] earlier indicated, the Basic Law as formulated in 1949 made a clear delineation between the powers of the federal and the Länder governments, and this division was very specific with regard to tax revenue and collection. Originally the intention was to allocate taxation powers either to the federation or to the Länder, with the federation receiving income from customs duties and sales taxes, and the Länder from income and corporate taxes. However, and in marked contrast to Switzerland, the Basic Law gave to the federal government the concurrent right to legislate in any tax area should the needs of the government require additional funding. This provision, which did not require Bundesrat approval, was a short-term expedient: the Basic Law also required the financial constitution to be revised after 1952. Given the urgent reconstruction tasks facing Germany it was not all surprising, therefore, that the federation legislated to access income and corporate tax revenues.

In addition, Article 106/4 of the Basic Law provided for horizontal equalization or a programme of redistribution from the richer to the poorer Länder

---

[2] The first part of this section relies partly on Mackenstein and Jeffery (1999).

(*Finanzausgleich*). Article 106/3 of the Law sanctioned supplementary vertical federal grants in education, health care, and welfare. The logic of these provisions was clear for Article 106/3 also required the Bonn government to safeguard 'uniformity of living conditions within the territory of the federation'. Only horizontal and vertical redistribution could achieve this result. What eventually transpired after the 1952 revision of the constitution was eventually concluded in 1955 was a *de facto* sharing of income and corporate taxes between the Länder and Bonn. Horizontal redistribution was limited by the political clout of the richer Länder in the Bundesrat, which also insisted that the poorer Länder should rely increasingly on vertical federal grants to make up the shortfall. The outcome was a system of intergovernmental finance that was quite far removed from the original 1949 objectives. Instead of a separated system, a shared, interdependent structure evolved with the federation taking on more and more of the responsibilities originally earmarked for the Länder. Increased public spending also resulted from the system, especially as the stated objective was to bring the poorer Länder up to 90 per cent of the national per capita income.

In its essentials, this system prevailed until 1969 when a major constitutional revision occurred under the leadership of the CDU/SPD Grand Coalition. In essence these reforms took German federalism even further away from the 1949 model, for they left increased scope for further incursion of the federal government into the affairs of the Länder. The main provisions were:

(1) a formalization of the shared taxation system: income and corporate taxes were to be shared on a 50/50 basis. In addition, the Länder received 37 per cent of VAT receipts of which 75 per cent were allocated on a per capita basis and 25 per cent according to an income equalization formula;
(2) a new programme of federal supplementary grants to enable the poorer Länder to reach at least 98 per cent of the financial capacity—government income per head of population—of the federation average; and
(3) refinements of the horizontal equalization programme so as to bring all Länder up to the average financial capacity of the federation.

Although these reforms worked well during most of the 1970s, by 1980 it was clear that the system contained certain structural flaws. Originally, North Rhine-Westphalia, Baden-Württemberg, Hamburg, and Hesse had shared most of the financial burden of equalization. By the 1980s, however, economic dislocation and change had reduced this number to just two: Hesse and Baden-Württemberg. In other words, the stated aim of the system, which was to bring all the Länder up to a similar level, had failed. The relatively poor Länder remained relatively poor and were even joined by others such as Bremen during the 1970s. As Wolfgang Renzsch (1998: 130–1) notes:

Due to the greater number of Länder receiving assistance than providing it, the balance became unstable between the two groups, and the answer to the question of fiscal equalization was becoming increasingly oriented toward, and often gave clear preference to, the Länder entitled to receive assistance. Overall, however, the system of fiscal equal-

ization and other measures, despite being intensified, could not free the poorer Länder
. . . from . . . rising social costs, decreasing resources for the development of infrastructure, increasing borrowing and interest payments.

A lack of balance in the equalization system led several of the richer Länder
to by-pass the federation and finance a number of programmes on their own.
At the same time the poorer Länder became even more dependent on federal
supplementary grants. Finally, disputes between individual Länder and Bonn
were increasingly taken to the Federal Constitutional Court. Interestingly, the
Court generally favoured a policy of judicial restraint in these and other cases
involving federal-Land relations, arguing on narrow, technical grounds rather
than on the basis of broad constitutional principle (Blair and Cullen 1999).

It was in this context that the unification process began in 1990. Absorbing
the eastern Länder was a daunting task. They contained some 17 million
people—almost 30 per cent of the west's population—and the eastern per
capita income was a meagre 30 per cent of the west's. Following unification,
the GNP per capita in Germany sank by one sixth or down to 85 per cent of
the pre-unification level (quoted in Renzsch 1998: 127). Given these facts, it is
not surprising that both the federation and the Länder decided on an emergency transition period of four and half years during which exceptional payments would be paid to the east financed out of government borrowing.
Hence the German Unity Fund of DM115 billion was established of which 20
billion would be financed out of savings and the remaining 95 billion out of
equally shared Länder-federation borrowing. In the event, the structural economic problems of the east were such that this amount had to be supplemented periodically.

The next four years were characterized by intense negotiations culminating
in a settlement on 1 January 1995 which marked the full incorporation of the
eastern Länder into the equalization and grant system. At first each Land put
forward its own proposals, all of which favoured the proposing state! After
much wrangling the decision on a new system came down to a choice between
a plan proposed by the federal minister of finance, Theo Waigel, and one proposed by Bavaria. Waigel's proposal would have involved a sharing of the burden of eastern subsidies between the richer western Länder and the federal
government (for details, see Mackenstein and Jeffery 1999: 166). The richer
Länder who mobilized behind the Bavarian alternative dismissed this out of
hand. When faced with support for the Bavarian plan by all the Länder the
federal government capitulated. In essence, this plan proposed no fundamental change to the old pre-unification system. However, in order to bring the
eastern Länder up to an income level approaching the federation average, a
dramatic shift in the distribution of VAT receipts was instituted. In future a full
45 per cent of VAT receipts would be allocated to the Länder: up from the
existing level of 37 per cent. The difference would be allocated directly to the
eastern Länder to bring them up to 92 per cent of the federation average. Only
after this redistribution would the inter-Länder equalization programme

become operative, the objective of which was to bring the eastern Länder up to 95 per cent of the average. Finally, federal supplementary grants would be enhanced but not in ways which would undermine the *status quo ante* and leave the western Länder substantially worse off. However, these grants would be substantial as they were designed to bring the eastern states up to 99.5 per cent of the average government income for the whole federation—after the effects of all the other grant programmes.

What this effectively meant was that the burden of financing the east was shifted further on to the federal government—although through VAT receipts the citizens of the richer Länder would, of course, be paying a disproportionate amount of the cost. Crucially, however, the finances of the western Land governments would be protected. Table 6.2 shows just how important the federal contribution was to be. In 1995, the western Länder contributed just 20 per cent of the total, made up of a small VAT component, DM12.8 billion from horizontal redistribution and DM2.1 billion from the residual German Unity Fund.

Table 6.3 shows the combined redistributive effect of the two main grant programmes: equalization and federal supplementary grants. Note that while, in terms of percentage of Land Gross State Product (GSP), the eastern states receive very substantial benefits from other Länder and the federal government, the net costs even to the richest western Länder is very small—1 per cent of GSP in Hesse and 0.52 per cent in Baden-Württemberg and Bavaria. The latter figures are almost identical to that operative before unification.

General agreement exists to the effect that this system is administratively flawed. Given the very serious and continuing problems of the east, the pressure for further federal largesse and greater inter-Länder equalization continues to build. This has led the federal government to cut back on supplementary grants to the western Länder, raising new taxes which are not shared with the Länder and encouraging the Länder to take on a more independent role in financing some programmes (see the discussion in Mackenstein and Jeffery 1999: 169). The upshot has been a revival of the fiscal politics of the 1980s. Today, however, the much greater economic disparities between the

Table 6.2. Financial equalization flows, 1995 (DM millions)

Measures	Federal level	Western Länder	Eastern Länder
VAT redistribution	−17,500	−900	18,400
Horizontal inter-Länder transfers		−12,800	12,800
Federal supplementary allocations	−26,740	7,770	18,790
German Unity Fund annuities	2,100	−2,100	
Other	−7,775		7,775
Total	−49,915	−8,030	57,945

Source: Mackenstein and Jeffery (1999: Table 7.1).

Table 6.3. Distribution of Federal Vertical and Länder Horizontal Grants,[a] Federal Republic of Germany, 1996

Land	Schl.H.	Hamb	Nied	Brem	NorWe	Hesse	Rhein	Baden	Bayer	Saar	Berlin	Brand	Meck	Saxony	L. Sax	Thür	Total
Total grants (DM billions)	0.41	−0.49	1.8	2.75	−3.12	−3.25	1.2	−2.53	−2.87	2.5	8.0	3.7	2.8	6.47	4.11	3.23	37.4
Grants per capita (DM)	665	−349	422	2,470	−174	−541	302	−245	−239	232	2,305	1,456	1,560	5,990	1,500	1,292	457
Grants as % of GSP[b]	0.41	−0.39	0.63	7.4	−0.48	−1.0	0.78	−0.52	−0.52	6.3	6.2	8.0	9.3	13.2	8.5	7.7	1.2

[a]Vertical grants: Supplementary grants; Horizontal Grants: the Interstate Equalization Programme.
[b]Gross state product.

Source: Grant data computed from Statistik Bund (1997) and GSP data.

Länder mean that the disputes are more conflictual and difficult to resolve. This accepted, the economic condition of the eastern Länder is such that they can be addressed only through national action. The scene is set, therefore, for a further nationalization of German politics.

Territory, Politics, and German Federalism

From the discussion thus far, it might be inferred that, at least until unification, some variety of territorial politics existed in the Federal Republic. Disputes within the Bundesrat between the richer and poorer Länder over federal funding and horizontal equalization certainly suggest this. However, as Gerhard Lehmbruch showed some years ago, those parties dominating the Bundesrat have used that advantage either to support the incumbent government drawn from the Bundestag or to oppose the incumbent government's national legislative programme (Lehmbruch 1978: 151). The latter scenario applied during the 1969–82 period when the CDU/CSU held a majority in the upper chamber while the SPD/FDP dominated the lower chamber. Moreover, as Pridham and Jeffery (1973) have shown, Land and Bund elections were increasingly inter-linked during the post war years: voters at the Land level voted on land rather than local/regional issues. Organizationally, the main parties also developed structures that greatly facilitated the articulation of national concerns at the state and local levels. For all intents in purposes, therefore, Germany had developed a *national* party system. The same parties operated at the state and national levels; extensive organizational connective tissue between different levels existed; party discipline was fully developed in both national legislatures.

As earlier catalogued, the 1980s represented some retreat from this position. Disputes over federal grants and equalization intensified and the partial 'untangling' of federal and Land tasks reduced the interdependence between the two branches of government. In addition, the party system, while hardly transformed, did show signs of significant change. The Greens emerged as a fourth force in national politics and the electorate became increasingly volatile. Electoral trends in land and national elections also became less synchronized. Finally, a more intrusive role for the European Union began to impact on federal-Land relations. Many Länder governments interpreted the enhanced EU in terms of a removal of some Länder powers to Brussels and thus represented a strengthening of that body most responsible for influencing EU decision-making: the national government.

While all this is true, these changes were insufficient to change the basic characterization of German federalism. It remained grounded primarily on cooperation in the context of a nationalized party and political system. This apparently enduring quality derives form the simple fact that the territory of postwar Germany was remarkably homogeneous economically, culturally, and ethnically. Those divisions that did exist—for example, between native

Germans and immigrant labour—had no significant territorial dimension. Indeed, by most measures, the Federal Republic was more homogeneous than any of the other states discussed in this book. All this was to change with unification and the absorption of a dramatically poorer country in the form of East Germany. What then have been the effects of unification on the dynamics of German federalism? Most commentators agree that the character of intergovernmental relations has changed significantly. As was shown in the last section, new strains in what Germans call the fiscal constitution became increasingly manifest during the 1990s. As judged by objective indicators, however, the absorption of the eastern Länder was achieved with relatively few strains. As earlier chapters have shown, 'stateness' problems are usually articulated through changes in the party system. Party change is, in turn, reflected in those national institutions in which the states have some representation—often the upper house of the national legislature. If unresolved within the existing institutional structure, dissident regions or interests will call for constitutional change that may or may not resolve the problem. In the worst-case scenario, secession or disintegration may ensue. None of these outcomes occurred in the German case. Let us look at each of these measures in turn.

The Party System and the Role of the Bundesrat

Students of German political parties are agreed that while unification has certainly changed the system it did not transform it (see Roberts 1997: Ch. 12). Remarkably, the same 'west German' parties continue to dominate almost all of the Länder. The established parties, notably the CDU and SPD, created bases in the eastern Länder and won electoral support with relatively little opposition from other parties. Only one party, the Democratic Socialists (PDS), which is the successor to the old Communist Party, is a definably eastern party and its support is limited. In the 1998 Bundestag elections it received 5.1 per cent of the vote, up very slightly from the 1994 election. Admittedly, the PDS showing in the east averaged around 20 per cent, but it came second to the two main parties only in Brandenburg.[3] And only in Saxony-Anhalt, where it is in informal coalition with the SPD, does it play a role in government (see Table 6.4).

In other words, the distinctive economic and cultural status of the east has not led to a territorial fracturing of the party system as has occurred in Canada and prevailed in the United States for much of its history. Indeed with five parties now represented in the Bundesrat—CDU/CSU SPD, FPD, Greens, and PDS—and an increasingly volatile electorate, the potential for a clearly defined territorial politics may have even been reduced. During the fiscal battles of the 1980s cross-Länder coalitions were created to facilitate a united front against the federal government. Following unification, although some coincidence of

[3] It polled 21.% in Brandenburg, 24.8% in Mecklenburg, 19.7% in Saxony, 20.1% in Saxony-Anhalt, 21% in Thüringen, and 16.7% in Berlin (www.statistik-bund.de/wahlen/info98).

Table 6.4. Party alignments in the Bundestag and the Bundesrat, May 1998

Party alignments in the Bundestag

	Government parties	Opposition parties	Other
	CDU/CSU, FDP	SPD, Greens	PDS[a]

Government composition in the Länder

Land (Bundesrat votes)	Aligned with the federal government	Cross-cutting federal government and opposition	Aligned with the federal opposition	Other
Baden-Würrtemberg (6)	CDU–FDP			
Bavaria (4)	CSU			
Berlin (4)		CDU–SPD		
Brandenburg (4)			SPD	
Bremen (3)		SPD–CDU		
Hamburg (3)			SPD–Green	
Hessen (5)			SPD–Green	
Lower Saxony (6)			SPD	
Mecklenburg-West Pomerania (3)		CDU–SPD		
North Rhine-Westphalia (6)			SPD–Green	
Rhineland-Palatinate (4)		SPD–FPD		
Saarland (3)			SPD	
Saxony (4)	CDU			
Saxony-Anhalt (4)				SPD–(PDS*)
Schleswig-Holstein (4)			SPD–Green	
Thüringia (4)		CDU–SPD		
Total Bundesrat vote (69)	16	18	31	4

[a]While the PDS is also, of course, in Bundestag opposition, its GDR past puts it 'beyond the pale' in terms of federal-level cooperation with the wider Bundestag opposition. In the narrower east German context, however, it is widely regarded as a legitimate expression of eastern interests, and therefore, in Saxony-Anhalt at least, a partner for (limited) cooperation.

Source: Jeffery (1999: Figure 3).

interest did develop among the smaller Länder and eastern Länder or among the western Länder and richer Länder, they failed to form lasting coalitions constructed on the basis of territorial separateness (see Jeffery 1999: 160).

This is confirmed by the behaviour of the majority parties in the Bundesrat. After 1994, when the SPD and the Greens held a majority in the chamber, they exercized their veto no more than when the CDU/CSU enjoyed a similar position in the 1976–80 period (Table 6.1). Although some of these votes involved Länder-specific issues (Jeffery 1999: 159), national issues were as important. In other words there is no real evidence that unification has produced the sort of territorial politics that represents anything other than an embryo of a 'stateness' problem in Germany.

Constitutional Reform

Not surprisingly, unification did produce constitutional change. Following a report by a joint Bundesrat/Bundestag commission, a Constitutional Reform Act was passed in 1994 whose main purpose was to rationalize the federal system in the wake of unification. Constitutional reform affected four areas: the participation of the Länder in European affairs; some sorting out of federal-Land responsibilities with regard to both legislation and administration; territorial reform; and reform of financial equalization. Only with regard to the role of the Bundesrat in EU matters, however, were the reforms fundamental. As Schneider (1999: 77) notes, as far as legislative responsibilities are concerned 'real shifts of competence between federation and Länder did not come to pass'. Administrative changes were also small, and ambitious plans for territorial change, and in particular the proposal to combine Berlin with the adjacent Brandenburg, fell foul of a popular referendum. Changes affecting some of the smaller Länder, in particular Hamburg, have yet to be implemented (Leonardy 1999: 286). As our earlier discussion of fiscal federalism showed, no fundamental change in the architecture of intergovernmental fiscal relations occurred. Instead, the concerns of the richer western Länder shifted the burden of funding unification on to the federal government. One aspect of the constitutional reforms in this area at least attempted important change. This was the abandonment of the 'uniformity of living conditions' clause with a replacement clause promising 'equivalence' of living conditions. However, the change was cosmetic rather than substantive and the 'uniformity' requirement remained for the apportionment of tax revenues (Leonardy 1999: 297).

The extension of the Bundesrat's veto power to European matters was of a quite different order. As Schneider records:

. . . the Bundesrat has emerged as the real 'winner' in the constitutional reform process . . . the Bundesrat no longer participates only in the legislation and administration of the federation, but also now directly 'in matters of the European Union' . . . The Bundesrat has thus become one of the most important focal points and pivots of German participation in the process of the European Union. It also has a new 'European Chamber,' to which each Land sends one member, which can act on behalf of the Bundesrat plenary with equivalent decision-making authority. (Schneider 1999: 78–9)

Apart from this extension of the powers of the Bundesrat, the 1994 reforms were primarily technocratic in nature. Their aim was not to alter fundamental federation-Land power relations but to rationalize relations in the light of unification. Most commentators agree that they did not go far enough; many believe that German federalism now displays serious structural problems in the areas of legislative competence, fiscal relations, and Land jurisdictional boundaries (Leonardy 1999). These same commentators predict intensifying pressures for constitutional reform early in the new century.

Summary and Conclusions

Germany is, of course, an unusual federation. The Länder did not come together voluntarily in order to avert an external threat by providing a common defence.[4] In this sense, the German case is fundamentally different from the Swiss, Canadian, and American cases. Instead, the occupying powers required the creation of a democratic and federal republic to govern the territory of West Germany. The particular shape of the federal system arrived at by the Land minister-presidents reflected a number of important German political and bureaucratic traditions. These included—Berlin apart—utilization of historically established city and regional jurisdictions, a devolved system of administration, and a uniform civil and tax code. In addition, the creation of an upper house as a representative or council of the states echoed similar arrangements in Bismarck's Reich and in the Weimar Republic. In these respects the variety of German federalism enshrined in the Basic Law was not new at all. The real novelty came in the form of a democratically accountable parliamentary system. Eventually this was to produce a stable and effective political party system rooted in a surprisingly strong and resilient civil society.

As catalogued, between 1950 and 1982 German federalism was characterized by an increasing degree of centralization. This showed itself in a gradual encroachment of the federal government into areas where originally it was expected the Länder governments would act. In addition what were intended as separate taxing and spending powers soon became shared powers. Finally, opposition by the richer Länder to horizontal equalization led to the growth of federal supplementary grants allocated in the main to the less well-off states. Enhanced federal power was facilitated by a stable and increasingly centralized party system. The same parties operated at all levels and the Bundesrat acted more as a second legislative chamber than as council of the states.

---

[4] However, given the Soviet threat there was of course a compelling defence logic behind the creation of a West German state. But a unitary state would have served NATO's defence needs as well as a federal system.

This system was subject to new strains and tensions during the 1980s as the differential effects of economic dislocation on the Länder revealed the inadequacies of an equalization system devoted to 'uniformity of living conditions'. Further problems resulted from some fragmentation of the party system and increased electoral volatility. In comparative perspective, however, these developments did little to challenge the integrity of the system. Economic and cultural homogeneity ensured that no individual Land or groups of Länder were persistently opposed to federal policy across a range of issue areas— although the richer Länder did form a political bloc organized to resist territorial redistribution. In this sense, no discernible stateness problem existed in pre-unification Germany. Interestingly, institutional arrangements were amenable to the development of such a problem. The Bundesrat veto could have been the focus of opposition for disgruntled Länder, but it was used sparingly and only rarely involved fundamental differences between the Länder and the federal government. The major reason for this moderation was, of course, that the major political cleavages in German society were not territorial but ideological.[5] Hence national parties mobilized voters at all levels of government on the basis of the electorate's stand on such issues as the role of the state in *German* society, not in Bavarian or North Rhine-Westphalian society.

Remarkably, unification failed fundamentally to alter this situation. In spite of the fact that the eastern Länder were—and remain—very poor in relation to the rest of Germany, they were incorporated without great political upheaval and in the absence of fundamental constitutional change. In the realm of intergovernmental fiscal relations, transferring the main burden of subsidy from the Länder to the federal government facilitated incorporation. What this meant, of course, was that taxpayers throughout Germany, but particularly richer taxpayers in the west, bore most of the cost. While they hardly accepted this burden with equanimity, they nonetheless accepted it.

In essence, the territorial dimension in German fiscal politics appears to be confined mainly to the housekeeping concerns of the Land finance ministries. For Land governments, so long as the costs of horizontal transfers from the richer to the poorer Länder are kept to an acceptable minimum, the burden of unification remains tolerable. Higher taxes for most Germans may be a source of discontent, but in terms of political action disquiet has not been transferred into the institutional structure of German federalism in ways which create long-lasting territorial alliances.

In 1992 McEvoy quipped that 'Unifying Germany was the easy part. The real challenge is to unite the Germans' (quoted in Roberts 1997: 174). As it turned out, however, it proved remarkably easy to unite the Germans. No better evidence of this is needed than the essentially unchanged party system. Only the PDS is a specifically eastern party—although even the PDS has attempted to build a base in the west—and it has limited electoral support. Unlike Canada or the *post bellum* United States south, no great territorial

---

[5] On the decline of ideology in the SPD, see Conradt (1996: Ch. 5).

cleavage has emerged with political parties serving as the main agents for the articulation of sectional or regional grievances.

As Charlie Jeffery (1999: 161–4) has noted, unification has none the less changed the nature of German federalism. It is now less consensual in style and more competitive and heterogeneous. The Länder are now more assertive but less inclined to form lasting cross-border Land alliances. Crucially, however, the more abrasive and conflictual politics typical of post-unification Germany is mediated by political parties whose appeal is based on ideology and interest rather than region and territory.

7

Switzerland: Dispersing Power for National Unity

The Swiss cantons regard themselves as having been there before the Confederation, and as having created the federation by a voluntary act . . .

Christopher Hughes, 1975

Constitutional Origins: The Politics of Collective Security

SWISS constitutional history has been shaped by its geography. Following the decline of the Holy Roman Empire, linguistically and culturally distinctive alpine valleys came together to provide for a common defence against the imperial ambitions of Germans, Austrians, and French, or Burgundians. The first of such efforts dates from 1291 when the small forest communities of Uri, Shwyz, and Unterwalden created a 'perpetual league' or a confederation to provide for mutual security. (Codding 1961: 21). Over the next two centuries the number of cantons in the confederation grew to ten by 1500. With few exceptions the confederation was successful in winning limited wars with a succession of enemies. Internal tensions were, however, never far from the surface; and this was particularly true following the Reformation, when the populations of many of the German-speaking cantons were converted to Protestantism. Religious wars broke out in 1529, 1531, 1656, and finally in 1712 (Gillard 1955: Ch. 2). These conflicts established a religious dualism that persists to this day.

Constitutionally, the confederation was little more than a mutual defence pact. The only confederacy-wide institution was the Diet, made up representatives of the cantons, which met infrequently and operated according to a unanimity rule. In addition, decisions had to be ratified by each canton government. Even on the eve of the French Revolution, Switzerland did not have a government in the modern sense. The enforcement of confederacy decisions depended on the approval of all the cantons who remained sovereign in all the crucial areas of governance including citizenship, macroeconomic policy, external trade, and security. However, under the direction of Napoleonic France, Switzerland did acquire a centralized unitary government between 1798 and

1803—a development that led to great internal unrest and strengthened Swiss commitment to self-determination (Bonjour, Offler, and Potter 1952: 225–30). Recognizing the problem, Napoleon restored elements of the old confederation in 1803 and, following the defeat of the French in 1815, the cantons chose to return to confederal arrangements. However, between that date and the ratification of a new constitution in 1848, the country was torn with strife between radical, mainly urban, Protestant forces and conservative, mainly Catholic and rural interests. Although there was a clear religious dimension to this conflict, it also followed the broader European division between liberals intent on advancing democracy and the sovereignty of the people, and conservatives determined to maintain the old order based on hierarchical social relations.

Liberal ideas triumphed following a short and almost bloodless civil war precipitated by the apparent secession of the Catholic cantons from the confederation (Bonjour, Offler, and Potter 1952: 264–7). The ensuing constitution was formally ratified in September 1848 and, as amended in 1874, forms the basis for the modern Swiss constitution. Fifteen-and-a-half cantons approved the constitution and six-and-a-half rejected it. The latter accepted the arrangement because there was no viable alternative, and certainly not one that could guarantee their security against hostile powers. The Swiss 'founding' experience was different from the American mainly because the Swiss did not feel the need to differentiate themselves from the political system of a recent occupying power. Instead, the main concern was accommodating religious and linguistic diversity among the 25 cantons and half cantons—increased to 26 in with the creation of the Jura in 1979. To this end they created a highly decentralized constitutional structure. Legislative power was divided equally between the popularly elected National Council and the Council of the States made up of two representatives from each canton. The two chambers are known as the Federal Assembly, which also elects each of the other branches, the executive and judiciary. There is no one-person executive. Instead the Federal Council is made up seven heads of government departments while the Supreme Court is made up of 39 full-time and 40 substitute federal judges. Cantonal power is, thus, exercized through the Council of States directly on the other two branches. And unlike the United States Senate, the cantons have kept control of the method of election of Council of States members who, in constitutional terms at least, remain representatives of the cantons in national government.

In addition, the constitution is much more specific on the allocation of powers between the different levels of government than is the US Constitution (Table 7.1). As in the US, federal powers are enumerated, but unlike the American case so are some cantonal powers including, originally, control of state-church relations and the police. Moreover, the constitution requires that any change in these substantive powers be subject to constitutional amendment. Indeed, Article 3 of the constitution requires that all future responsibilities be vested in the cantons unless a constitutional amendment is approved:

Table 7.1. Constitutional allocation of responsibilities according to level of government

Exclusive Federal Competence (Article 49)	Foreign affairs[a]
Federal Competence (Article 50)	Defence, citizenship,[b] political asylum, status of foreigners, civil and penal law, social protection, economic order, money and currency, energy, national transportation, telecommunications
Cantonal Competence (Article 51)	Public order, public welfare, establishments of health care, schools and education, church/state relations, land use planning, highways, water and utilities

[a]But cantons can enter into international agreements with their immediate neighbours.
[b]But in citizenship and a number of other areas the cantons and/or local governments play a major part in the administration and details of policy. Swiss passports, for example, omit mention of place of birth and instead mention 'commune of family origin', which may date back many centuries.
Source: The Constitution of Switzerland (Berne, 1997).

The cantons are sovereign, in so far as their sovereignty is not limited by the federal constitution, and exercise all those rights, which have not been transferred to federal power. (Quoted in Steinberg 1996: 77)

At first sight, this looks similar to the US Tenth Amendment:

All powers not delegated to the United States by the Constitution, nor prohibited by it to the States are reserved to the States respectively or to the people.

In practice, however, the two amendment procedures have operated very differently. Only in the case of the adoption of a federal income tax and with regard to civil rights and liberties have US federal powers been constitutionally enhanced (McKay 1997: Ch. 4). In all other cases, Congress has simply passed laws greatly increasing federal power in a wide range of areas from social security through education and law enforcement to medical care. No specific allocation of these responsibilities to the federal government has been constitutionally sanctioned.[1] In the Swiss case, however, constitutional approval has been necessary for all major enhancements of federal powers including social security, the federal highways programme, environmental policies, agricultural subsidies, and aid for higher education (Linder 1998: 42–3). The cantons' role in this process is twofold. First, they are represented in the Council of States where a majority in necessary to enact all legislation, and second, an approving referendum vote in a majority of the cantons has to be held before an amendment is passed. Hence, enshrined in the Swiss system is the concept of the *Standemehr* or the requirement that citizens approve major changes in a majority of *countries* or cantons. Indeed a *double majority* is

---

[1] However, in some cases judicial interpretation has been necessary.

needed for constitutional change, which also requires a majority of the Swiss *people* to approve a measure. As will be developed later, the referendum device has also been used as an instrument for the expression of cantonal and regional power.

As a result of these multiple veto points, constitutional amendments are often attempted several times. In some cases they are never adopted. In almost every case the process is prolonged and in many cases the final version of the amendment is usually a watered down version of the original. (Linder 1998: 85–6).

A final feature of the original 1848 document is that a three level citizenship—communal, cantonal, and national—is constitutionally enshrined. The national constitution establishes that every citizen of a canton is a Swiss citizen, and every cantonal constitution establishes that all its citizens are also citizens of a commune, or *gemeinde*. In none of the other countries under discussion in this book is what has been called 'complex self-identification' (see Lancaster 1999) constitutionally established—although it is, of course, present in the European Union.

As with all the countries under discussion in this volume, the Swiss founding constitution represented a compromise between provincial interests and nationalizing forces. In this particular case most of the nationalizing forces were liberal, urban, and Protestant, while those opposing the centralization of power were conservative, rural, and Catholic. Liberals insisted on the presence of anti-clerical provisions in the constitution, which the Catholics accepted only on the condition that most aspects of church-state relations were devolved to the cantonal level. In addition, the institution of numerous checks and balances on central power ensured the continuation of cantonal sovereignty. Even so, religious conflict continued for several decades after 1848. In 1874 the constitution was revised in part to strengthen the federal government's role in military affairs and in part further to strengthen anti-clerical provisions (Codding 1961: 34). While the Protestant/urban Catholic/rural cleavage was to remain a prominent feature of Swiss political life for many decades—and indeed remains so to this day—it has never manifested itself in ways which threaten the viability of the system.

Institutional Adaptation: Socialism, Security, and Cantonal Sovereignty, 1874–1950

As Steinberg (1996: 51) notes, during the nineteenth century 'Swiss national identity developed slowly and painfully as a process of conflict resolution'. And many of those living in conservative Catholic communes continued to deny that there was any such thing as a Swiss identity. Between the end of the century and 1918 two further political cleavages emerged which were to shatter the old order in many European states, but which were accommodated with relative ease in Switzerland. There was, first, the idea of 'nation', or *Volk*, that was gaining influence throughout Europe and especially among German speakers. German Swiss were no less influenced by this development and by the outbreak of World War I most German-speaking Swiss identified firmly with the Reich and the German cause while French speakers identified with the Allied side. None the less, and in strict compliance with the checks on majority rule inherent in the constitution, Switzerland adhered to neutrality for the duration of the war. More threatening to the viability of the regime was the emergence of revolutionary socialism in Switzerland, which culminated in the general strike of 1918. Led by the Socialist Party (SP), the strike was organized to demand better working conditions including a maximum working week. In addition, the SP called for the introduction of proportional representation for all federal elections. With their vote concentrated in urban areas and spread thinly elsewhere, the socialists were at a considerable electoral disadvantage in relation to the radicals, the party of the 1848 constitution. Although the strike failed—it was put down by federal troops—almost all of the strikers' original demands were met. Proportional representation was accepted—19-and-a-half cantons voted in favour; a 48-hour week was introduced; and in 1919 work began on the strengthening of the social security system and on institutionalizing worker participation in industrial plants. By the end of the 1930s the SP had won a 'permanent' place on the Federal Council. Moreover, many of the originally very radical socialist demands were transformed into complex and consensual manager-worker agreements, which effectively replaced the strike as a weapon of collective bargaining. These arrangements persist to this day (Steinberg 1996: 59–63).

While it impossible to assign a particular weight to the role of political institutions in the accommodation of first religious then nationalist and finally socialist challenges to the regime, it is clear that they played a major part. Proportional representation had long been a feature of local and cantonal politics, so its acceptance at the national level was a natural progression. The so-called 'magic formula' for the composition of the Federal Council, whereby all the main political parties are informally guaranteed representation in relation to their electoral support, was adapted to include the SP. Above all, the fact that none of the challenges to the system developed along exclusively territorial lines owes much to the fact that ideologically, religiously, and linguistically distinctive cities and regions have always enjoyed full representation at the centre, and have been able to wield an effective veto over unacceptable federal legislation. In other words, cantonal and communal sovereignty was—and remains—remarkably well protected. As Bird (1986: 32) puts it: 'The policy goal of the political-legal system . . . is, in principle, to maximise the sovereignty of each jurisdiction in a democratic setting and to maintain traditions, languages and customs.'

Few events demonstrate Swiss respect for cantonal sovereignty so well as the granting of cantonal status to the Jura in 1978–9. Unusually among the Swiss cantons, the Jura region, which was—and remains—predominantly Catholic and French-speaking, was incorporated into the Protestant and German-speaking Berne canton at the 1815 Congress of Vienna. Thus Berne became a 'multicultural' canton and over the decades also became increasingly dominated by the German-speaking population. Separatist movements had been active for most of the nineteenth century, and indeed there were six distinctive separatist movements active between 1820 and the 1970s (Jenkins 1986: Ch. 7). In the 1960s a Jurassian Liberation Front (*Front de libération jurassien*) was formed which engaged in sporadic acts of violence. More-mainstream parties worked to resolve the problem through constitutional means and in particular to reconcile the divisions between separatists and voters loyal to the Berne canton. Eventually, it was agreed that any solution would have to involve not only the people of the Jura region but also the Berne canton and the whole of Switzerland. Accordingly, at the initiative of the Bernese government a series of what Linder calls 'cascade votes' were taken in every commune of the Jura. Where a majority emerged for the creation of a new canton, a fifth of the electorate could demand a second vote. Once the boundaries of the new canton were set, a third vote was allowed for those communes lying at the border of the new canton. Eventually, the whole of the Berne electorate voted in favour of the cascade voting system, followed by a vote in all cantons. The vote was 1.3 million for and 28,000 against, with large 'yes' votes in all Swiss cantons (Linder 1998: 66–7). In this way the new canton was created by what might be called a cumulative series of approving ballots. While some linguistic and religious problems remain within the Jura region, and at least three other cantons also have internal divisions based on language and religion,[2] the Jura experience does show how a potentially dangerous division was resolved using uniquely Swiss consensus-building devices.

Equalization and the Limited Accrual of Central Power, 1950–2000

In contrast to most other countries of western Europe, Switzerland was slow to accumulate a significant public sector in the post-war decades. As late as 1970 the total public sector accounted for just 21.3 per cent of GDP compared with 33 per cent for eight comparable European states.[3] And while by 1977 this total had increased to 30.4 per cent, the gap between Switzerland and other states remained over 12 per cent (Bird 1986: Table 2.2). Even then, two unique features marked expansion of the Swiss public sector. First, although as in other countries transfer payments made up the bulk of the increase, the Swiss social security system was and remains highly devolved. It grew out of what the Swiss call the 'third sector', or a system of trade union and other voluntary associations which traditionally had provided for social assistance (for a discussion, see Butschi and Cattacin 1993). When, in the 1960s and 1970s, wel-

---

[2] Fribourg, Valais, and Graubunden. See the discussion in Jenkins (1986: Ch. 11).
[3] Denmark, Finland, France, Greece, Ireland, Netherlands, Sweden, and the UK.

fare provision was expanded it did so by adapting the decentralized third-sector provision already in place. As a result, the cantons and communes, who in turn used third-sector institutions, were left with the responsibility for administering welfare. They also retain discretion over eligibility and benefit levels. Thus social assistance for the needy remains remarkably decentralized in Switzerland. Federal involvement is minimal and local control is jealously guarded against central encroachment (see Segalman 1986: Ch. 5). In the case of social *insurance* the federal government is much more involved and national standards and national administration do apply in the case of old-age pensions, disability payments, and other insurance schemes. In total these payments do represent a major item on the federal budget, but they are financed directly by employee and employer payroll taxes (Segalman 1986: Ch. 3).

Second, and again in contrast to other states, most of the Swiss public-sector growth occurred at the cantonal and commune level. In proportional terms, the federal government's role actually decreased in the 1950–80 period. In 1960 confederation own-source revenue accounted for 45 per cent of total government revenues. By 1980 this had declined to 35 per cent, while the cantonal/commune share increased from 55 per cent to 66 per cent (Bird 1986: Table 2.5). Remarkably, this trend continued into the mid-1990s. In 1995 total federal revenue came to 32.7 per cent of total government spending and cantonal/commune revenue was 67.3 per cent (International Monetary Fund 1997: Tables A and B).

This unique pattern of public sector growth stems directly from the fact that the Swiss cantons enjoy something approaching total tax sovereignty. They are constitutionally prohibited only from imposing inter-cantonal double taxation or 'prohibitive' taxes on trade and industry and providing 'unjustified' *ad hominem* tax relief. In addition, the cantons and the federal government cannot tax each other's institutions (Articles 46.2, 31.8, 42, and 39.5 of the Swiss Constitution). In addition, *any* change in federal taxation, including tax rates, has to be approved through constitutional amendment. Indeed the main federal taxes—a wholesale sales tax and a portion of the income tax—were originally adopted in wartime as 'emergency' measures. They were formally incorporated into the constitution only in 1958; and the relevant amendment not only fixed federal tax rates but also subjected them to a 'sunset' provision: they have periodically to be renewed or they pass from the statute books (Bird 1986: 28). As will be shown later, a cumbersome amendment procedure in which the cantons can play a major role has had the effect of greatly restricting the role of the federal government in Swiss public policy.

A further unique feature of Swiss federalism is that, in spite of the existence of considerable inter-cantonal inequalities in wealth and income, the federal government has played a relatively small role in equalization. It was not until 1959 that the first law specifically designed to reduce such inequalities was passed—although the federal government began to provide the cantons with specific-purpose grants for such services as roads several decades earlier. By the mid-1990s four major transfer programmes were in place, at least one of which was designed to compensate for the inequalities that result from variations in cantonal incomes and tax structures:

1. Specific-purpose federal grants, or *Beitrage*. Used primarily in higher education and agriculture, these grants are conditional and tied to rigid rules. This is one of the few areas where the federal government exercises significant control over the direction and nature of public policy. These grants constitute around 22 per cent of all federal grants. Interestingly, as in the EU, agriculture is the single largest federal programme—18.3 per cent of the total in 1996 (*Finances publiques en Suisse, 1996* 1998: Table D.4.5)
2. A second category, refunds, or *Ruckvergutungen*, are also specific-purpose grants but are designed as federal compensation for cantonal or local implementation of federal and cantonal programmes. These include federal roads, civil defence, and aspects of social security. In 1996 these made up 38 per cent of all grants, with federal roads taking the lions share (*Finances publiques en Suisse*, 1996, Table D.4.5)
3. Investments, or *Investitionsbeitrage*. These investment subsidies are tied to formal popular petitions from citizens who request federal help for specific improvements, such as the restoration of historic buildings. The smallest of all the federal subsidies, they are designed to maintain minimum standards in a limited range of areas.
4. The redistribution from the federal government based on cantonal financial capacity, or *Péréquation financière* (PF). This is a specifically equalizing tax-sharing device whereby shared cantonal/federal taxes are redistributed on the basis of a complex formula based on revenue per capita, the canton's GDP per capita, the cantonal tax effort, and the canton's expenditure requirements (Spahn 1997: 115–16). This formula results in transfers to the poorer cantons and, in some cases, a tax redistribution away from the richer cantons. In this sense there is a strong horizontal element to the programmes. Typically, the PF amounts to around 20–25 per cent of all grant programmes.

These grant programmes have evolved over a long period in response to changing economic, political, and social circumstances. As noted, explicit attempts to reduce inequalities between the cantons began with the 1959 federal law on equalization that was designed to compensate those cantons whose tax effort was below the average. At no time, however, have the Swiss attempted to establish 'uniformity of living conditions' among the cantons. Instead they have striven simply to reduce the more obvious inequalities resulting from complex and highly differentiated tax regimes. In this respect their philosophy of intergovernmental relations is very different from that prevalent in Germany, where the achievement of equal living standards between the Länder is constitutionally enshrined (see Mackenstein and Jeffery 1999: 153–64).

As can be seen from Table 7.2, all federal grants constituted just 3.4 per cent of Gross State Product (GSP) in 1995 and varied from 1.6 per cent of GSP in

Table 7.2. Swiss federal grants:[a] distribution by canton, per capita, and as percentage of gross state product, all grants and *péréquation* grants (Swiss francs), 1995

Canton	Zur	Bern	Luz	Uri	Schw	Wald Ob/Ni	Glar	Zoug	Freib	Soleu	Bale St/Co	Schaf	Apen E/I	St. G	Aarg	Thurg	Tess	Vaud	Valais	Neue	Gene	Jura	Gris	TOTAL/AVERAGE
Total (total) grant, SF bns	1.01	1.58	0.51	0.19	0.18	0.11	0.18	0.15	0.54	0.26	0.48	0.11	0.12	0.47	0.55	0.24	0.53	0.95	0.78	0.4	0.47	0.33	0.54	10.68
Grant PC (av.)	852	1,657	1,514	5,257	1,517	2,894	1,651	1,615	2,382	1,113	1,142	1,477	2,127	1,068	1,041	1,092	1,758	1,550	2,434	534	1,184	4,911	2,866	1,502
PF grant PC	-322	510	263	1,400	34	498	285	-847	648	205	-402	471	643	137	-8	124	390	84	1,187	774	-382	1,471	579	276 (av.)
Grant % GSP	1.6	4.5	4.1	14.2	3.9	3.6	3.7	2.4	6.6	5.5	2.3	3.4	6.5	2.8	2.5	3.0	4.7	3.7	9.8	6.8	2.5	16.9	7.7	3.4 (av.)
PF % GSP	-0.76	1.34	0.71	3.8	0.08	1.3	0.63	-1.26	1.8	0.9	-0.88	0	1.87	0.35	0	0.33	1.04	0.2	4.0	2.2	-0.79	5.01	1.55	

PF: the *Péréquation Financière*, which is the only formula-driven equalization programme based on horizontal redistribution through tax sharing.

[a] All federal grants as defined by Federal Finance Administration (1996).

Source: Computed from data in Administration fédérale des finances (1996).

Zurich to 16.9 per cent in the Jura. In comparative perspective, this figure is quite low. The equivalent figures for comparable countries are: Australia 8 per cent, Canada 4.8 per cent, and Germany 5.2 per cent—all figures are for 1995. Only in the USA is the figure lower: 2.7 per cent in 1991, although it exceeded 5 per cent during the mid-1970s (ACIR 1993: Table 1).

Table 7.3 shows that the relationship between grants and cantonal income per capita is really quite loose. A poorish canton such as Thurgau, for example, receives relatively little in the way of subsidy compared with the much richer Geneva. These discrepancies are explained by the fact that many of the grant programmes—for example, in such areas as infrastructure—do not necessarily correlate with cantonal income. Because the share of direct federal transfers to cantons which is not based on their financial capacity is larger than that which is, the richer cantons are, paradoxically, made richer as a result of financial compensation. This has led Swiss experts frequently to argue that the official taxonomy of the cantons' financial capacity is unsatisfactory.

Table 7.3. Ranking of Swiss cantons by gross state product per capita, *péréquation* grants per capita, and all grants per capita, 1995

Canton/half-canton	Ranking by GSP Per capita	*Péréquation* ranking Grant per capita	All grants ranking Grant per capita
Zoug	1	23	12
Zurich	2	21	23
Geneve	3	22	17
Bale City/Country	4	20	18
Glaris	5	14	11
Schaff.	6	17	16
Argovie	7	19	22
Vaud	8	18	13
Schwyz	9	12	14
Soleure	10	16	19
Saint-Gall	11	15	21
Obwald/Nidwald	12	11	4
Tessin	13	8	9
Grisons	14	6	5
Berne	15	9	10
Lucerne	16	10	15
Uri	17	2	1
Thurgau	18	13	20
Fribourg	19	5	7
Neuchatel	20	4	6
Appenzell/E. & I.	21	7	8
Valais	22	3	3
Jura	23	1	2

Source: As for Table 7.2.

Indeed, given the very considerable disparities in inter-cantonal income and wealth—for example, in 1995 canton Zug had more than twice the income per capita of the Valais—perhaps the most striking feature of the Swiss system of intergovernmental transfers is just how little it has changed over time. Unlike Germany, which has gone to great lengths to compensate the poorer east German Länder following unification, or the Canadians who provide the lower-income eastern provinces with substantial federal aid, the Swiss have done little to reduce inter-cantonal inequalities. Moreover, stasis in the Swiss system applies to an apparent inability both significantly to reduce inequalities and to execute major institutional reforms of any sort. It is highly unlikely, for example, that the Swiss could easily implement the sort of reform of intergovernmental relations which have occurred in the US in the last 20 years. As we saw in Chapter 4, these have involved a major devolution of powers to the states, as well as quite dramatic changes in the level of federal aid— for example, between just 1979 and 1983, federal aid to the states declined form 15 per cent of federal spending to under 10 per cent (ACIR 1993: Table 1). Similarly, the relative ease with which Germany incorporated the relatively impoverished eastern Länder into the intergovernmental equalization programme was facilitated by an amenable institutional structure (See Chapter 6, pp. 93–98). Such an adaptation would be nigh impossible to implement in Switzerland, even though inter-cantonal inequalities almost rival those in unified Germany.

When attempting to explain the apparent conservatism of the Swiss system, we have first to look at institutional arrangements. Put simply, changes in public policy in Switzerland have to follow a sometimes tortuous route involving the building of consensus at many levels: horizontally between cantons and between federal institutions, as well as vertically between levels of government and between voters and governments.

This applies *tout force* to the only explicitly equalizing programme, the PF. For while the PF distribution follows inter-cantonal inequalities quite faithfully, the actual redistributive effect is very small. As Table 7.2 shows, expressed as a percentage of GSP only in Uri, the Valais, and the Jura are the figures significant. Interestingly, these figures are quite close to those represented by EU structural and cohesion funds as a percentage of the GNP of such countries as Greece and Portugal.[4]

Reform Attempts: The Case of the *Péréquation Financière*

The barriers to reform in the Swiss system are well demonstrated by the current debate over the future of the PF. Starting in the early 1990s, federal officials began producing proposals for the wholesale reform of Swiss intergovernmental grants. The effort was executive led: the seven-member

---

[4] Structural funds accounted for 3.5% of Portuguese GNP in 1992 (Tsoukalis 1993: 245).

Federal Council was responsible for the proposals, labelled the *Nouvelle Péréquation Financière* (NPF) (*La Nouvelle Péréquation Financière* 1996). These recommendations were in line with those proposed both by the Federal Finance Administration and the Permanent Conference of Cantonal Directors of Finance. Ostensibly, they were motivated by three considerations: the needs to reduce the cost of the programme, to strengthen cantonal autonomy, and to increase redistributive efficiency. As was shown in the last section, the PF has done little to reduce inter-cantonal inequalities. At the same time, because the distribution formula is based on actual spending at the cantonal level it encourages an incremental increase in the size of federal grants.

As first announced in 1994, the specific objective of the reform was to replace federal subsidies hitherto based on cantonal financial capacity with a new inter-cantonal perequation programme based on 'unattributed' resources. To this end the reforms involved three specific objectives:

(1) A reduction in vertical transfers or subsidies—federation to canton—and an increase in horizontal transfers—canton to canton;.
(2) a shift in the grant element of the programme so that grants are given not on the basis of financial capacity but on the basis of the actual usage of the designated services by the cantons. These federal grants are given in such areas as higher education and roads; and
(3) a reallocation of federal direct taxes so that the proportion attributed on the basis of the differential financial capacity of the cantons is increased.

Federal Council documents argue that in total these reforms will increase what they call 'allocative efficiency' by reducing the cost of programmes. Contracts tied to specific needs rather than allocative formulae will achieve this. At the same time, the redistributive element will be more finely honed to service the needs of the most indigent cantons.

There is no question that if fully implemented these reforms would involve a radical departure from existing practice. This is because in order to achieve them it would be necessary to tackle five key aspects of the intergovernmental system. First, the reforms would require the untangling of the tasks performed by the federation from those performed by the cantons. Currently these are jointly performed in 50 areas. Of these, 29 would be untangled with the federation acquiring exclusive competence in eight and the cantons in 21. The main areas affected are social security, health, research, the armed services, and national roads. The principle of subsidiarity would be the main criterion employed in this untangling process.

Second, inter-cantonal cooperation should be reorganized to increase efficiency. Cantons in receipt of services by another canton should compensate the donor canton adequately and some services should be pooled to exploit economies of scale. While the federation should play no direct financial role in this area, it should help resolve inter-cantonal conflict and it should require the cantons to contract-out services in certain key areas such as metropolitan transport and cultural facilities.

Third, in those areas where the cantons and the federation share responsibilities through joint funding and administration of programmes, the NPF reform would replace the present system based on the payment by the federal government of a proportion of the total costs of a service with a global lump sum, or block grant, which would be fixed for a prescribed period. In this way, the cantons would have an incentive to reduce costs and only where these were 'excessive' would the federal government increase the block grant.

Fourth, the NPF reforms are designed to increase the financial autonomy of the cantons. This is implicit in some of the reforms mentioned above and in particular the untangling of federal and cantonal tasks. That said, because cantonal financial autonomy is very jealously guarded in Switzerland, any reform would have to pay lip service to the idea. In some respects, of course, including the new block grant system, cantonal autonomy would *not* be protected.

Finally, the NPF would replace the existing perequation based on financial capacity—a mix of financial costs and resources—with a new index of resources based on taxes levied on (1) personal income and wealth; (2) company profits and capital; and (3) taxes on motor vehicles. In total, these taxes represent over 90 per cent of national tax revenue and over 60 per cent of cantonal revenue. This new system would, above all, reduce intercantonal inequalities by requiring resource-rich cantons to transfer funds to the poorer cantons. The ultimate aim would be to reduce disparities by 20 per cent and ensure that every canton is up to at least 80 per cent of the Swiss average. Aware that inter-cantonal transfers alone would not achieve a great deal, the reformers also proposed the institution of a complementary grant from the federal government to the poorer cantons to ease the burden on the richer cantons and, in their terms, 'to comply with the principle of subsidiarity'.

According to the reformers, these changes would be both politically advantageous—federalism would be revived, and economically advantageous—they estimated that for the year 1996 the NPR could, hypothetically, save around 3 billion Swiss francs (SF), amounting to 1.8 billion savings for the federation and 1.2 billion for the cantons. However, this figure assumes that the reforms are fully implemented by that date—a target not envisaged even in the most optimistic scenario—and that the 'untangling ' of responsibilities involves *all* federal grants to the cantons as well as horizontal transfers. As will be discussed below, this is a wholly unrealistic assumption.

Aware of just how sweeping these reforms were, the Federal Council set an indefinite timetable for their full implementation. Stage One, which would be achieved 'not before the year 2000', would involve a series of constitutional changes. As was discussed earlier, any major change in taxation in Switzerland requires constitutional change. Stage Two, to be implemented some time after 2000, would involve only the NPF *au sens étroit,* or the redistribution based on cantonal financial capacity. Stage Three, for which no date is set, would apply the reforms to all federal transfers which fund the joint canton/federally performed tasks.

Perhaps the most interesting feature of these proposed reforms is that while the avowedly major objective is a reduction in inter-cantonal inequalities, in fact increases in allocative efficiency—that is, a more rational distribution of resources resulting in lower costs—are the top priority. It is interesting in the sense that it presents a different picture from the traditional interpretation of Swiss *cooperative* federalism. This is not entirely new since references to the *competitive* nature of federalism can be found in the 1994 document: 'In a federal system, the regional collectivities are in competition with each other, which forces them constantly to improve their efficiency in the provision of public services. One can note here an analogy with the market economy'(NPF 1996: 43).

The 1996 document on the NPF spells out the priority of allocative efficiency not only by replacing all forms of subsidies with block grants in order to 'encourage' cantons to cut costs, but also by the way in which a closer inter-cantonal cooperation is envisaged. For example, whereas the poorer cantons' contribution for using the hospital or university facilities of richer cantons had always been based on their financial capacity, it is now proposed to base it on cantonal usage. Hence the market price of those services will improve allocative efficiency, but not redistribution.

The NPF also plans to compensate for the higher federal costs of untangling the tasks between the federation and the cantons—only partly covered by cuts in federal subsidies—by reducing the cantonal share of direct federal taxes (DFT) to make up the difference of 620 million SF—a notional figure for fiscal year 1996 (Frey and Spillman 1996: 14). By reducing tax sharing, the NPF is proposing to cut what some experts see as the best way potentially to improve redistribution (NPF 1996: 61). If the share of DFT that currently accrues to the cantons is not contributing enough to equalization, it is, as we saw earlier, because that share is inefficiently attributed on the basis of cantons' differential financial capacity. This was explicitly recognized by a official report on PF published in 1991 by the Federal Finance Administration which then argued that to redress the balance in favour of cantonal financial capacity-based tax sharing would be the most efficient way to improve PF through DFT But the equalization potential of a different tax-sharing basis appears to have been lost in the 1996 document, where it is replaced by horizontal transfers—rich to poor cantons—with some compensation by the federation disguised to raise the resources of the poorer cantons to 87 per cent of the Swiss average. Although the complexity of the new mechanism does not make it easy to assess its precise redistributive effect, it is difficult to understand why the overall cantonal share of DFT would simply be cut by 620 million SF, instead of using tax-sharing more fully as an equalizing device.

Put another way, the Federal Council's proposals are essentially technocratic in design. In this sense, they are typical of federally inspired reforms that strive to impose some degree of rationality on a system whose institutional and political complexity all too often results in a high degree of both complexity and resistance to change (see Bird 1986: 25–35). Yet, judging from past

Swiss experience, equalization as such should not provoke much resistance from the poorer cantons as 'fiscal equalisation is much less important in Switzerland than in most other federal countries' (Bird 1986: 62). Indeed, all previous attempts to introduce greater fiscal harmonization, such as the creation of an exclusively federal income tax with participation of the cantons in the proceeds, have always been defeated. Resistance to change is more likely to come from the potential impact of the NPF on cantonal autonomy. Since closer cantonal cooperation is a key factor in the cost-efficiency priority of the NPF, it is proposed to give to the Federal Council the power (1) to impose on the cantons an obligation to contract in five of eight areas earmarked for inter cantonal cooperation where this would help reduce costs, and (2) to resolve the inter cantonal conflicts which subsequently might arise. If implemented, these measures would clearly affect inter-cantonal autonomy and as such they are highly unlikely to be accepted. Since they are an essential element of the NPF, cantonal approval of the reform is doubtful, at least in its present form.

Dispersing Power for National Unity

One reason for the stasis characteristic of the Swiss system is that constitutional and institutional arrangements greatly limit the power of central institutions. *A priori* it would be expected that the defence of state—cantonal—interests would primarily be the responsibility of the Council of States—the *Standerat*—which is elected strictly on a territorial basis: the 46 members are made up of two representatives from each canton, just one from the half cantons. The cantons rather than the confederation decide on the electoral rules governing their election. Not only is the Council of the States territorially based, it is also a genuine partner in the legislative process. Absolute equality between the two chambers is observed. As a result, cantonal approval is required for all major changes in intergovernmental relations. However, the Swiss party system is not unlike the American in the sense that the same parties operate at all levels; but they are highly decentralized through the cantons and the communes. Also like the American system, this decentralization does, in theory, facilitate the representation of distinct territorial units by giving disproportionate power to small rural cantons (for a discussion see Steinberg 1996: Ch. 3). In practical terms, these institutional arrangements mean that just 9 per cent of the Swiss population, representing eleven-and-a-half of the smallest cantons, have a theoretical veto on all national legislation (Linder 1998: 74). Comparisons with the evolving federal arrangements in the European Union are interesting in this respect. Under the qualified majority voting (QMV) rule in the EU Council of Ministers, 71 per cent of the votes are required for new measures. Thus 30 per cent of the Council members can block 'legislation'. Should the eight smallest countries making up this 30 per cent vote together, they would constitute a blocking minority of 13.7 per cent of the EU population. In this regard state power is, in theory, more devolved in Switzerland than in the EU—although this does not apply to taxation that in the EU is subject to a unanimity-voting rule.[5]

In reality, however, cantonal sovereignty is little more protected through representation in the Council of the States than state power in the US is protected through the Senate. Instead the rural/small canton bias in the Council's electoral arrangements means that for most of the time it is dominated by centre-right parties whose representatives usually vote as *national* actors on *national* issues. As in the US, organizational decentralization in the party system tends to encourage contrasting voting stances at different levels of government. The same parties operate at all levels but local and cantonal party representatives may have little in common with national party politicians. This point is well demonstrated by recent votes in the Federal Assembly on international issues. In both houses, members have generally supported Swiss membership of the UN, the EU and other international organizations. Majorities in favour have generally been as great in the Council of States as in the Federal Assembly. However, such measures have often subsequently fallen foul of popular votes, with a clear territorial divide between the isolationist German-speaking eastern and rural cantons and the more internationalist western, French-speaking cantons (Kobach 1997).[6] In this sense, cantonal power is expressed not so much through the Council of States as through direct democratic devices including the popular referendum held at the cantonal level. *National* political institutions are generally distrusted and in the German-speaking cantons the *Neinsager*—nay-sayer—vote is common. This is expressed as popular opposition to federal decisions, which are seen as out of touch with ordinary voters. As Kobach (1997: 204) perceptively notes 'direct democracy tends to divorce policies from parties in the eyes of the voter'. Such instruments as the 'magic formula' and the very loose organizational structure of the parties aggravate this dissociation. Therefore, large majorities in the national legislature and in the Federal Council can, and are, overturned by the voters.

An additional direct-democratic institution is the requirement that all significant federal legislation is subject to a sort of 'hearing' by the cantons. If the cantons are opposed to the legislation, it is abandoned or modified in ways that satisfy the objections. Direct-democratic institutions, including popular referendums and petitions, are thus intricately woven into the fabric of decision making, and indeed these are obligatory for all constitutional changes (see the discussion in Linder (1998: Ch. 3). As already indicated, all tax changes are subject to constitutional approval. Finally, a complex system of

[5] In fact, of course, neither the Swiss cantons nor the Council of Ministers vote solidly by size of jurisdiction. However, the smallest eleven-and-a-half Swiss cantons do generally vote together sufficiently to account for around 20–25% of all votes in the Council of States. It is estimated that Swiss membership of the EU will require about a 59% support among the voting population (Linder 1998: 75). Most of the splits in the Council of Ministers take a north vs south rather than small state vs large state dimension. As a result, votes tend to be approximately in proportion to population.

[6] Since 1977 decisions on Swiss membership of supranational organizations have been subject to referendum approval.

power sharing is in place, including the so-called 'magic formula' on the composition of the Federal Council that gives the leading political parties a guaranteed representation.

While none of these constraints amounts formally to a requirement for unanimity on important changes, they do mean that a substantial concurrent majority, often greatly in excess of 50 per cent, is required. In many instances change takes place only when a broad consensus—established both horizontally across federal institutions and, crucially, vertically between the voters, the cantons and the federal government—has been built up over a long period.

This may help explain why, in contrast to many comparable countries, as the Swiss public sector has grown, the proportion of income and spending accounted for by the central government has actually shrunk (Linder 1998: Fig. 2.1). While the power of the cantons can be exaggerated—some observers interpret their power in terms of social class and economic rather than territorial interest (see Church 1989)—there is no doubt that decision-making is very significantly more decentralized than in other federal systems. The cantons also devolve significant powers, including taxing powers, to the municipalities or the communes much as, in the EU, governments in Germany, Spain, and elsewhere devolve taxing power to lower level units. In addition, the Swiss have in place an elaborate system of what they call *fédéralisme d'exécution*, or 'implementation federalism', which, as in Germany, mandates the cantons and the communes to implement programmes funded by the federal government. This phenomenon helps explain the somewhat higher levels of federal spending in the Swiss system than what might be expected given its decentralized structure and limited public sector size (Table 7.4).

A final and crucial point is that the Swiss have long consciously attempted to preserve the ethnic, linguistic, and cultural identity of the cantons. Constitutional provisions and a system of highly decentralized direct democracy ensure this. Again, this is unique to Switzerland. In Germany, Australia, and the US no institutional devices exist to this end. In the case of Quebec, they do—but only in defiance of a *Canadian* ethos of ethnic and cultural multiculturalism (see the discussion in Chapter 4, pp. 48–52).

Given these institutional and political constraints, the prospects for implementation of the NPF are slight. Indeed, this is recognized by the Federal Council itself, whose documents provide for an open-ended timetable even for the first stage of implementation. What instead is likely to transpire is more of the same: no wholesale reform of the system, with policy changing incrementally following much discussion and consultation. In sum, the hallmarks of the system—conservatism and a complex and often inequitable distributive pattern—are likely to continue.

Three further points relating to the role of political parties in this complex institutional structure need to be made. First, and as already noted, party-based coalition building is more difficult in Switzerland than in any comparable country. For although the same parties operate at commune, cantonal,

Table 7.4. The structure of government budgets in Switzerland, 1993

Budget item	Confederation	Cantons	Communes	Total[a]
	% of consolidated total			
Outlays	37.5	48.5	35.0	100.0
Revenues	33.1	44.6	32.8	90.5
Deficit	4.4	4.0	2.3	9.5
	% of GDP			
Outlays	11.6	15.0	10.8	30.9
Revenues	10.2	13.8	10.1	28.0
Deficit	1.4	1.2	0.7	2.9

[a]Single items may not add up due to the elimination of double-accounting for the total. Budgeted figures may not coincide with financial accounts.

Source: Spahn (1997: Table 6.1).

and national levels, the decentralized institutional structure tends to weaken the connective tissue between federal, cantonal, and local party politicians. As a result the national parties 'are coalitions of cantonal parties which in turn are coalitions of communal parties' (Steinberg 1996: 113). It is, therefore, more appropriate to talk of 'families' of parties rather of discrete and distinctive parties. Hence the Radicals have traditionally represented a family consisting of the Swiss Liberal, Radical Democrat, and Democratic Parties; and the Social Democrats are also a broad church of left and left-of-centre interests (see the discussion in Gruner and Pitterle 1983).

Second is the fact that the devolved nature of Swiss political parties relates closely to the widespread use of direct democratic devices. As Gruner and Pitterle (1983: 31) note:

Swiss parties can truly be called the 'children of popular rights', that is products of the referendum and the initiative. It is not the relatively weak Parliament but these instruments of Swiss direct democracy that provide the counterweight to an otherwise too powerful national executive. Through repeated successes with the referendum and the initiative, 'outsider' parties and groups are able to accumulate political capital, which in time they can use to procure access to the ruling elite.

However, the Swiss national Council is not made up of numerous parties each with a distinctive local or cantonal base. Instead the parties group themselves into officially recognized factions. After the 1999 elections, for example, seven factions dominated the assembly, four of which—the Social Democrats, Radicals, Christian Democrats, and the Swiss People's Party—had dominated Swiss politics since 1919. The 1999 election was notable because of the success of the conservative and isolationist Swiss People's Party, which increased its representation in the Council from 29 seats to 44 scoring 22.5 per cent of the vote.[7]

Third, quite apart from the factional basis of the main parties, the number of veto points in the decision-making structures, including the need to enact constitutional amendments in order to expedite major policy change, has greatly weakened the ability of parties in national government to produce programmatic reforms. As can be seen from Table 7.5, the fact that centre-left parties have managed to muster more than simple majorities in the National Assembly in almost every electoral cycle between 1947 and 1953—the very period when the role of the central state increased so dramatically in other countries—has not translated into a significant increase in the role of the federal government. Indeed, on the contrary, in proportional terms this role actually decreased.

Table 7.5. Representation of centre-left[a] parties in the Swiss National Assembly, 1947–1983

Year	% of seats
1947	55.5
1951	53.6
1955	54.6
1959	53.6
1963	54.0
1967	52.5
1971	50.0
1975	53.0
1979	52.5
1983	51.0

[a]Social Democrats, Radicals (FDP), and Workers' Party.

Source: Computed from data provided by the Swiss Parliament, http://www.parlament.ch/Dveroeffentli chungen/Ru

Simple majorities are ineffective, of course, in the absence of corresponding majorities in the Council of States, among the legislatures in a majority of the cantons and, through direct-democratic devices, among a majority of the Swiss people. Perhaps the most interesting question in this context is the extent to which voting in the Council of States represents a specifically *territorial* politics, which is in conflict with an ideological politics in the National Assembly or with popular opinion. In fact a form of territorial politics does operate but not in the same way as it has in Canada or Germany or did, historically, in the US. For one thing, the major parties have no specifically

[7] http://www.parliament.ch/D/Veroeffentlichungen/Ru.

territorial appeal based on particular cantons. Instead, the conservative parties have greater support in the smaller rural cantons; and the centre-left parties have strength in the larger urban cantons. Because they can so easily exercise a veto at the national level through the use of popular referendums, the smaller cantons have had no need to create oppositional sectional parties in the style of the southern Democrats in the US or the Parti Quebecois. Indeed, as has already been shown, members of the Council of States may not truly reflect public opinion in their home cantons. This is more likely to be reflected in popular votes. As can be seen from Table 7.6, the eleven-and-a-half smallest cantons that are able to exercise an effective veto have done just that in a number of important areas of public policy over the last several decades. Moreover, the slow depopulation of many of these cantons, together with a growing urban population in the larger cantons, means that population threshold of this veto power is gradually being lowered. This almost certainly has had, and will continue to have, the greatest impact on international policy, including such issues as Swiss membership of the EU, where voters in the conservative cantons are likely to remain insistent on Swiss neutrality. As far as opposition to changes in federal taxation are concerned, the picture is more complex as any implied or actual increases in taxation is likely to meet the resistance of the business community as well as conservatives generally. Of course, the smaller, poorer cantons would welcome increased federal largesse in the form of intergovernmental grants, but, as the discussion of the PF reforms showed, these very same cantons would resist any changes in intergovernmental fiscal relations that were seen to compromise cantonal sovereignty. Aware of these problems, the Swiss are constantly proposing major constitutional changes whether it be in the case of particular policy areas, such as the PF, or basic constitutional arrangements, such as the composition of the Council of States. Most of these are doomed to failure if only because 'Changing the rules of federalism is a game to be played under the existing rules of federalism, and there is no reason for minorities to renounce their long-held minority rights when asked to do so' (Linder 1998: 76).

Table 7.6. Federalist against democratic rule: practical veto power of small cantons in five votes

Year/issue	No-votes from 11.5 smallest cantons as % of all votes
1955, protection from tenants	25.3
1970, federal finances	24.0
1973, federal education	21.7
1975, federal economic policy	20.5
1983, federal energy policy	20.0

Source: Linder (1998: Table 2.5).

Summary and Conclusions

It has become almost axiomatic that the Swiss political system is exceptional (see, for example, the discussion in Church 1989). Swiss exceptionalism derives mainly from the fact that, uniquely among mature democracies, the veto points in the system both operate within political institutions and are imposed on elected representatives through the extensive use of direct-democratic devices. Hence cantons and communes restrain the federal government, as does bicameralism, a collective executive, and judicial review. And interwoven into this already complex decision making environment are constitutionally mandated opportunities for the people to participate through referendums and initiatives. Territorial politics are at the heart of Swiss politics. From the very beginning the Swiss have striven to protect the linguistic, religious, and cultural distinctiveness of diverse, often quite isolated communities, while at the same time granting the federal government sufficient autonomy to provide for national security. Later, the responsibilities of the federal government were extended to include most of the functions of the modern state, but always on terms acceptable to the cantons. Institutionally, the Swiss have created a system that provides for multiple veto points on all important national decisions, many of which have a territorial dimension. Although cantonal interests are formally represented in the *Standerat*, it would be misleading to label the Council a genuine 'Council of the States' given that the political parties operate in the chamber more on the basis of ideology and economic interest than on the basis of distinctive territorial units. In this sense, the *Standerat* operates much as do other upper houses discussed in this volume. Indeed, only the German Bundesrat approximates to qualifying as a genuine Council of the States.

The cantons do none the less exercize important restraints on national power. As was shown in the case of intergovernmental fiscal relations, cantonal approval is needed for any policy change which significantly affects cantonal autonomy. The articulation of cantonal interests operates both constitutionally and through custom and established practice. Crucially, in those policy areas that have the most potential to undermine cantonal sovereignty, and in particular taxation and international relations, there is a *constitutional* requirement not only for national legislative approval but also for popular approval by canton. It is through this double majority mechanism that cantonal autonomy is best protected. Often, popular opinion, especially in the smaller, rural cantons, is more conservative than that expressed through national representatives in the Council of States, where the representatives are more influenced by national party political cues than by sectional interests.

In spite of claims that the Swiss system results in a dissociated mosaic of public policies, the degree of *consensus* on the need for moderated, devolved policies suggests that the Swiss are prepared to pay the price in policy complexity and confusion in the name of national unity. Put another way, in contrast to the situation in Canada and elsewhere, the Swiss do have a conception of national interest that is rooted in constitutional and institutional arrangements. As will be discussed in the next two chapters, the Swiss experience may hold important lessons for the ways in which the European Union develops over the next several decades.

8

The Federal Experience in Comparative Context

The problem which all federalized nations have to solve is how to secure an efficient central government and preserve national unity, while allowing free scope for the diversities, and free play to the members of the federation. It is . . . to keep the centrifugal and centripetal forces in equilibrium, so that neither the planet States shall fly off into space nor the sun of the Central government draw them into its consuming fires.

Lord Bryce

C HAPTERS 3–7 showed the varied and complex historical experience of the five established federations. Constitutions and institutions have been amended and adapted through time in response to changing distributions of state and central power. The purpose of this chapter is to place these experiences in comparative context both through comparison within the sample countries and between this sample and the European Union. Discussion will follow the sequence of the individual country chapters. Hence comparison will concentrate on original constitutional design, institutional adaptation, the role of political parties in adaptation, and finally the significance of the fiscal dimension.

The EU in Comparative Context I: Constitutional Design

All five of the federal states under discussion in this book were conscious creations designed to overcome historically specific economic and political problems. In the case of the United States and Switzerland, these related primarily to security concerns. Security issues were also important in explaining the creation of the Canadian and Australian federations, although economic considerations also loomed large. The German case is distinct from the others because of the role played by occupying powers. Security questions, and in particular the need to stem a revival of German nationalism, were paramount, but this agenda was imposed from outside rather than agreed among a collection of separate, independent states. Indeed, the status of the founding states in Germany was very different from that of the states/provinces/cantons in the other cases. For although the Länder did formally exist in 1949, they had no long-established history as democratically elected regional governments. In all the other cases, representative regional government was well established by the time a federal system was adopted (Table 8.1). Interestingly, at least in temporal terms, the democratic experience of these regional units was not so dramatically different from that of a number of European states at the time of the signing of the Maastricht Treaty (Table 8.1). Of course, the countries that make up the EU are modern states with policy responsibilities and institutional structures of accountability and control that are not fully comparable with the situation in colonial America, Canada and Australia or even with the

Table 8.1. Democratic experience of state/regional governments at the time of accession to a federal state and EU States in 1999

Established federations	Years of democratic experience
Australia	42: 1859–1901
Canada	27: 1840–67, Upper Canada only
US	8: 1781–89 plus variable experience of colonial assemblies
Switzerland	33: 1815–48 plus 100s of years of variable experience by canton
Germany	3: 1946–9 plus variable experience of Länder during the Weimar period

EU states	Years of democratic experience
Austria	46, 61 since adoption of constitution but with a break during Nazi era
Belgium	161 since adoption of constitution in 1830
Denmark	142 since adoption of present constitution
Finland	71 since adoption of present constitution
France	121 since creation of the 3rd Republic
Germany	42 since adoption of constitution
Greece	17 since first competitive election in 1974 following military rule
Ireland	69 since adoption of present constitution
Italy	43 since adoption of present constitution
Luxembourg	72 since adoption of universal suffrage, 132 since adoption of constitution
Netherlands	114 since spread of suffrage in late nineteenth century, 152 since adoption of present constitution
Portugal	17 since creation of new constitution
Spain	13 since creation of new constitution
Sweden	84 since universal male suffrage
UK	107 since adoption of near universal male suffrage

Note: The criterion for democratic experience is the adoption of representative institutions and competitive elections with a wide degree of—although not necessarily universal—male suffrage.

Sources: various, including Lane, McKay, and Newton (1997).

longer established Swiss experience. This accepted, what all these federal structures have in common—voluntary association and some degree of democratic
control—provides for a better subset of comparison for the EU than any other
group of states.

Apart from Germany, none of the federations created a constitution from
scratch. In this respect, their experience was not dissimilar to that of the EU,
where state building has been incremental and remains incomplete. In the US
case, the equivalent process was much shorter, but even the Americans lived
for eight years under the Articles of Confederation. In the case of Switzerland,
of course, the process was extremely lengthy lasting as it did from 1291 to
1848 or possibly 1874. The point of these comparisons is, of course, to empha-
size that federation building in these countries proceeded through the
voluntary association of democratic states. Negotiation, compromise, and
bargaining were necessary before a final constitutional formula was reached.
The institutional relationships arrived at in each of the founding constitutions
were shaped by the needs of the time. The EU has been through—and indeed
continues to go through—much the same process. And just as scholars have
argued long and hard over the reasons for the creation of such federations as
the United States and Canada (for a summary see Riker 1964: Part 2; and the
discussion in McKay 1999b: Ch. 2), so they argue over the origins of the EU.
Although the historical circumstances at the inception of the EEC/EU are very
different from those surrounding the creation of the established federal states,
they can at least be placed in the same analytical categories. Security considerations were paramount during the early to mid-1950s and economic considerations dominated discussions in the 1980s and 1990s. In recent years the
perception that Europe needs a single market in goods, labour, and services
operating in a low-inflation, fiscally sound environment has almost certainly
been the main driving force behind the moves towards 'ever closer union'.
Analysis in earlier chapters showed that almost the same imperatives—specifically, the removal of interstate trading barriers—were, if not the dominating
issues, then certainly crucial issues at the inception of the United States,
Canada, Australia, and 'modern'—that is, post-1848—Switzerland. Even in the
German case, the creation of a single German market and hence a potentially
powerful German economy was an important consideration for the framers of
the Basic Law in 1949.

None of this is to deny that accounting for the origins and development of
the EU is contentious. A large and rich literature has produced a number of
competing explanations drawing on integration theory, realist, and liberal
intergovernmentalist perspectives (for a summary see Moravscik 1998: Chs 1
and 2). None of these explanations draws on systematic comparison with
existing federations, however, and this in spite of the obvious parallels repeatedly outlined in earlier chapters. Empirically, one of the main differences
between the EU and the other cases is that the EU's founding 'constitution'
has been forged out of a series of intergovernmental meetings rather than a
constitutional convention resulting in a single authoritative document. Of the

four treaties that make up the EU constitution,[1] one, the Treaty of European Union, can lay claim to being the most important because both symbolically and functionally it granted to the EU the most state-like characteristics. Hence the transfer of most macroeconomic functions to the Union, the creation of European citizenship, and the important symbolism inherent in the change of name from EC to EU all suggest that the framers at Maastricht were in the business of creating a federal-like political entity. However, in another sense Maastricht highlights the distinctiveness of the EU experience: in Europe policy has typically preceded institution building; in the other federations institution building preceded policy. From the very beginning European integration was propelled forward through functional integration. First coal and steel, then agriculture, then the single market, and finally a single currency were the driving forces behind the various treaties. Institutional arrangements were always secondary to these functional policy concerns. In an important sense this is the source of the democratic deficit. For in other federations the sorting out of policy responsibilities between different levels of government was part and parcel of the original constitutional design. Of course, functional concerns—notably security and macroeconomic management— were vital considerations during this process, but in all cases the creation of democratically accountable central institutions was seen as the *sine qua non* for effective central policy making and implementation in these and other areas. In the EU, by way of contrast, sometimes-intrusive central policy responsibilities have been the inspiration for the strengthening of central accountability through the creation of more democratically representative institutions. We will return to these points in a later section.

The EU in Comparative Context II:
Institutional Adaptation

As earlier chapters showed, changing economic and political circumstances have, over time, forced the amendment, compromise, and reinterpretation of original constitutions. The subsequent development of central government-state relations has thus been a function of the interaction of original constitutional arrangements with economic and political change. Crucial to the eventual shape of these relations has been the ways in which actually or potentially rebellious states and regions have been able to articulate grievances through participation in central decision making. Table 8.2 provides a schematic outline of the ways in which states are represented in central decision making and in the constitutional amendment process in five federations and the EU.

---

[1] Treaty of Rome, Single European Act, Treaty on European Union, Treaty of Amsterdam. The EU actually had its origins in the European Coal and Steel Community (ECSC) in 1951. For an account, see Milward (1994).

Table 8.2. Representation of states[a] in central decision-making and constitutional change in five federations and the European Union

Country	De facto veto power of upper house	Territorial dimension to veto voting	Role of first ministers conferences	Frequency of amendment attempts	State legislative approval for constit. change	State popular approval for constit. change
US	yes	no	none	low	yes	no[g]
Canada	no	n/a	high	medium	yes	yes
Australia	yes	no	medium	low	yes	yes
Germany	yes[b]	sometimes	medium[d]	low	yes	no
Switzerland	yes	sometimes	none	high	yes	yes
EU	yes[c]	yes	high[e]	high[f]	yes	sometimes[h]

[a] Member states in EU.
[b] Limited to certain issue areas.
[c] Council of Ministers.
[d] Federal-Länder Inter-ministerial Committees
[e] Intergovernmental Conferences.
[f] Through successive treaties.
[g] But state conventions can be called to approve a constitutional change with two-thirds and Congress approving.
[h] Through a popular ratification by referendum of EU treaties in some countries.

All the systems but the Canadian accord a veto power to upper houses, but only in the EU is both the principle and practice of this power based on territorial considerations. Hence voting in the Council of Ministers is almost always reported in terms of national—or state—interest. This sometimes applies in the German Bundesrat and the Swiss Standerat, but, as the discussion in Chapters 6 and 7 showed, in neither chamber do territorial interests and alliances dominate proceedings. First Ministers Conferences have emerged as an important forum for provincial pressure on the central government in Canada, and indeed they have been crucial in setting the agenda for constitutional change. In Australia, equivalent conferences carry less weight, although they do act as a forum for the airing of state grievances. Land interests on Germany also make use of intergovernmental conferences—the interministerial committees—but these operate as part of an ongoing system of codetermination.

A further indicator of state power is the extent to which states are incorporated into arrangements for constitutional change. There are two dimensions to this dynamic. There is, first, the extent to which constitutional change is attempted; and second, the significance of the amendment attempts. Table 8.2 shows the pattern for the former but not the latter. In Canada attempts at constitutional change have been frequent, but because of the deep difference of interest between English-speaking and French-speaking Canada few have been successful. In Switzerland amendments attempts are common, as they are, in a quite different context, in the EU. Because of the double concurrent majority built into the Swiss amendment process, constitutional amendments are often unsuccessful. Although it is difficult to talk unambiguously of equivalent processes in the EU, the adoption of successive treaties represents an approximate functional equivalent. In both Switzerland and the EU, a wide range of policy areas and institutional arrangements is reviewed in the amendment process. In effect, the states have an effective veto over changes in the allocation of policy to different levels of government and in basic constitutional relationships, although in Switzerland this veto power is carefully spelt out in the constitution.

As far as the importance of amendment attempts is concerned, it is a truism that most amendments to a constitutional are likely significantly to alter existing power relations including federal-state relations. However, in Switzerland almost any policy change involving a change in central-cantonal relations requires an amendment as Article 3 of the constitution reserves all powers to the cantons unless specifically given to the federal government. And, of course, all amendments are subject to both referendum and cantonal approval.

In all of our sample federations state approval is required for constitutional change, although this point becomes almost moot in those systems, such as the American and Australian, where constitutional change has been rare. The final column in Table 8.2 measures whether, formally or by custom and tradition, popular approval in the various states is required for the validation of amendments. What is interesting about this measure is the unique position of Switzerland and the EU, for, as mentioned, only in the Swiss case does the constitution require approval from the upper house, state legislatures, *and* a popular vote by canton. In the EU, the approval mechanism does, of course vary from state to state, but only in the Danish case is referendum approval constitutionally established. Moreover, it could be argued that many of the decisions of the Council of Ministers, including unanimity decisions such as the imposition of minimum VAT rates, are not, again with the exception of Denmark, subject even to national/state legislative approval (see the discussion in Abromeit 1998: 21–2). Put another way, some of the decisions which in Switzerland are subject to the constitutional amendment double concurrent-majority rule are in the EU solely within the domain of the Council of Ministers, albeit through unanimous voting approval. We will return to this point in the next chapter.

The pattern of state representation outlined in Table 8.2 has, in the case of the established federations, developed over many decades or even many centuries. In every instance, the status of provinces and states in relation to the central government has diverged from the intentions of the original framers. Both in Australia and the United States, the senates were designed to function as 'councils of the states'; but neither ever performed as such. Instead, the Australian Senate became, at least until the introduction of proportional representation in 1949, a chamber dominated by the party in control of the House of Representatives and the government. Since then it has continued to be dominated by party interests, albeit not always the same ones as those in control of the government. In no sense does it function as a states' house. Similarly, the US Senate never functioned as a council of the states. The 'doctrine of instructions' whereby senators' actions were bound by the directives of state legislatures was never very effective and quickly fell into disuse. The breakdown of the Union in the 1860s was precipitated by dissident state legislatures, not by the Senate. And in the *post-bellum* period, the southern senators organized their legislative agendas on the basis both of ideology and of territory and section. Even in Germany, where the Bundesrat was unambiguously designed as a states' house, it has evolved into a second house for the articulation of national party based interests—but with a territorial dimension. A similar development has occurred in Switzerland, where the Standerat has developed into a chamber dominated by the centre-right parties rather than become a genuine house of the states.

The Canadian Senate was never intended as a house of the states and the absence of a central legislative forum for the representation of provincial interests had led dissident provinces, and especially Quebec, to seek redress by other means. One of these alternatives has been the development of *ad hoc* First Ministers Conferences, which in Canada have taken on a special importance in agenda setting and settling disputes between the federal government and the provinces. Indeed, the Conference has now been accorded formal constitutional status. The approximate functional equivalent to the Canadian

example also exists in Australia and, more significantly, in the EU, where successive intergovernmental conferences are scheduled for the specific purpose
of setting an agenda for constitutional and policy change.

Only in Switzerland is it possible to claim that the original framework of the
1848 and 1874 constitutions has not been radically altered through re-inter-
pretation and amendment—although even here the system has acquired a
degree of centralization. Interestingly, the popular approval or referendum
device has not been subject to great change over time. Referendums were
important at the inception of the Swiss and the Australian systems and have
continued to be so ever since. By way of contrast, state legislative—or sometimes state convention—approval for original constitutional change in
Germany and the US was there at the origins and remain the norm to this day.
Only in Canada has the referendum device been deemed a necessary—and
very recent—innovation as an imprimatur of constitutional change. And, as
will be developed later, this transition followed a long period where 'stateness'
problems dominated Canadian politics.

The EU in Comparative Context III: Adaptation and the Role of Political Parties

Students of political party systems tend to classify parties in terms of fragmentation or number of parties operating in national legislatures, ideological
polarization between the most extreme national parties, and the degree of
convergence between the two main national parties (Duverger 1963; Hix
1998: 41–4). However, in the absence of a territorial dimension, none of these
measures tells us a great deal about the relationship between stateness problems and institutional design. Fragmented party systems—Switzerland—may
be politically stable while less fragmented systems—Canada—may be in constitutional crisis. Political polarization may be greater in stable systems—
Germany—than in less stable systems—Belgium. The distance between the
two main parties also tells us little, as this is usually small in developed democracies.

Territorially based taxonomies tell us much more. Figure 8.1 shows the territorial dimensions to party systems in the five federations and the European
Union. Organizational and ideological centralization measures the extent to
which *across all jurisdictions* the main parties are centralized in both organizational and ideological terms. In every case these are correlated: decentralized
parties are more ideologically diffuse, and centralized parties more ideologically united. Spatial unity measures the degree to which the same parties
operate both at the national level and at the state or provincial level. Hence
the Australian system is dominated by two centrally concentrated parties
which operate at all levels. While Australia has the most unified party system
it is not as centralized as, say, the Danish system, given that the National—previously Country—Party has its support concentrated in a few states. Both

Switzerland and the US are characterized by organizationally and ideologically decentralized parties, but in both countries the same parties generally operate at all levels. In Germany the party system, while broadly retaining its pre-unification structure, has lost spatial unity and organizational-ideological cohesion since 1990. Similarly, the Canadian party system has fragmented over the last 70 years so that today different parties operate in some provinces from those dominant at the national level.

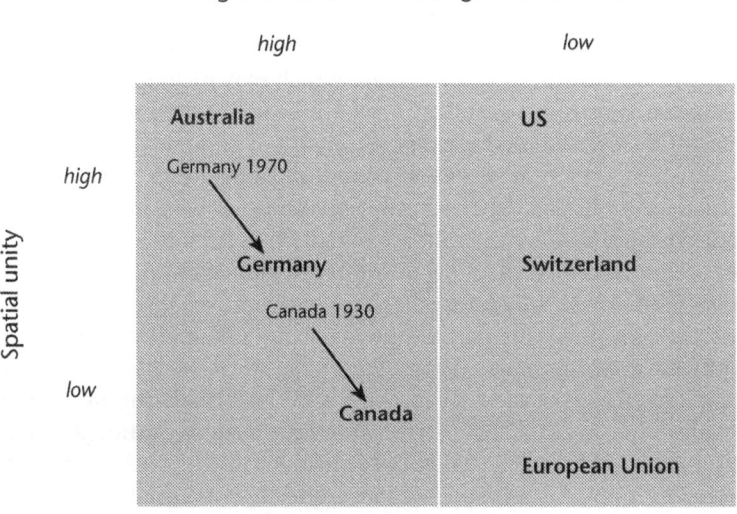

Organizational and ideological centralization

FIGURE 8.1. The territorial dimension to party systems in five federations and the European Union, 2000

The EU is very much an outrider in this taxonomy. There are no union-wide parties worthy of the name; and while it is possible to identify ideological 'families' of parties across countries, considerable variation within these families exists (see Hix and Lord 1997: Ch. 4). As numerous commentators have noted, the absence of genuinely European parties places limits on the legitimacy of EU government measured whether in terms of its scope, its activities, or its moral authority (see Hix 1998, and sources cited there). This is, perhaps, the most important implication of the experience of the five federations for the EU. Party systems broadly reflect the strength of regional and national loyalties. When institutional arrangements fail accurately to reflect these loyalties at the appropriate level, stateness problems can emerge. Hence for many decades the centralized institutional structure of American national government led to centralizing policies advanced by a centralizing national political parties. These were unacceptable to sectional interests in the south, whose access to central decision making remained limited. Ultimately, the southern states felt obliged to secede rather than to accept northern policies on trade and slavery. After the civil war, an uneasy peace between north and south was maintained only through the successful manipulation of parliamentary rules by southern senators and representatives, which served as a southern veto on unacceptable national policies.

In Canada, parliamentary arrangements and an impotent upper house also facilitated centralizing policies, but instead of a constitutional breakdown dissident regions, and in particular Quebec, have used *ad hoc* institutions such as the First Ministers Conference to bargain for the devolution of power. Provincial political parties, quite distinct in organization and purpose from the national parties, have brokered this compromise. Even so, Canada's constitutional system is far from being stable. Remaining stateness problems are such that a new constitutional settlement, which may include the secession of Quebec, is still a distinct possibility. Such a prospect is nigh inconceivable in Australia where regional identities are secondary to national identities. This is reflected in the party system, whose centralized operations have long overcome any decentralist tendencies in the constitution. As in modern America, and notwithstanding the regional base of the small National Party, party differences are grounded in ideology and interest rather than in territory. The Swiss case is the most difficult to place in comparative context. With a few minor exceptions, the same parties operate at the national and the cantonal levels, but most of the major parties are made up of locally and regionally based factions. These coalitional factions are looser than the decentralized party coalitions characteristic of the American system, although they do resemble the distinctive factional politics characteristic of the US south in the 1940s (see Key 1949). As was stressed in Chapter 7, Swiss parties are generally regarded as weak because they are subject to the numerous checks and balances imposed by federalism and direct democracy. In other words, institutional arrangements erected for the express purpose of protecting distinctive cultural, religious, and linguistic cantons have shaped the Swiss party system.

The EU in Comparative Context IV: The Fiscal Dimension

As was catalogued in earlier chapters, distributional issues are often at the heart of conflicts between central and state governments; and of these none is as important as intergovernmental fiscal relations. However, when one attempts to place this subject in comparative quantitative context, numerous data problems arise. One common measure is state and local government own-source revenue as a percentage of total government revenue (Table 8.3). According to these data, Australia and Germany are the most fiscally centralized and Switzerland and the least. While the variation between the sample federations is substantial, the real statistical outrider is the EU, where own-source revenue—agricultural levies and customs duties—amounted to a meagre 0.2 per cent of total government revenue in 1995. Of course, these figures hide tax-sharing arrangements which are well established in Germany and

Switzerland. Indeed, the lion's share of EU income is based on a form of tax sharing—a percentage of national VAT revenues—albeit one involving the actual collection of tax only at the member-state level. These figures also imply that because in some countries—and notably Australia—the state and local share is decreasing, then central power must be on the wane. This is not necessarily so, however. Indeed, as was shown in Chapter 5, this decrease must be explained more by the adoption of neo-liberal policies than by any desire to devolve power to state and local government.

Table 8.3. State and local government own-source revenue as a percentage of total government revenue, 1987 and 1995

	1987	1995
Australia	21.0	28.5
Germany	25.4	24.1
US	40.1[a]	41.3
Canada	45.0	45.2[b]
Switzerland	68.0[c]	69.7
EU[d]	99.7	99.8

[a]1988
[b]1994
[c]1991
[d]EU figure based on all member state and EU taxes except EU own-source income–agricultural levies and custom duties. EU data also based on 40.1% of EU total GDP in taxation in 1987 and 42% in 1995.

Sources: International Monetary Fund (1997); *Budget of the European Union 1998–99* (1998).

When intergovernmental grants are taken into account the pattern remains broadly the same (Table 8.4). At first sight it would appear that the Swiss cantons and communes actually transfer monies back to the federal government. However, the Swiss data exclude social security, which is a major transfer programme. This item was excluded because the Swiss themselves exclude it from their data. As we saw in Chapter 7, social support has a very special status in Switzerland, with the cantons and communes playing a major role. Of course, these data include all intergovernmental transfers as measured by a single statistical source, the International Monetary Fund's *Government Finance Statistics Yearbook*, which is based on a standardized survey form sent to all the relevant government departments. Unfortunately, the data are not always reliable and are sometimes not compatible with the statistics issued by competing national and state departments in the same countries. Moreover, they exclude the specifically equalizing component in intergovernmental transfers. Comparing equalization data in a systematic manner is also beset with methodological problems, not least the fact that some countries employ vertical redistribution, some horizontal redistribution, and some both. In addition, in one country, the United States, there is no formula-driven equalization programme worthy

Table 8.4. State and local expenditure as a percentage of total expenditure 1987 and 1995 including intergovernmental grants and excluding defence

	1987	1995
Australia	42.0	43.0
Germany	43.7	40.5
USA	50.1[a]	51.2
Canada	58.5	59.7[b]
Switzerland[c]	67.6[d]	64.2
EU	99.5	99.07

[a]1988
[b]1994
[c]Swiss data exclude social security.
[d]1991

Source: International Monetary Fund (1997); Administration fédérale des finances (1998).

of the name. It is nonetheless possible to compare programmes in four of the states with the EU by concentrating on the redistributive effect of strictly equalizing programmes on the most needy component states. Thus, Table 8.5 shows the effects of such programmes on the poorest three component states.

Two points stand out from these data. First, they confirm that the Australian federal government is the most fiscally intrusive of the sample, with Germany and Canada following closely behind. Second, the Swiss do the least in the way of redistribution among the sample of four established federations. Indeed, at 4.3 per cent of state GDP in the three poorest cantons, the Swiss pattern is quite close to that of the EU, where the figure for Greece, Portugal, and

Table 8.5. Average level of equalizing federal grants as a percentage of gross state product in the poorest three states in four federations and the European Union, 1995

Australia	15.1[a]
Canada	16.4[b]
Germany (1996)	10.3[c]
Switzerland	4.3[d]
EU (1992)	2.9[e]

[a]Tasmania, South Australia, Northern Territory.
[b]Newfoundland, Prince Edward Island, and New Brunswick. Yukon and North West Territories are excluded because of their very small populations.
[c]Saxony, Mecklenberg, and Lower Saxony.
[d]Uri, Jura, and Valais.
[e]Greece, Portugal, and Ireland.

Note: US data are excluded because there is no formula-driven equalizing federal programme.

Sources: Switzerland: Administration fédérale des finances (1998); Germany: Satistik Bund (1997); Canada: Statistics Canada (1996); Australia: Commonwealth of Australia (1994; 1995); EU: Wishlade (1996: 32).

Ireland was 2.9 per cent in 1992. Of course, the data refers *only* to formula-driven equalizing programmes. Actual federal aid is significantly higher in all cases bar the EU through centrally directed social security, infrastructure, and other social programmes which often by-pass state governments. The EU data do, of course, exclude agricultural subsidies. The unusual status of the Swiss case, and the parallels between Switzerland and the EU, are brought out by a more systematic comparison of fiscal arrangements in the sample countries. Table 8.6 provides just such a schematic comparison. State tax conformity refers to the extent to which states within federations employ the same taxes and uniformity measures whether tax levels are broadly the same or whether they diverge. Only Switzerland and the EU grant to their component states something approaching complete tax autonomy—although the EU's minimum VAT rate in theory represents more of limit on regional tax autonomy than applies in Switzerland. Tax harmonization would, of course, take the EU further down the road of central fiscal control. Three of the sample countries also coordinate the collection of taxes in one authority. In the US, Switzerland, and the EU, federal taxes are collected by the federal government, and state and local taxes by state and local authorities. This is an important indicator of fiscal autonomy, as is central control of state borrowing. Again, the position of the EU is interesting in this context because, under the terms of the Stability and Growth Pact, members of the Euro-zone are limited to running a budget deficit of no more than 3 per cent of GDP, which can be exceeded only under exceptional economic conditions (Von Hagen and Eichengreen 1996). To be fair, in practice state and provincial governments in the US, Canada, and Switzerland do not abuse their freedom to borrow; and if they did, something like the Stability Pact or the Australian Loan Council might well be introduced. But the fact remains that the institutional constraints on member state government borrowing in the EMU are formally greater than in several established federations.

Institutionalization of the state role refers to the extent to which, in fiscal matters, state interests are formally represented in central government. State influence on the centre measures the state role in practice, whatever the institutional and constitutional arrangements. The general role of states in central decision making was covered earlier in the chapter; and the pattern for fiscal relations is broadly the same as in other issue areas. However, the parallelism between the US and Switzerland comes into sharp relief in the fiscal area. In both political entities the barriers to changes in central levels of taxation are formidable and in both countries the component states—or voters the component states— have an effective veto over tax matters. Hence in both the state influence on centre is categorized as 'very strong'. In reality, of course, the unanimity rule employed in the EU Council of Ministers on tax matters is a stronger restriction on the central authorities than is the double concurrent-majority rule applicable in Switzerland. None the less, both rules are strong and place Switzerland and, in fiscal matters at least, the EU in a separate category from the other federations.

Table 8.6. Fiscal arrangements and the state role in national tax decisions: five federations and the European Union

	Australia	US	Canada	Germany	Switzerland	EU
State tax conformity	Yes	Very little	Yes[a]	Yes	None	None
State tax uniformity	Yes	No	Very little	Yes	No	No—except min.VAT rate
Single tax admin. and collection	Yes	No	Yes[a]	Yes	No	No
Independent tax role of centre	Large	Large	Medium	Large—but with tax sharing	Small	Very small
Extent of formula-led redistribution	High	Low	High	High	Low	Low
Central control of state borrowing[c]	Yes[d]	No	No[e]	Yes	Yes	Yes[b]
Institutionalization of state role	Yes[d]	Yes	No[e]	Yes	Yes	Yes
State influence on centre	Weak	Weak	Strong	Strong	Very strong	Very strong

[a]Quebec has a distinctive base for the level and administration of the individual income tax.
[b]Through the Stability and Growth Pact.
[c]Excluding state constitutional limitations and conventions rather than rules.
[d]Formally, but the upper house acts as an additional arm of the national government.
[e]But meetings of first ministers have become *de facto* institutionalised.

A further parallel between the two states exists in the general area of social welfare, although it is not as pronounced as in the fiscal realm. One of the defining characteristics of citizenship in the modern state is the acceptance of a redistributive welfare role for central governments (see the discussion in Scharpf 1997). With few exceptions, citizens accept the fact of redistribution across regions and across social groups. Hence voters in the south of England rarely question the reallocation of their tax pounds to voters in the north. And, was shown in Chapter 6, even in the much more extreme case of a unified Germany affluent tax payers in the west have accepted redistribution to poorer citizens in the east. Such redistributions are not always acceptable, however, as the Canadian case shows. Indeed, resentment on the part of French-speaking Canadians that Quebec may be a net loser in the distribution of federal largesse was not always founded in fact.

Put another way, stateness problems are likely to be aggravated not only by an intrusive central role in equalizing grant programmes but also in social security payments that are paid direct to individuals.

Although social security was not a major focus of earlier chapters, Chapter 7 did note the unusual context of social support programmes in Switzerland. Uniquely among the five countries, social support—welfare or social assistance—has always been primarily a state and local responsibility. Even social insurance—mainly old-age pensions—which in terms of spending and benefit levels is effectively federalized is subject to considerable influence by state and local interests. Table 8.7 places the Swiss experience in comparative context. Note that, at over 50 per cent of all federal spending, social welfare expenditure appears high in Switzerland. However, almost this entire sum consists on spending on social insurance; and, of course, the Swiss federal government actually spends less on domestic policy as a percentage of GDP than does any

Table 8.7. Patterns of social welfare spending and administration in five federations, mid-1990s

	Central govt. social welfare expend. as % of total domestic central expend.	State and local social welfare expend. as % of total social welfare expend.	State and local influence on central social welfare legislation	State and local role in administration of programmes
Australia	36.3	9.2	low	low
Canada	42.0	37.3	low	medium[a]
Germany	48.4	22.5	low/medium	high
US	35.1	28.6	low	low/high[b]
Switzerland	51.6	20.3	high	high

[a]Mainly Quebec.
[b]Low for social security, high for welfare following 1996 legislation.

Sources: Statistics: International Monetary Fund (1997); categories: see text.

of the sample countries. Indeed, in 1997 the Swiss federal government spent a mere 11.7 per cent of GDP. Spending by all levels of government came to 39.4 per cent of GDP. The great variety of cantonal and local programmes that is rooted in the slow evolution of social assistance in Switzerland is not dissimilar to the great variety of programmes characteristic of the EU member states. We will return to the significance of this point in the next chapter.

Conclusions

Clearly the experience of some of the sample countries is very different indeed from that of the EU. It would be difficult, for instance, to find much in common between Australia and the EU, whether the comparison was based on history, politics, or constitutional design. But something might be learnt even from the Australian case. From the very beginning the Australian federal government assumed a dominant fiscal role that included controls on state taxing and borrowing powers. The resulting fiscal centralization has aggravated the abrasive, confrontational nature of an Australian politics often dominated by the role of the federal government in grant distribution. Perhaps fortunately, highly centralized political parties that take their cues from ideology and interest rather than territory articulate the debate on this role. While in Australia territorially defined identity is weak, in the EU it is strong. It is therefore difficult to imagine any scenario where fiscal centralization in the EU would not precipitate territorial conflicts, some of which could lead to stateness problems (for an account of competing scenarios under European Monetary Union, see McKay: 1999*a*).

   As can be inferred from the analysis so far, the experience of the other sample federations is more rather than less relevant for the EU. This applies in particular to Switzerland, which is easily the most decentralized of the five federations. Over many decades, the overriding concern of the Swiss has been to restrain central power in order to preserve the linguistic, cultural, and religious identities of the cantons. To this end they have constructed a constitution whose main purpose has been to extend central authority only when a double majority of the Swiss people and the Swiss cantons permits it. An elaborate system of direct democracy coupled to a highly codified constitution has assured this. While the Swiss system can be criticized for being inefficient and/or politically conservative, few can question its success it limiting the power of the central state. What then are the implications of the Swiss experience and that of the other federations for constitutional design in the EU?

9

Designing Europe

Two features stand out about . . . questions of [EU] constitutional choice. First, they are irreducibly normative, in the sense that the answers that are given to them rely implicitly or explicitly on political principles or values . . . . Second, these normative issues are intertwined with questions of institutional analysis. Evaluating alternative institutional proposals cannot be done without understanding how the existing decision-making institutions of the EU actually work and what the feasible range of alternatives to current practice might be.

Albert Weale and Michael Nentwich, 1998

Territory, Identity, and Power: The EU in Comparative Perspective

ULTIMATELY, problems of governance in the European Union are problems of territory. Stateness problems may well develop given the continuing transfer of power to a higher governmental authority with limited legitimacy in the eyes of the citizenry in the various member states. Until the adoption of the Single European Act (SEA) and, more significantly, the Treaty on European Union, direct comparisons between the EU and existing federations were usually viewed as inappropriate. Both the legal status and the functional role of the EC were more akin to those of a supranational organization than a nation state. However, most commentators agree that the changes wrought by the SEA and Maastricht have moved the EU into a position closer to that of developed federation than a mere supranational organization. The extensive academic commentary on the constitutional and political status of the EU is evidence enough that it is inappropriate merely to label the EU a customs union or supranational organization (see, *inter alia*, Abromeit 1998; Schmitter 1996; Weale and Nentwich 1998). There is, moreover, good reason to suppose that the government of the EU will become stronger and more intrusive, at least over the medium term. This can be inferred from the philosophy of *acquis communautaire* or the assumption that all the integration achieved to date is irreversible and the related drive towards 'ever closer union of the peoples of Europe'. The latter is, of course, enshrined in the Treaty on

European Union (Article 4). The former view is widely shared among leading actors in the EU ranging from members of the Commission and the EP to judges on the European Court of Justice (see the discussion in Abromeit 1998: 254–7). More telling, perhaps, are the implications of recent transfers of power, and in particular monetary policy, to the EU level. Potentially, EMU brings the participating countries into closer contact not only economically but in the longer run also politically. This is because EMU may accelerate fiscal harmonization and centralization, which in turn will bring into sharper relief the costs and benefits of centrally organized redistribution (see McKay 1999a: 474–7 and sources cited). Even in the absence of fiscal redistribution, the 'one size fits all' inherent in EMU may not be able to broker asymmetry in the economic performance of different member states; and indeed, if Euroland is not an optimal currency area it may actually increase such asymmetries. Differential inflation, growth, and unemployment rates may lead nationally based political parties to focus electorates' discontent on the EU rather than national level (McKay 1999a: 477–81). Finally, EMU may oblige—and indeed in some cases already has obliged—national governments to reform welfare states and inflexible labour markets (Mussa 1997; McKinnon 1997). Again, such a process effectively 'nationalizes', or 'supranationalizes', these policy areas, which again may provoke parties to transfer electorates' attention to the EU level.

Of course, we can only speculate on the likely outcome of these changes, some of which will become apparent only when the economies of the EU are subject to an external economic shock or when a significant downturn in the level of economic activity occurs (see the discussion in Feldstein 1997). But the point is that whatever the specific economic and political consequences, EMU has increased the power of the EU central state and thus the state-like characteristics of EU institutions. Given that the potential problems of EMU are almost always portrayed in spatial or territorial terms, EMU also has the potential for the growth of stateness problems within the territory of Euroland.

As was outlined in earlier chapters, fiscal relations are often at the centre of disputes between central and regional governments; and as will be argued below, the experience of these countries suggest that a strong case exists for limiting the scope of EU fiscal responsibilities.

Either directly or indirectly it is the broadening policy responsibilities of the EU that has provoked so much scholarship on the democratic deficit (DD). While the DD has always been rooted in institutional relationships, and in particular the fact that the unelected Commission rather than the elected EP produces a large volume of EU legislation, most agree that the deficit has increased in recent years (see the discussion in Andersen and Eliassen 1996). In essence, the DD is deemed to have increased because among the citizenry of most European countries there is an insufficient sense of European identity to legitimize the moral authority and the scope of new EU responsibilities (for a summary see Beetham and Lord 1998). While identity varies from country to country and region to region, only 5 per cent of a 1998 sample of all citizens in the EU considered themselves 'European only' compared with 44 per cent who placed their identity in national terms alone (Eurobarometer 1998). These findings are broadly compatible with a large body of survey based research on this subject over the last several decades (for a summary, see Van der Eijk and Franklin 1996).

This accepted, citizens in some countries and regions, and especially in those such as Belgium where national identity is poorly developed, have acquired multiple identities which some observers have labelled 'complex self-identification' (Lancaster 1999). As was shown in earlier chapters, the institutions of federalism together with the operations of party systems have often acted as mediating agents for the articulation of multiple identities. Nowhere is this clearer than in Switzerland, whose political institutions were originally constructed, and have since been continuously adapted, to mirror the local, cantonal, and national identities of the Swiss. In contrast, Canadian political institutions have generally failed to reflect the multiple identities of many Canadians. Parliamentary democracy tied to strong, nationalizing parties and the absence of adequate means for the representation of the provinces in national decision making have led to serious stateness problems, which even after more than 130 years of governance have yet to be resolved.

It could be argued that, in terms of accommodating multiple citizen identities, the flaws in American constitutional design were even more egregious. A centralized institutional structure and the relative absence of mechanisms for the representation of the states in national decision making helped precipitate a bloody civil war. The ensuing political settlement resolved the issue but only at the expense of possibly contributing to the immiseration of the region and the subjugation of its African-American population for almost 100 years. In the case of Australia, the territorial issue has been less important in part because territorially differentiated identity is largely absent in that country. None the less, the adversarial nature of intergovernmental relations, especially as they relate to fiscal policy, is largely the product of an institutionally and politically centralized system. In Germany what at first sight appears to be a relatively decentralized institutional structure has been utilised by centralizing parties exploiting a strong sense of national identity. Although ameliorated by a complex system of devolved administration, the importance of centrally negotiated national standards reflects the strength of national identity. This value has prevailed even in the face of the trials and tribulations of unification.

The European Union and Institutional Design

The experience of these countries shows that, in order to avoid stateness problems, institutional arrangements should accommodate not only the prevailing pattern of complex self-identification but also the balance between regional and national identification. Obviously this is no easy task especially given the fact that identification changes over time and given that adapting institutional arrangements to reflect such changes is always problematical. In the case of the EU, however, there is at least the advantage that we are dealing with a nascent rather than a fully developed federation. There is also the advantage that close to universal agreement exists on the need for reform of existing institutions. Much of the debate on institutional design has dwelt on the need to strengthen the role of the European Parliament. There has thus been an assumption that the EU should evolve into the classic parliamentary model of governance: a powerful lower house held responsible and represent-ative through party government (for an overview, see Weiler, Haltern, and Mayer 1995; Falkner and Nentwich 1995). Critics have rightly pointed out that a number of alternatives exist including presidential arrangements (Hix 1998) and direct democracy (Abromeit 1998). Others have been concerned to place the reform of the EU and the correction of the DD in analytical and the-oretical context (Weale and Nentwich 1998). While all of these contributions must of necessity be comparative—meaningful reform of EU institutions can be discussed only by reference to the experience of other countries—none has relied on deeper comparisons of the EU with the historical experience of a range of established federations. What follows is a list of reforms/observations deriving from the analysis provided in Chapters 3–8. Naturally some of these overlap with the suggestions provided by other observers. However, a more systematic use of comparison, albeit with a limited number of countries, should enrich rather then simply duplicate these efforts. Given the complex-ity of EU institutions and the ways in which they interact with national gov-ernments, it is possible to produce an almost infinite number of alternative institutional scenarios whether or not they are drawn from careful compari-son. Indeed, many of such efforts to date are both well thought out and plau-sible (see in particular Abromeit 1998). For this reason the analysis here will be confined to the implications that can be drawn directly from the experience of the five sample countries. In this context, three institutionally specific and two general points will be made.

1. *Classical parliamentary government may be an inappropriate model for future governance in the EU.* As others have noted, the simple majoritarian principle inherent in parliamentary government can work well in systems where national identity is developed. When, however, identities are rooted in regions, states, or provinces, majoritarianism can aggravate legitimation prob-lems (Weale 1998: 49–50; Hix 1998). Given the poorly developed sense of European identity across most EU states, an EP vested with real legislative pow-ers might well lose legitimacy among a range of national electorates who per-ceive European elections as second- rather than first-order elections (see Gable 1998: 333–54). Less discussed in the literature are situations where national identity is well developed in some regions but not in others. Empirically, this is much more common.[1] Hence in Canada citizens in Quebec have a poorly

---

[1] Indeed, it is often the major source of stateness problems as the examples of the UK—in Northern Ireland—Spain, Russia, and Indonesia show.

developed national identity in relation to the rest of Canada. Historically, majoritarian parliamentary arrangements did little to accommodate the needs of the Quebecois. Crucially, Canada's problems were aggravated by the enhanced role of the federal government resulting from the adoption of Keynesian economics and the welfare state. In other words, when the perceived needs of the union were changed by intellectual fashion and majority opinion, an institutionally powerful federal government was able to enhance central power irrespective of the wishes of territorially defined minorities. It seems more likely that rather than develop asymmetrically in this way, European identity will remain quite poorly developed at least amongst the larger member states. If so, the more appropriate comparator case for the EU is Switzerland. The citizens of individual cantons or groups of cantons are not somehow more 'Swiss' than others. Instead, the citizenry have worked hard to organize political and institutional arrangements in such a way that cantonal sovereignty is protected and central power contained. The major task for the EU is to safeguard national sovereignty through equally novel institutional design. A much-strengthened EP catering to the interests of territorial majorities would fail to provide such a safeguard.

2. *A strong case exists for maintaining the dominant position of the Council of Ministers including its territorial base but in the context of a new EU constitution.* Problems of governance in Canada have also been aggravated by the fact that the political system operates in a *de facto* unicameral context. In the absence of formal state representation at the centre, the potential for the lower house to use its majority in ways unacceptable to territorial minorities is enhanced. In very different contexts, party dominance of the Australian and US senates has long prevented those chambers from acting as a representative of state interests—although, in recent decades at least, the absence of strong regional sentiment has reduced the need for effective state representation. The Swiss Standerat and German Bundesrat both act as councils of the states, but, in both, party and ideology have supplemented exclusively territorial considerations. While the EU formally lacks an upper house, the Council of Ministers is widely regarded as a functional equivalent. In that body territory is all, whether decisions are taken unanimously or by QMV. Given the great ethnic and linguistic heterogeneity of the European Union and the very limited sense of European identity, a powerful case exists for the maintenance of the territorially based veto power of the Council of Ministers. This is especially so should the powers of the EP be strengthened and should party alignments develop along ideology and interest rather than territorial lines. The Canadian, German, and US experience suggests that, once regionally based politicians gain access to central power through representation in upper houses, their incentive structures change in ways that favour national over state and regional interests. While this transition is rarely complete—even in the face of unification, the integrity of the German federalism has not been wholly undermined by the growth of party power—it could be argued that only the institutions of direct democracy have ensured the continuing and

effective representation of the Swiss cantons in national decision making. In the EU the Council of Ministers is the key institution working in defence of member state interests. At present the unanimity decision rule applies to a relatively wide range of areas.[2] Many of these are, however, functionally equivalent to constitutional change in other countries. This certainly applies to enlargement and membership of international organizations. A case exists, therefore, for codifying these key areas in a new EU constitution and subjecting them to a formal amendment process (on the need for a new constitutional settlement, see Bellamy, Bufacchi, and Castiglione 1995).

3. *Codification should include all areas relating to taxation and controls on member state spending and borrowing. Constitutional amendments should additionally be subject to supermajoritarian approval procedures.* It follows that the new constitution has to be highly decentralist in nature. The subsidiarity principle which, in part at least, employs an efficiency criterion—'the scale and effects' clause in the Article 3b of Title II of the Maastricht Treaty[3]—should be replaced by a 'stronger' guarantee of member state sovereignty similar to that provided by Article 3 of the Swiss constitution. Any extension of central power should be based not on what is economically or bureaucratically efficient, but on what is constitutionally mandated. Hence state rights should be protected by a clause such as:

The member states are sovereign, in so far as their sovereignty is not limited by the EU constitution, and exercise all those rights which have not been transferred to EU institutions.

---

[2] The list of issues areas subject to unanimous vote is actually quite long and includes:
- any action not specifically authorized under the EU treaties;
- revision of EU treaties;
- admission of new members;
- proposals for new programmes or institutions that will include, some, but not all, EU countries;
- defence;
- manufacture and sale of arms;
- decisions of principle on common foreign policy;
- international agreements;
- citizen's rights, laws against discrimination;
- police and judicial cooperation in criminal matters;
- visa, asylum, and immigration—this may move to majority voting in 2004;
- free movement of people, residence rights;
- social security, protection and representation of workers;
- use of EU money for promoting employment;
- new EU or national subsidies to industry;
- obligatory harmonization of tax legislation;
- financial assistance to a member in serious economic trouble;
- the 'excessive deficit' procedure of the monetary union;
- external trade in services and intellectual property;
- measures to promote culture and history;
- allocating structural and cohesion funds to poorer EU regions, environmental matters primarily concerning taxation, energy, or town planning;
- transport measures with a 'serious effect' on particular regions;
- changes in rules, regulations, and seats of EU institutions including the parliament, commission, court of auditors, court of justice, and central bank; nomination of their top officials; and
- sources of EU budget revenue.

Listed in *The Economist*, 13 November 1999: 52.

[3] For full text, see Chapter 2, footnote 1.

The onus for an extension of central power therefore lies unambiguously on constitutionally mandated change. And, as in the case of Switzerland, any substantive shift in the balance of central and regional power should be subject to constitutional amendment. What specifically might represent a shift in the balance of power? A good starting point would be those areas presently subject to unanimous vote in the Council of Ministers including the excessive deficit procedure of EMU, fiscal harmonization, new taxes, and the allocation of structural and cohesion funds to poorer EU regions. As was clearly demonstrated in earlier chapters, fiscal matters are usually at the heart of central-local conflict in established federations. Often central economic power accumulates because founding constitutions fail to specify the limits to the federal government's taxing and regulatory capacity. Such has certainly been the case in Canada, Australia, Germany, and the United States. In two of these examples, Canada and the United States, serious stateness problems ensued. Only in Switzerland is the central government's powers codified to the point where substantive changes in federal taxation and other areas of responsibility require constitutional amendment. The urgent need in the EU, then, is to specify the territorial division of responsibility by jurisdiction and to codify it in the new constitution. Once this list is codified, it could be changed only by a formal amendment to the constitution. Again as in Switzerland, the amendment procedure should involve some form of super-majoritarianism or a double vote by QMV in the Council and a majority vote in the EP, both to be approved by a popular vote in each of the member states. Given the great linguistic, cultural, and ethnic heterogeneity of the EU, a case could be made for some form of concurrent majority or QMV being instituted for the popular vote, possibly a majority in two-thirds or three-fifths of all the member states. In this way it would be very difficult to extend central power beyond that enshrined in the constitutional settlement. Crucially, any such extension would be subject to voter approval in concurrent majority of member states. In addition, some member states might decide to opt out of a particular aspect of EU jurisdiction, as has been the case with the UK and EMU. Precedents for this do exist in other federations. For example, special arrangements have been made for Quebec in the Canadian social security system and for territories in both Canada and Australia. Again, a popular opt-out vote in the affected member state could be constitutionally mandated.

The key question, of course, is specifying exactly which areas should be subject to these procedures and which not. At the moment, EU constitutional conferences are the only means whereby major changes in EU treaties can be proposed. In the ten years between 1990 and 2000 three such conferences were held, and the philosophy underpinning the *acquis communautaire*, together with the prospect of further enlargement, implies that this sort of constitutional ad hocery will continue into the foreseeable future. Conference agenda setting is greatly influenced by the *acquis communautaire* philosophy: the assumption is always how EU institutions can be strengthened and EU responsibilities extended (on Maastricht, see Dyson and Featherstone 1999; on

Amsterdam, see Moravcsik and Kalypso 1998). Yet the experience of constitution building in other federations suggests that, in order to avoid legitimization problems, a constitutional settlement eventually has to reached that
clearly defines the limits to central power and provides the states with guarantees of sovereignty. No such settlement has thus been concluded in the
European Union.

This analysis raises two general points. First, there is the problem of the *efficiency* of the decision rules employed. As Dahl and others have pointed out,
federalism and social contract theory suggest that the more complex and heterogeneous the polity, the more likely are the decision rules employed to
move in the direction of unanimity (Dahl 1964; see the discussion in Abromeit
1998: 118–19). Decision making pathologies may result including logrolling
and the pork barrel. As Weale (1998: 56) puts it: 'the reason is that with per-
fect information and low transaction costs, rational egoists will have an incentive to misrepresent their preferences to get the bribe of being induced to join
the proto-winning coalition, and under imperfect information, log rolling will
produce specific and visible benefits'. Empirical evidence from the Federal
Republic of Germany suggests that in some federal systems just such an outcome has ensued (Chapter 6; see also Scharpf 1988). However, the example of
Switzerland shows that super-majoritarianism linked to territorially defined
referendums is as likely to result in *non-decisions* as in logrolling and the pork
barrel. For example, attempts to expand the scope of government in
Switzerland have often fallen foul of the constitutional barriers. Swiss public
spending, and especially federal government spending, has been held to lower
levels than in any comparable country, even though left and centre-left parties have held majorities in the lower house over many electoral cycles. Similar
constitutional arrangements in the EU might produce the similar results.[4] In
other words, the price of maintaining the legitimacy of the EU—and in particular, perhaps, an enlarged EU—may be the imposition of severe limitations
on the scope of the central government.

As in Switzerland this may produce protestations to the effect that state—or
member state—autonomy in fiscal and other areas results in a 'tax jungle', or
less than Pareto-optimal economic arrangements. But such outcomes may be
preferable to the emergence of stateness problems and territorial disintegration. Present arrangements, where most day-to-day legislative initiatives
emanate from the Commission and where constitutional adaptation proceeds
on an ad hoc basis, do of course already result in decision pathologies including logrolling, the pork barrel, and corruption (Marks 1992; 1996). The formal
allocation of a range of policy issues in a new constitution would not in itself
remove these problems, but it might well prevent them spreading, especially
if popular approval was required for any new or greatly enhanced spending
programme.

---

[4] Indeed they already have, given the unanimity vote in the Council.

The second general point concerns the relationship between the institution of direct democratic devices and questions of justice and equity. A common criticism of direct democracy is that it produces both incompetent and conservative decision making. However, this point is not always easy to demonstrate empirically. The most extensive analysis of the use of referendums and initiatives in the American states concludes that although they do have a conservative impact in fiscal terms—taxes are typically reduced rather than increased—the rights of minorities are not always threatened by direct democracy (Bowler, Donovan, and Tolbert 1998). In some instances—for example, the medical use of marihuana—liberal outcomes have resulted and in some not. The key variable would appear to be the tolerance level of small, homogeneous communities, not the instruments of direct democracy themselves (Bowler, Donavon, and Tolbert 1998: Ch. 12). A similar pattern would appear to apply in Switzerland: conservative votes, including the denial of votes for women in 1959, derived from the veto power of smaller rural cantons. When one compares these cases with the EU, two points stand out. First, there is no equivalent to these communities among the member states in the EU. Smaller members are not notably more conservative than larger members. Second, in the EU we have little reason to believe that the 'federal government' will come to represent liberal progressive opinion battling against backward regressive states or groups of states. This, typically, has been the position with the Swiss and American federal authorities in relation to some cantons and states. As far as the guarantee of basic rights for citizen is concerned, and in contrast to the historical development of Switzerland and the US, EU member states employ broadly similar civil rights and liberties standards. Instead, most of differences between the EU states concern distributional and regulatory issues—the very issues that tend to produce conservative outcomes following popular votes in the US and Switzerland. Yet these and other federations function relatively well even with state fiscal autonomy, variations in employment laws, and, in the case of Switzerland and the USA, quite large differences in the size and administration of social assistance programmes. It has, of course, already been established that the institution of a popular vote mechanism for EU constitutional amendments would likely result in conservative outcomes in fiscal and distributional policy. This is the price that would have to be paid to pre-empt legitimization and stateness problems. Economists in general, and those working on fiscal federalism in particular, may bemoan the resulting 'inefficiencies'; but in the longer term the more egregious of these may be corrected. Certainly this is the lesson of the Swiss experience. As Richard Bird (1986: 242–3) noted some years ago:

. . . the Swiss experience demonstrates [that] when people are left to decide for themselves what they want to do and when, their decisions tend on the whole to be rather conservative. The status quo is retained until it becomes absolutely obvious to all that the situation requires change. At least in Switzerland, however, desired changes eventually get made. Although the pace of change and some of the details may not be very appealing to intellectual elites, it is by no means clear that concurrence with intellectual fashion is an appropriate criterion for evaluating the efficacy of either economic or political institutions.

None of this is to deny that the use of referendums involves biases most of which favour already advantaged social groups (see the discussion in Abromeit 1998: Ch. 6). But what is being proposed is not the introduction of 'strong democracy' or the institutionalization of direct democratic devices on a day-to-day basis across a wide range of policies (Barber 1984), but merely the requirement that EU constitutional amendments be subject to approval by a territorially defined concurrent majority. Even if such an innovation involves class bias, this is surely preferable to the situation where central power may accrue, almost by default, without the consent of the citizens of the component states.

Conclusions

Although some EU member states already subject EU treaties to approval by referendum, to *require* all member states to do so and greatly to extend the issue areas where such votes apply represents a major and possibly unachievable political change. Each member state has a distinctive political tradition and political culture and in some—Germany, for example—judicial interpretation of treaties is constitutionally more important than is popular approval (Gustavsson 1998). To elevate the popular vote to prime position would, therefore, require amendments to the Basic Law. Constitutional change would, indeed, be required in almost all of the EU member states before the suggested reforms could be implemented. But given the scale of the economic and political changes—and especially EMU and enlargement, which are already in place or are timetabled—the existing EU constitution has to be reformed. Among the institutions and issues in need of attention are the number and selection of EU Commissioners, voting rights in the Council, defence, and the whole area of fiscal reform and harmonization.

While the reforms suggested in this chapter might be considered politically unrealistic or even utopian, the experience of the five sample federations shows that failure to adapt constitutional arrangements in ways that accurately reflect levels of regional and national identity can have damaging consequences. Stateness problems can ensue that can, variously, involve jurisdictional battles, constitutional crises, and, in the worst scenarios, secession and even civil war. The more extreme of these outcomes seems highly unlikely in the EU, which remains a nascent rather than fully developed federation. It is nonetheless moving in the direction of ever more intrusive central power—and this in a context where all agree that federation-wide citizen identity is poorly developed. Over the next several decades the most urgent task for the EU is arriving at a new and permanent constitutional settlement. In this endeavour, constitutional framers should look first to the experience of those

democratic countries with the longest experience of federal political arrangements. Something can be learnt from all five of the countries under discussion
in this book, but perhaps most can be learnt from the very decentralized institutions of the Swiss confederation. Where identity is localized and interstate
heterogeneity great, a powerful case exists for the creation of devices that are
specifically designed to limit the accumulation of centralized political power.

REFERENCES

Abromeit, Heidrun (1998). *Democracy in Europe: Legitimising Politics in a Non-State Polity*. New York and Oxford: Berghahn Books.

Administration fédérale des finances (1996). *Finances Publiques en Suisse, 1995*. Berne: Administration fédérale des finances.

——(1998). *Finances Publiques en Suisse, 1996*, Vol. 18. Berne: Administration fédérale des finances.

Advisory Commission for Intergovernmental Relations (ACIR) (various years). *Significant Features of Fiscal Federalism*. Washington, DC: ACIR.

Ahmad, Etisham (1997). *Financing Decentralised Expenditures: An International Comparison of Grants*. Cheltenham and Brookfield, MA: Edward Elgar.

Aitkin, Don, Jinks, Brian, and Warhurst, John (1988). *Australian Political Institutions*. Melbourne: Longman Cheshire.

Alston, Lee J. and Ferrie, Joseph P. (1999). *Southern Paternalism and the American Welfare State: Economics, Politics, and Institutions in the South, 1965–1965*. Cambridge and New York: Cambridge University Press.

——Eggertsson, Thrainn, and North, Douglass C. (eds) (1996). *Empirical Studies in Institutional Change*. New York: Cambridge University Press.

Anderson, F. J. and Bonsor, N. C. (1986). 'Regional Economic Alienation: Atlantic Canada and the West', in K. Norrie (ed.), *Disparities and Interregional Adjustment*. Vol. 64 of the research studies for the Royal Commission on the Economic Union and Development Prospects or Canada. Toronto: University of Toronto Press, 64–91.

Anderson, Svein S. and Eliassen, Kjell A. (1996). *The European Union: How Democratic Is It?* Thousand Oaks, CA and London: Sage.

Anton, Thomas (1983). 'The Regional Distribution of Federal Expenditures', *National Tax Journal*, 36: 429–42.

Barber, Benjamin (1984). *Strong Democracy: Participatory Politics for a New Age*. Berkeley and Los Angeles: University of California Press.

Beckton, Clare F. and Mackay, A. Wayne (1986). 'Institutional and Constitutional Arrangements: An Overview', in Clare F. Beckton and A. Wayne MacKay (eds), *Recurring Issues in Canadian Federalism*. Toronto and London: University of Toronto Press, 1–76.

Beer, Samuel H. (1977). 'Political Overload and Federalism'. *Polity*, 10: 5–17.

——(1993). *To Make a Nation: The Rediscovery of American Federalism*. Cambridge, MA: Harvard University Press.

Beetham, David (1991). *The Legitimation of Power*. London: Macmillan.

——and Lord, Christopher (1998). 'Legitimacy and the European Union', in Albert Weale and Michael Nentwich (eds), *Political Theory and the European Union: Legitimacy, Constitutional Choice and Citizenship*. London and New York: Routledge, 15–33.

Begg, David, *et al.* (1993). *Making Sense of Subsidiarity: How Much Centralisation for Europe?* London: Centre for Economic Policy Research.

Belanger, M. and Campeau, J. (1991). *Rapport de la Commission sur l'avenir politique et constitutionnel du Quebec*. Montreal: Government of Quebec (27 March).

Bell, Winifred (1965). *Aid to Dependent Children*. New York: Columbia University Press.

Bellamy, Richard, Bafucchi, Vittorio, and Castiglione, Dario (eds) (1995). *Democracy and Constitutional Culture in the Union of Europe*. London: Lothian Foundation Press.

Bidwell, Charles (1993). *Maastricht and the UK*. London: PACE.

Billington, Monroe (1984). *Southern Politics Since the Civil War*. Malabar: Krieger.

Birch, Anthony H. (1989). *Nationalism and National Integration*. London: Unwin Hyman.

Bird, R. M. (1986). *Federal Finances in Comparative Perspective*. Toronto: Canadian Tax Foundation.

Blair, Phillip and Cullen, Peter (1999). 'Federalism, Legalism and Political Reality: The Record of the Federal Constitutional Court', in Charlie Jeffery (ed.), *Recasting German Federalism: The Legacies of Unification*. London and New York: Pinter, 119–54.

Bonjour E., Offler, H. S., and Potter, G. R. (1952). *A Short History of Switzerland*. Oxford: Oxford University Press.

Bothwell, Robert C. (1996). *Canada and Quebec: One Constitution, Two Histories*. Victoria: University of British Columbia Press.

——Drummond, Ian, and English, John (1989). *Canada Since 1945*, 2nd edn. Toronto: University of Toronto Press.

Bowler, S., Donavan, T., and G. R. Potter (eds) (1998). *Citizens as Legislators: Direct Democracy in the United States*. Columbus: Ohio State University Press.

Brecht, Arnold (1967). 'American and German Federalism: Distribution of Powers', in Aaron Wildavsky (ed), *American Federalism in Perspective*, Boston: Little, Brown, 185–9.

Brzinski, Joanne B., Lancaster, Thomas D., and Tuschhoff, Christian (eds) (1999). *Compounded Representation in Western European Federations*. London and Portland: Frank Cass.

Budget of the European Union, 1998–99 (1998). Brussels.

Burgess, Michael (ed.) (1990). *Canadian Federalism: Past, Present and Future*. Leicester and New York: Leicester University Press.

Butschi, Danielle and Cattacin, Sandro (1993). 'The Third Sector in Switzerland: The Transformation of the Subisdiarity Principle'. *West European Politics*, 16: 362–79.

Cammisa, Marie (1968). *From Rhetoric to Reform: Welfare Policy in the United States*. Boulder, CO: Westview Press.

Carty, R. K. and Stewart, David (1996). 'Parties and Party Systems', in Christopher Dunn (ed.), *Provinces: Canadian Provincial Politics*. Peterborough, Ontario: Broadview Press, 63–94.

Cash, William J. (1969). *The Mind of the South*. New York: Vintage.

Church, Clive H. (1989). 'Behind the Consociational Screen: Politics in Contemporary Switzerland'. *West European Politics*, 12: 35–54.

Codding, George Arthur Jr (1961). *The Federal Government of Switzerland*. Boston: Houghton Mifflin.

Commonwealth of Australia (1994). *Budget Papers: Commonwealth Financial Relations with Other Levels of Government, 1993–4*. Canberra: AGPS.

——(1995). *Budget Papers: Commonwealth Financial Relations with Other Levels of Government, 1994–5*. Canberra: AGPS.

——(1999). *Budget Papers: Commonwealth Financial Assistance to the States*. Canberra: AGPS.

Conradt, David P. (1996). *The German Polity*, 6th edn. London: Longman.

Cox, Gary W. and McCubbins, Mathew D. (1993). *Legislative Leviathan: Party Government in the House*. Berkeley: University of California Press.

Dahl, Robert (1964). *A Preface to Democratic Theory*. Chicago: University of Chicago Press.

Deeg, Richard E. (1994). 'Germany's Länder and the Federalisation of the European Union'. Paper delivered at the annual meeting of the American Political Science Association: New York:

Duchacek, Ivan D. (1970). *Comparative Federalism: The Territorial Dimension of Politics*. New York: Holt, Rinehart, and Winston.

Dunn, Christopher (ed.) (1996). *Provinces: Canadian Provincial Politics*. Peterborough, Ontario: Broadview Press.

Duverger, Maurice (1963). *Political Parties: Their Organisation and Activity in the Modern State*. New York: Wiley.

Dyson, Kenneth and Featherstone, Kevin (1999). *The Road to Maastricht: Negotiating Economic and Monetary Union*. Oxford and New York: Oxford University Press.

Elkins, Stanley and McKitrick, Eric (1993). *The Age of Federalism: The Early American Republic, 1788–1800*. New York and Oxford: Oxford University Press.

Ethier, Mireille (1986). 'Regional Grievances: The Quebec Case', in K. Norrie (ed.), *Disparities and Interregional Adjustment*. Vol. 64 of the research studies for the Royal Commission on the Economic Union and the Development Prospects for Canada. Toronto: University of Toronto Press.

Eurobarometer, 49 (1998). Brussels.

European Economy 1993 (1993). Brussels.

Falkner, G. and Nentwich, M. (1995). *European Union: Democratic Perspectives After 1996*. Vienna: Service Fachverlag.

Fehrenbacher, Don E. (1976). *The Dredd Scott Case: Its Significance in American Law and Politics*. New York and Oxford: Oxford University Press.

Feldstein, Martin (1997). 'The Political Economy of the European Economic and Monetary Union: Political Sources of an Economic Liability'. *Journal of Economic Perspectives*, 11: 23–42.

Fenno, Richard F. Jr. (1973). *Congressmen in Committees*. Boston: Little, Brown.

Frey, R, Spillman, A., Dafflon, B., Jeanrenaud, C., and Maier, A. (1994). 'Tâches de la péréquation financière dans l'état fédéral', in R. Frey, *La péréquation financière entre la Confédération et les cantons*, Expertise relative aux aides financière et indemnités de la Confédération en faveur des cantons mandatée par l'administration fédérale des finances et la Conférence des Directeurs Contonaux des finances. Berne and Lucerne, 1–54.

Gable, Mark (1998). 'Public Support for European Integration: An Empirical Test of Five Theories'. *Journal of Politics*, 60: 333–54.

Gagnon, Alain G. (1990). 'Quebec-Canada Relations: The Engineering of Constitutional Arrangements', in Michael Burgess (ed.), *Canadian Federalism: Past, Present and Future*. Leicester and New York: Leicester University Press, 95–121.

Galligan, Brian (1995). *A Federal Republic: Australia's Constitutional System of Government*. Melbourne and Cambridge: Cambridge University Press.

Gillard, Charles (1955). *A History of Switzerland*. London: Allen and Unwin.

Government of Victoria, Federal State Relations Committee (2000). *Report on Australian Federalism: The Role of the States*, http://www.home.vicnet.au/~fsrc/Report2/

Gruner, Erich and Pitterle, Kenneth J. (1983). 'Switzerland's Political Parties', in Howard R. Penniman (ed.), *Switzerland at the Polls: The National Elections of 1979*. Washington, DC: American Enterprise Institute, 30–59.

Gustavson, Sverker (1998). 'Defending the Democratic Deficit', in Albert Weale and Michael Nentwich (eds), *Political Theory and the European Union: Legitimacy, Constitutional Choice and Citizenship*. London and New York: Routledge.

Hamilton, Alexander, Jay, John, and Madison, James (1961). *The Federalist*, ed. Benjamin F. Wright. Cambridge, MA: Harvard University Press.

Hix, Simon (1998). 'Elections, Parties and Institutional design: A Comparative Perspective on European Union Democracy'. *West European Politics*, 21: 19–52.

——and Lord, Christopher (1997). *Political Parties in the European Union*. Basingstoke: Macmillan.

Holmes, Jean and Sharman, Campbell (1977). *The Australian Federal System*. Sydney and London: Allen and Unwin.

Huitt, Ralph K. (1965). 'The Internal Distribution of Influence: The Senate', in David Truman (ed.), *The Congress and America's Future*. Englewood Cliffs, NJ: Prentice Hall, 91–117.

International Monetary Fund (1997). *Government Finances Statistics Yearbook 1997*. Washington, DC: International Monetary Fund.

Irving, Helen (1999). *The Centenary Companion to Australian Federation*. Melbourne and Cambridge: Cambridge University Press.

Jeffery, Charlie (1999). 'The Role of the Bundesrat', in Joanne B. Brzinski, Thomas D. Lancaster, and Christian Tuschhoff (eds), *Compounded Representation in Western European Federations*. London and Portland: Frank Cass, 130–66.

——and Savigear, Peter (eds) (1991). *German Federalism Today*. Leicester: Leicester University Press.

Jenkins, John R.G. (1986). *Jura Separatism in Switzerland*. Oxford: Oxford University Press.

Johnson, Neville (1998). 'Territory and Power: Some Historical Determinants of the Constitutional Structure of the Federal Republic of Germany', in Charlie Jeffery (ed.), *Recasting German Federalism: The Legacies of Unification*. London and New York: Pinter, 23–39.

Katz, Richard and Mair, Peter (1995). *How Parties Organize*. Thousand Oaks and London: Sage.

Key, V. O. (1949). *Southern Politics in State and Nation*. New York: Knopf.

Kincaid, John (1996). 'From Dual to Coercive Federalism in American Inter-governmental Relations', in John S. Jun and Deil S. Wright, *Globalisation and De-centralisation*, Washington, DC: Georgetown University Press, 29–47.

King, Anthony (1996). *Running Scared: Why American Politicians Campaign Too Much and Govern Too Little*. New York: Basic Books.

Klatt, Hartmut (1999). 'Centralising Trends in West German Federalism 1949–1989', in Charlie Jeffery (ed.), *Recasting German Federalism: The Legacies of Unification*. London and New York: Pinter, 40–57.

Kobach, Kris W. (1997). 'Spurn they Neighbour: Direct Democracy and Swiss Isolationism'. *West European Politics*, 20: 185-211.

Krelove, Russell, Stotsky, Janet G., and Vehorn, Charles L. (1997). 'Canada', in Teresa Ter-Minassian (ed.), *Fiscal Federalism in Theory and Practice*. Washington, DC: International Monetary Fund, 201–55.

Lancaster, Thomas D. (1999). 'Complex Representation and Compounded Representation in Federal Systems', in Joanne B. Brzinski, Thomas D. Lancaster, and Christian Tuschhoff (eds), *Compounded Representation in Western European Federations*. London and Portland: Frank Cass, 59–89.

Lane, Jan-Erik and Ersson, Svante (1991). *Politics and Society in Western Europe*, 2nd edn. London and Thousand Oaks, CA: Sage.

——McKay, David, and Newton, Kenneth (1997). *Political Data Handbook: OECD Countries*, 2nd edn. Oxford: Oxford University Press.

La Nouvelle Péréquation Financière (NPF) *entre Confédération et cantons—lignes directrices. Rapport de l'organisation de project instituée conjointement par le Département fédéral des finances et par la conférence des directeurs contonaux des finances* (1996). Berne et Lucerne: Report of the Federal Department of Finance and the Conference of Directors of Finance of the Cantons.

Leff, Carol Skalnik (1999). 'Democratisation and Disintegration in Multinational States: The Break up of the Communist Federations'. *World Politics*, 51: 205–35.

Lehmbruch, Gerhard (1978). 'Party and Federation in Germany: A Developmental Approach'. *Government and Opposition*, 13: 151–77.

——(1989). 'Institutional Linkages and Policy Networks in the Federal System of West Germany'. *Publius*, 19: 221–35.

Leonardy, Uwe (1989). 'Forty Years of German Federalism: Past Trends and New Developments'. *Publius*, 19: 185–202.

——(1999). 'The Institutional Structure of German Federalism Towards 2000: To Be Reformed or Deformed?', in Charlie Jeffery (ed.), *Recasting German Federalism: The Legacies of Unification*. London and New York: Pinter, 285–311.

Leslie, Peter (1993). 'The Fiscal Crisis of Canadian Federalism', in Peter Leslie, Kenneth Norrie, and Irene K. Ip, *A Partnership in Trouble: Renegotiating Fiscal Federalism*. Ottawa: C. D. Howe Institute, 1–86.

Lijphart, Arend (1969). 'Consociational Democracy'. *World Politics*, 21: 207–25.

——(1977). *Democracy in Plural Societies: A Comparative Exploration*. New Haven: Yale University Press.

Lindberg, L. and Scheingold, S. (1970). *Europe's Would-be Polity*. Englewood Cliffs, NJ: Prentice Hall.

Linder, Wolf (1998). *Swiss Democracy: Possible Solutions to Conflict in Multi-Cultural Societies*. London and New York: Macmillan, St. Martin's Press.

Linz, Juan and Stephan, Alfred (1992). 'Political Identities and Electoral Consequences: Spain, the Soviet Union and Yugoslavia. *Daedalus*, 121: 123–39.

——(1996). *Problems of Democratic Transition and Consolidation: Southern Europe, South America and Post-Communist Europe*. Baltimore: Johns Hopkins University Press.

Lipset, Seymour Martin (1996). *American Exceptionalism: A Double Edged Sword*. New York: Norton.

Lloyd Brown, John (1990). 'The Meech Lake Accord in Historical Perspective', in Michael Burgess (ed.), *Canadian Federalism: Past, Present and Future*. Leicester and New York: Leicester University Press, 176–204.

Mackenstein, Hans and Jeffery, Charlie (1999). 'Financial Equalisation in the 1990s: On the Road Back to Karlsruhe?', in Charlie Jeffery (ed.), *Recasting German Federalism: The Legacies of Unification*. London and New York: Pinter, 155–76.

McConnell, Grant (1969). *The Decline of Agrarian Democracy*. New York: Scribner's.

McKay, David (1981). 'The Rise of the Topocratic States: US Intergovernmental Relations in the 1980s', in Douglas E. Ashford (ed.), *Financing Urban Government in the Welfare State*. London and New York: Croom Helm and St Martin's Press.

——(1989). *Domestic Policy and Ideology: Presidents and the American State, 1965–1987*. Cambridge and New York: Cambridge University Press.

——(1996). *Rush to Union: Understanding the European Federal Bargain*. Oxford and New York: Oxford University Press.

——(1997). *American Politics and Society*, 4th edn. Oxford: Oxford University Press.

——(1999a). 'The Political Sustainability of European Monetary Union'. *British Journal of Political Science*, 29: 463–85.

——(1999*b*). *Federalism and European Union: A Political Economy Perspective*. Oxford and New York: Oxford University Press.

McKinnon, Ronald I. (1997). 'EMU as a Device for Collective Fiscal Responsibility'. *American Economic Review: Papers and Proceedings*, 87: 227–9.

McMinn, W. G. (1994). *Nationalism and Federalism in Australia*. Melbourne and Oxford: Oxford University Press.

McRoberts, Kenneth (1997). *Misconceiving Canada: The Struggle for National Unity*. Toronto and Oxford: Oxford University Press.

Mansell, Robert and Schlenker, Ronald (1995). 'The Provincial Distribution of Federal Fiscal Balances'. *Canadian Business Economics*, Winter: 1–22

Marks, Gary (1992). 'Structural Policy in the European Community', in Alberta M. Sbragia (ed.), *Europolitics: Institutions and Policy Making in the 'New' European Community*. Washington, DC: Brookings Institution, 191–224.

——(1996). 'Exploring and Explaining Variation in Cohesion Policy', in Lisbet Hooghe (ed.), *Cohesion Policy: The European Community and Sub-National Government*. Oxford: Oxford University Press. 388–422.

——Nielsen, François, Ray, Leonard, and Salk, Jane (1996). 'Competencies, Cracks and Conflicts: Regional Mobilization in the European Union', in Gary Marks, Fritz W. Scharpf, Philippe C. Schmitter, and Wolfgang Streek, *Governance in the European Union*. Thousand Oaks, CA and London: Sage, 40–63.

Matthews, Donald (1960). *US Senators and Their World*. New York: Vintage.

Matthews, Russell and Grewal, Bhajan (1997). *The Public Sector in Jeopardy*. Melbourne: Centre for Strategic Economic Studies, Victoria University.

Mayhew, David (1974). *Congress: The Electoral Connection*. New Haven: Yale University Press.

Milward, Alan S. (1994). *The European Rescue of the Nation State*. London: Routledge.

Moravscik, Andrew (1998). *The Choice for Europe: Social Purpose and State Power from Messina to Maastricht*. Ithaca and London: Cornell University Press.

——and Kalypso, Michael (1998). 'Federal Ideas and Constitutional Realities in the treaty of Amsterdam'. *Journal of Common Market Studies, Annual Review*, 36: 13–38.

Morison, Samuel Eliot and Commager, Henry Steele (1962). *The Growth of the American Republic, Volume 1*. New York and Oxford: Oxford University Press.

Muller, Steven (1967). 'Federalism and the Party System in Canada', in Aaron Wildavsky (ed.), *American Federalism in Perspective*. Boston: Little, Brown, 144–61.

Mussa, Michael (1997). 'Political and Institutional Commitment to a Common Currency'. *American Economic Review: Papers and Proceedings*, 87: 217–20.

Nathan, Richard P. (1996). 'Overview Essay on Federalism and Social Policy', unpublished paper. Princeton: University of Princeton.

Norrie, Kenneth H. (1991). *A History of the Canadian Economy*. Toronto: Harcourt Brace Jovanovich Canada.

——(1993). 'Intergovernment Transfers in Canada: An Historical Perspective on some Current Policy Choices', in Peter Leslie, Kenneth Norrie, and Irene K. Ip, *A Partnership in Trouble: Renegotiating Fiscal Federalism*. Ottawa: C. D. Howe Institute, 87–129.

Ornstein, Norman J., Mann, Thomas E., and Malbin, Michael J. (1992). 'Committees', in Robert L. Peabody and Nelson W. Polsby (eds), *New Perspectives on the House of Representatives*. Baltimore: John Hopkins University Press, 113–41.

Ornstein, Norman J., Mann, Thomas E., and Malbin, Michael J. *Vital Statistics on Congress, 1997/98* (1998). Washington, DC: American Enterprise Institute.

Painter, Martin (1998). *Collaborative Federalism: Economic Reform in Australia in the 1990s*. Melbourne and Cambridge: Cambridge University Press.

Patterson, Samuel C. and Mughan, Anthony (eds) (1999). *Senates: Bicameralism in the Contemporary World*. Columbus: Ohio State University Press.

Petchey, Jeffrey D. and Shapiro, Perry (1997). '"One People One Destiny": Centralization and Conflicts of Interest in Australian Federalism', in David Wildasin, *Fiscal Aspects of Evolving Federations*. Cambridge: Cambridge University Press, 194–219.

Peterson, Paul E. (1995). *The Price of Federalism*. Washington, DC: Brookings Institution.

Polsby, Nelson W., Gallagher, Miriam, and Rundquist, Barry S. (1969). 'The Growth of the Seniority System in the House of Representatives'. *American Political Science Review*, 63: 789–99.

Pridham, Geoffrey (1973). 'A "Nationalisation" Process: Federal Politics and the State Elections'. *Government and Opposition*, 8: 455–72.

Provincial Economic Accounts, 1994/5 (1996). Toronto: Statistics Canada.

Renzsch, Wolfgang (1998). 'Financing German Unity: Fiscal Conflict Resolution in a Complex Federation'. *Publius*, 28: 127–46.

Rieselbach, Leroy (1986). *Congressional Reform*. Washington, DC: Congressional Quarterly Press.

Riker, William (1955). 'The Senate and American Federalism'. *American Political Science Review*, 49: 452–69.

——(1964). *Federalism: Origins, Operation, Significance*. Boston: Little, Brown.

——(1975). 'Federalism', in Fred I. Greenstein and Nelson Polsby (eds), *The Handbook of Political Science. Volume V: Government Institutions and Processes*. Reading, MA: Addison Wesley.

——and Schaps, Ronald (1957). 'Disharmony in Federal Government'. *Behavioural Science*, 2: 276–90.

Ripley, Randall B. and Franklin, Grace A. (1991). *Congress, the Bureaucracy and Public Policy*, 5th edn. New York: Dorsey Press.

Roberts, Geoffrey K. (1997). *Party Politics in the New Germany*. London and Washington, DC: Pinter.

Roy, Jayanta (ed.) (1995). *Macroeconomic Management and Fiscal Decentralisation*. Washington, DC: The World Bank.

Russell, Peter A. (1990). 'The Jurisdictional Pendulum within Canadian Federalism, 1867–1980', in Michael Burgess (ed.), *Canadian Federalism: Past, Present and Future*. Leicester and New York: Leicester University Press, 40–59.

Rye, Richard C. and Searle, Bob (1997). 'The Fiscal Transfer System in Australia', in Etisham Ahmad (ed.), *Financing Decentralised Expenditures: An International Comparison of Grants*. Cheltenham and Brookfield, MA: Edward Elgar, 144–83.

Scharpf, Fritz W. (1988). 'The Joint Decision Trap: Lessons From German Federalism and European Integration'. *Public Administration*, 66: 239–78.

——(1997). 'Economic Integration, Democracy and the Welfare State'. *Journal of European Public Policy*, 4: 18–36.

Scher, Richard K. (1997). *Politics in the New South: Republicanism, Race and Leadership in the 20th Century*, 2nd edn. New York: Sharpe.

Schlesinger, Arthur M. Jr.(1953). *The Age of Jackson*. Boston: Little, Brown.

Schlesinger, Rudolph (1998). *Federalism in Central and Eastern Europe*. London: Routledge.

Schmitter, Philippe C. (1996). 'Imagining the Future of the Euro Polity With the Help of New Concepts', in Gary Marks, Fritz W. Scharpf, Philippe C. Schmitter, and Wolfgang Streek, *Governance in the European Union*. Thousand Oaks, CA and London: Sage, 121–50.

Schneider, Hans-Peter (1999). 'German Unification and the Federal System: The Challenge of Reform', in Charlie Jeffery (ed.), *Recasting German Federalism: The Legacies of Unification*. London and New York: Pinter, 58–84.

Segalman, Ralph (1986). *The Swiss Way of Welfare*. New York: Praeger.

Shah, Anwar (1995). 'Intergovernmental Fiscal Relations in Canada: An Overview', in Jayanta Roy (ed.), *Macroeconomic Management and Fiscal Decentralisation*. Washington, DC: The World Bank, 233–55.

Shepsle, Kenneth A. (1994). 'The Institutional Foundations of Committee Power'. *Brookings Papers on Economic Activity*. Washington, DC: Brookings Institution.

Silvia, Stephen J. (1999). 'Reform Gridlock and the Role of the Bundesrat in German Politics', in Joanne B. Brzinski, Thomas D Lancaster, and Christian Tuschhoff (eds), *Compounded Representation in Western European Federations*. London and Portland: Frank Cass, 167–81.

Sinclair, Barbara (1999), 'Co-equal Partner: The U.S. Senate' in Samuel Patterson and Anthony Mughan (eds), *Senates: Bicameralism in the Contemporary World*. Columbus: Ohio State University Press. 32–58.

Skocpol, Theda (1995). *Protecting Mothers and Children: The Political Origins of Social Policy in the United States*. Cambridge, MA: Harvard University Press.

Smith, David E. (1990). 'Perennial Alienation: The Prairies West in the Canadian Federation', in Michael Burgess (ed.), *Canadian Federalism: Past, Present and Future*. Leicester and New York: Leicester University Press, 78–94.

Spahn, Paul Berndt (1997). 'Intergovernmental Grants in Switzerland and Germany', in Etisham Ahmad (ed.), *Financing Decentralised Expenditures: An International Comparison of Grants*. Cheltenham and Brookfield, MA: Edward Elgar, 103–43.

——and Fottinger, Wolfgang (1997). 'Germany', in Teresa Ter-Minassian (ed.), *Fiscal Federalism in Theory and Practice*. Washington, DC: International Monetary Fund, 226–48.

——and Shah, Anwar (1995). 'Intergovernmental Fiscal Relations in Australia', in Jayanta Roy (ed.), *Macroeconomic Management and Fiscal Decentralisation*. Washington, DC: The World Bank, 49–72.

Statistics Canada (1996). *Provincial Economic Accounts, 1994/5*. Toronto: Statistics Canada.

Statistik Bund (1997). *Land Finances*. Bonn: Statistik Bund.

Steinberg, Jonathan (1996). *Why Switzerland?* Cambridge and New York: Cambridge University Press.

Stewart, Gordon, Victor, Howard, and Jockel, Joseph T. (1996). *History of Canada Before 1867*. Lansing: Michigan State University Press.

Sturm, Roland (1998). 'Pa rty Competition and the Federal System: The Lehmbruch Hypothesis Revisited', in Charlie Jeffery (ed.), *Recasting German Federalism: The Legacies of Unification*. London and New York: Pinter, 197–216.

Swiss Parliament, http://www.parliament.ch/D/Veroeffentlichungen/Ru

Ter-Minassian, Teresa (ed.) (1997). *Fiscal Federalism in Theory and Practice*. Washington, DC: International Monetary Fund.

Tiebout, Charles M. (1956). 'A Pure Theory of Local Expenditure'. *Journal of Political Economy*, 74: 416–25.

Tsoukalis, Loukas (1993). *The New European Economy: The Politics and Economics of European Integration*. London: Pinter/Royal Institute of International Affairs.

Uhr, John (1999). 'Generating Divided Government: The Australian Senate', in Samuel C Patterson and Anthony Mughan (eds), *Senates: Bicameralism in the Contemporary World*. Columbus: Ohio State University Press, 93–119.

US Department of Congress (various years). *Statistical Abstract of the United States*. Washington, DC: US Department of Commerce.

——Bureau of the Census (various years). *Federal Expenditure by State*. Washington, DC: US Department of Commerce.

Van der Eijk, C. and Franklin, M. (1996). *Choosing Europe: The European Electorate and National Politics in the Face of Union*. Ann Arbor: University of Michigan Press.

Vipond, Robert C. (1991). *Liberty and Community: Canadian Federalism and the Failure of the Constitution*. Albany, NY: New York University Press.

Von Hagen, Jurgen and Eichengreen, Barry (1996), 'Federalism, Fiscal Constraints and European Monetary Union'. *American Economic Review*, 86: 134–8.

Wagenberg, Ronald, Soderlund, Wlater, Nelson, Ralph, and Briggs, Donald (1990). 'Federal Societies and the Founding of Federal States: An Examination of the Origins of Canadian Federation', in Michael Burgess (ed.), *Canadian Federalism: Past, Present and Future*. Leicester and New York: Leicester University Press, 7–39.

Ware, Alan (1996). *Political Parties and Party Systems*. Oxford and New York: Oxford University Press.

Watts, Ronald L. (1996). *Comparing Federal Systems in the 1990s*. Kingston: Institute of Intergovernmental Relations, Queens University, Ontario.

Weale, Albert (1998). 'Between Representation and Constitutionalism in the European Union', in Albert Weale and Michael Nentwich (eds), *Political Theory and the European Union: Legitimacy, Constitutional Choice and Citizenship*. London and New York: Routledge, 49–62.

——and Nentwich, Michael (eds) (1998). *Political Theory and the European Union: Legitimacy, Constitutional Choice and Citizenship*. London and New York: Routledge.

Weiler, J. H. H., Haltern, U. R., and Mayer, F. C. (1995). 'European Democracy and its Critique', in Jack Hayward (ed.), *The Crisis of Representation in Europe*. London: Frank Cass, 4–39.

Wildavsky, Aaron (ed.) (1967). *American Federalism in Perspective*. Boston: Little, Brown.

Williams, Colin H. (1995). 'A Requiem for Canada', in Graham Smith (ed.), *Federalism: The Multi-ethnic Challenge*. London and New York: Longman, 31–72.

Wilson, James Q. (1989). *Bureaucracy: What Government Agencies Do and Why They Do It*. New York: Basic Books.

Wishlade, Fiona (1996). 'EU Cohesion Policy: Facts, Figures and Issues', in Lisbet Hooge (ed.), *Cohesion Policy and European Integration*. Oxford: Oxford University Press, 27–58.

Young, Robert C. (1995). *The Secession of Quebec and the Future of Canada*. Toronto: University of Toronto Press.

INDEX

Lightning Source UK Ltd.
Milton Keynes UK
UKHW011824121218
333894UK00003B/194/P